JOHN OSBORNE

CASEBOOKS ON MODERN DRAMATISTS
VOLUME 16
GARLAND REFERENCE LIBRARY OF THE HUMANITIES
VOLUME 1404

CASEBOOKS ON MODERN DRAMATISTS
KIMBALL KING, *General Editor*

SAM SHEPARD
A Casebook
edited by Kimball King

CHRISTOPHER HAMPTON
A Casebook
edited by Robert Gross

HAROLD PINTER
A Casebook
edited by Lois Gordon

LANFORD WILSON
A Casebook
edited by Jackson R. Bryer

HOWARD BRENTON
A Casebook
edited by Ann Wilson

DAVID STOREY
A Casebook
edited by William Hutchings

PETER SHAFFER
A Casebook
edited by C.J. Gianakaras

DAVID MAMET
A Casebook
edited by Leslie Kane

SIMON GRAY
A Casebook
edited by Katherine H. Burkman

JOHN ARDEN AND
MARGARETTA D'ARCY
A Casebook
edited by Jonathan Wike

AUGUST WILSON
A Casebook
edited by Marilyn Elkins

JOHN OSBORNE
A Casebook
edited by Patricia D. Denison

DAVID HARE
A Casebook
edited by Hersh Zeifman

MARSHA NORMAN
A Casebook
edited by Linda Ginter Brown

JOHN OSBORNE
A CASEBOOK

EDITED BY
PATRICIA D. DENISON

First published by Garland Publishing, Inc.

This edition published 2011 by Routledge:

Routledge
Taylor & Francis Group
711 Third Avenue
New York, NY 10017

Routledge
Taylor & Francis Group
2 Park Square, Milton Park,
Abingdon, Oxfordshire OX14 4RN

First issued in paperback 2014

Routledge is an imprint of the Taylor and Francis Group, an informa business

Copyright © 1997 by Patricia D. Denison
All rights reserved

Library of Congress Cataloging-in-Publication Data

John Osborne : a casebook / edited by Patricia D. Denison.
    p.   cm. — (Garland reference library of the humanities ; vol. 1404.
Casebooks on modern dramatists ; vol. 16)
   Includes bibliographical references and index.
   ISBN 0-8240-7442-4
   1. Osborne, John, 1929–   . —Criticism and interpretation.
I. Denison, Patricia D. II. Series: Garland reference library of the humanities ;
vol. 1404. III. Series: Garland reference library of the humanities. Casebooks
on modern dramatists ; vol. 16.
PR6029.S39Z66   1997
822'.914—dc20   96-11610
                                                                                     CIP

ISBN 13: 978-1-138-88408-3 (pbk)
ISBN 13: 978-0-8240-7442-5 (hbk)

Cover illustration: John Osborne outside his London home in 1958. Slim Aarons/
NYT Pictures, 229 West 43d St., 9th fl., New York, NY 10036.

For Austin

Contents

ix   GENERAL EDITOR'S NOTE
Kimball King

xi   ACKNOWLEDGMENTS

xiii   INTRODUCTION
Patricia D. Denison

xxvii   CHRONOLOGY
Patricia D. Denison

3   THE HOUSE THAT JIMMY BUILT
Ronald Bryden

21   BEYOND ANGER: OSBORNE'S WRESTLE WITH LANGUAGE AND MEANING
David Galef

35   THE PERSONAL, THE POLITICAL, AND THE POSTMODERN IN OSBORNE'S *LOOK BACK IN ANGER* AND *DÉJÀVU*
Austin E. Quigley

61   OSBORNE ON THE FAULT LINE: JIMMY PORTER ON THE POSTMODERN VERGE
William W. Demastes

71   THE LOGIC OF ANGER AND DESPAIR: A PRAGMATIC APPROACH TO JOHN OSBORNE'S *LOOK BACK IN ANGER*
Luc M. Gilleman

91 THE ENTERTAINER AS A TEXT FOR PERFORMANCE
    Robert Gordon

115 LUTHER: THE MORBID GRANDEUR OF
    CORPOREAL HISTORY
    David Graver

127 FROM OUT OF THE SHADOW OF NICOL WILLIAMSON:
    INADMISSIBLE EVIDENCE
    Mark Hawkins-Dady

147 SEDUCED BY MERITOCRACY: CLASS AND SEXUALITY
    IN *A PATRIOT FOR ME*
    Robert F. Gross

167 "HONEY, I BLEW UP THE EGO": JOHN OSBORNE'S
    DÉJÀVU
    Sheila Stowell

175 JOHN OSBORNE, SUMMER 1993
    Kimball King

183 THE ANGRY YOUNG MAN WHO STAYED THAT WAY
    John Mortimer

187 A MEMORY OF JOHN OSBORNE
    Arnold Wesker

193 EULOGY FOR JOHN OSBORNE
    David Hare

197 BIBLIOGRAPHY
    Patricia D. Denison and Michal Lemberger

223 CONTRIBUTORS

227 INDEX

General Editor's Note

John Osborne, who died in 1994, will be remembered as a playwright who liberated modern British drama from genteel explorations of upper-middle class life and who opened the door to English social and political realities that few authors since Shaw had presented on stage. Osborne's initial fame rests on *Look Back in Anger*, which opened at the Royal Court Theatre on May 8, 1956 and subsequently dazzled audiences in Great Britain and around the world.

Osborne has written many other fine plays, and either *Luther* or *Inadmissible Evidence* may be his most challenging and mature work. But *Look Back in Anger* retains a mythological significance for the English and the new British theatre. Jimmy Porter, *Anger*'s legendary "angry young man," was identified with Osborne biographically and spiritually. Primarily, however, he stood for all the bright, disillusioned young men who found themselves disoriented and in pain a decade after World War II. Peter Barnes, Simon Gray, Peter Nichol, and, in fact, virtually all the major English playwrights writing today were stirred into action by Osborne. He moved from scathing political indictments of England and capitalism toward more psychologically and philosophically oriented drama. He was one of the most gifted playwrights of this century and a revered patron saint of a major dramatic movement. Compassionate and idealistic, Osborne was nevertheless easily moved to rage in defense of his principles.

Patricia D. Denison has collected an impressive variety of essays on this brilliant and controversial artist. Denison teaches at Barnard College in the departments of English and Theatre. Her scholarly interests focus upon the relationship between text, performance, and cultural context from the Renaissance to the present, with particular reference to English and American drama of the nineteenth century. She has published articles on Victorian and modern drama and the plays of James Herne, T.W. Robertson, and

Arthur W. Pinero. She recently completed a book on Arthur Pinero and late-nineteenth-century social drama.

The present volume surveys Osborne's rich canon, calls upon distinguished colleagues and critics to elucidate his purposes, and contains the touching eulogy David Hare delivered at Osborne's memorial service, as well as a thorough up-to-date bibliography of Osborne's impressive achievements.

Kimball King
General Editor

Acknowledgments

For their professional advice and personal kindness, I would like to thank Kimball King, General Editor, Casebooks on Modern Dramatists; Phyllis Korper, Senior Editor, Garland Publishing, Inc.; and Carol Buell, Production Editor, Garland Publishing, Inc. Significant support was provided by the Dana Grant and a Faculty Research Grant from Barnard College, Columbia University. Michal Lemberger, my research assistant, made important contributions to the bibliography. For her gracious correspondence and invaluable assistance with the chronology of her husband's life and work, I am grateful to Helen Dawson Osborne.

For their repeated reminders of the pleasures of living and learning off stage as well as on, I would like to thank my daughters, Laura, Rebecca, Caroline, and Catherine, and my husband, Austin.

John Osborne outside his London home in 1958. Slim Aarons/NYT Pictures, 229 West 43rd St., 9th fl., New York, NY, 10036.

INTRODUCTION
Patricia D. Denison

When T.S. Eliot reviewed the range of possibilities for literary achievement, he outlined two major options for ambitious writers and attempted to adjust the balance between them:

> We are inclined, in our judgements upon the past, to exaggerate the importance of the innovators at the expense of the reputation of the developers: which might account for what will seem, surely, to a later age, our undue adulation of Donne and depreciation of Milton.... It would not be desirable, even if it were possible, to live in a state of perpetual revolution.... There are times for exploration and times for the development of the territory acquired.[1]

Though Eliot is thinking primarily of poetry, he is also discussing Shakespeare, and the options of being an innovator or a developer seem equally pertinent to the case of playwrights. Forty years after John Osborne appeared on the theatrical scene, however, it remains unclear whether we can usefully situate his work in the context of such alternative means of advancing theatrical tradition. It would be difficult to make the case that Osborne as innovator wrote plays whose structure was widely imitated or that Osborne as developer wrote plays that extended an existing tradition, but he has somehow earned a secure place in every history of modern theatre as a writer who made a difference.

The essays in this volume review Osborne's complicated career and attempt to situate his plays in larger contexts that clarify their cumulative significance. Though William Demastes cites approvingly Sillitoe's remark that "John Osborne didn't contribute to the British Theatre: he set off a landmine called *Look Back in Anger* and blew most of it up," his positive contribution, as well as the negative one, is the focus of every essay's concern. For Ronald Bryden, in his thorough examination of Osborne's work from *Look Back in Anger* (1956) to *Déjàvu* (1991), the major difficulty is that of disentangling Osborne's "quality as a dramatist" from his role as a cultural critic of Britain's national consciousness in the years after the Second World War. Though Bryden comments at length on the autobiographical element in Osborne's plays, he sees Osborne at his best when "reflecting the divided mind and will of his country and generation." And what they are most divided about, he argues, is the relationship between innovation and tradition in English society, particularly as it bears upon the value of the postwar meritocracy that socialist-inspired reforms produced to counter the old aristocracy. Members of the new upwardly mobile grammar school/ university–educated elite soon found themselves confronting the recognition that, for many of the population, the new elitism was no more palatable than the old, and the innovative and traditional became difficult to distinguish. Consequently, it is "hard to know whether to call Jimmy Porter meritocracy's first protagonist or antagonist." The powerful but divided voice thus becomes Osborne's aesthetic trademark, and for many of his characters, cultural criticism becomes inextricably intertwined with self-evaluation.

Caught up in the confusion over social reform, Osborne keeps searching, Bryden argues, for a foundation for social and personal authenticity. In *The Entertainer*, he explores the music hall as a cultural institution whose authenticity draws upon a long established tradition of "common folk" before it was undermined by the influence of aristocrats or meritocrats. But efforts to locate a durable sense of personal authenticity in *Inadmissible Evidence*, *Time Present*, and *The Hotel in Amsterdam* bring the characters into increasing conflict with a convention of linguistic authenticity that bridges all classes and generations, helps sustain the phantasmagoria of misleading national myths, and does much to explain the prolonged career of England's artistic censor, the Lord Chamberlain, who was still approving plays for performance as late as 1968. The search for an authentic self and the search for an authentic language raise in different ways the issue of relating innovation to tradition, but both are linked to a third concern—that of finding an appropriate home. Location and setting thus achieve a particular importance in Osborne's plays, for home is often characterized as a site where truth ought to be spoken whatever the price entailed. As characters repeatedly discover, the price can be very high indeed. The Jimmy Porter of *Déjàvu*, Bryden argues, "can claim that he has made a home, a place where truth is spoken, even if his truths have driven away the children he evidently made it for."

David Galef addresses the same kinds of tensions in Osborne's work but enlarges the context in which Bryden situates them. He argues that though the communication gaps in Osborne's drama are usually assumed to represent social divisions, a close examination of the plays reveals semantic and epistemological rifts equivalent to those found in the work of Beckett and Wittgenstein. Though the plays are largely situated in England and explore the postwar English situation, that socio-historical context, for Galef, is only an instance of "an epistemological fissure" of much wider relevance.

Osborne's Martin Luther struggles, Galef argues, "not so much with the Word as with words," and he cites Osborne's remark that his primary concern is "how people relate to each other and to themselves." In this context it is Jimmy Porter's inconsistencies that loom larger than any of his emphatic judgments, and his divided self becomes the paradigm case for characters in subsequent plays. Galef cites approvingly Trussler's remark that Jimmy is neither adjusted to his era nor a spokesman for it, and argues that Osborne's characters occupy the Beckett territory of "postmodern protest against a self limited by language, a voice that ironically affirms what it speaks against." Again, it is the divided voice that demands attention, but the divisions are now situated in epistemological and not just social space. As a consequence, issues of innovation and tradition acquire, in this different context, a different relationship, and the divisions of the present recapitulate those of the past and foreshadow those of the future.

The sense of isolation and alienation exhibited by, for example, Archie Rice in *The Entertainer*, Alfred Redl in *A Patriot for Me*, and Bill Maitland in *Inadmissible Evidence* thus becomes symptomatic not just of England's divided consciousness, but of humanity's general situation: "Semantic slippage and faulty communication are, for Osborne, part of the human condition, and so the past is simply a paradigm for the present and the future." With several references to Wittgenstein's explorations of the problematics of language, Galef explores recurring patterns of semantic confusion and private experience in *The Hotel in Amsterdam*, *A Sense of Detachment*, and *West of Suez*, with Edward in the latter play observing: "Sometimes I don't feel I can understand a word of anything anyone says to me. As if they were as unclear as I am."

The difficulty, however, with plays that offer universal insights is their tendency to depict the world in repetitious terms and to function themselves as repetitious works. As Galef puts it, "One cannot pound this sort of drum too long without growing sick of the same noise or else slightly deaf." To pursue this line of inquiry beyond a certain point is to confront the implications of Wittgenstein's observation, cited by Isobel in *The End of Me Old*

Cigar: "Whereof one cannot speak, / Thereof one must be silent." But the counterargument is that to speak one's own language and voice one's own truth in an unreceptive world is, in its own way, a "courageous gesture in the face of meaninglessness." Where Beckett's characters often confront this situation in worlds that are unclearly situated, both socially and historically, Osborne depicts characters sliding toward the same dilemmas in a variety of social and historical milieus. These characters are sometimes the more bitter because they confront the failure of their own convictions to convince others in worlds where conviction and persuasion still seem to enjoy public currency.

These two expansive overviews of Osborne's career invoke two very different contexts, one firmly situating Osborne's work in a postwar English era, the other situating it in the more abstract context of humanity struggling with the problematics of language, relationships, and self. The other essays in the volume take more local aspects of Osborne's work and seek to relate in different ways the social and epistemological issues generated by the plays, thereby clarifying the differing ways in which Osborne links tradition to innovation.

Three of the essays explore Osborne's most famous play, *Look Back in Anger*. Austin Quigley, noting that the play "is widely regarded as a very important but not very good play," seeks to clarify its innovative strengths by exploring it in the light of the sequel, *Déjàvu*, a play that Osborne laconically refers to as "*Look Back II*." Where Jimmy Porter struggles in the first play with his parent's generation, he struggles in the second with his children's. Quigley uses this observation as a means of situating the idiosyncratic and inconsistent voice of Jimmy Porter as an intergenerational voice concerned with bridging the generational divisions it insists so emphatically upon. This bridging is not a means of diminishing generational difference but of clarifying the social and psychological contexts that historically situated relationships must both accommodate and address. For Quigley, the key context is neither national nor epistemological but cultural, and Jimmy becomes a threshold character in a play that both marks and magnifies a key moment of cultural transition.

Jimmy's divided allegiances and England's fragmentary social fabric thus serve to characterize a moment of larger cultural transition from narratives of Victorian and modern social coherence on an imperial scale to the more local and contingent social contracts characteristic of postmodernism. Citing postmodern theorists Hassan and Lyotard, who argue that eras do not simply succeed each other but coexist with each other for a while, Quigley points out that Jimmy's intergenerational perspective, visually rendered in the set of *Look Back in Anger*, forces him not only to straddle the irreconcilable values of Victorianism, modernism, and postmodernism, but to confront the shifts in scale upon which values are measured and constituted. The humor, irony, and parody of both plays become the means of multiplying perspectives for the audience and helping it grasp the peculiar relationship between tradition and innovation that emerges from a multilinear rather than a unilinear conception of history. "Strangely enough," Quigley argues, "it is Jimmy's very refusal to restrict his views to that of a single era, to unify his convictions into a single world view, or to align his actions with his assertions, that makes him serve as an unexpectedly successful site of engagement with the idiosyncratic shape of individual lives, the multilinear history of an evolving nation, and the contested development of a cultural process in a period of major transition." Arguing that "coherence . . . conceals as much as is revealed," the Jimmy Porter of *Déjàvu* seeks to generate in us all "the courage of uncertainty."

William Demastes also considers the postmodern implications of *Look Back in Anger*, but primarily in terms of the way Osborne contrasts his characters and addresses his audience. For Demastes, as for Quigley, *Look Back in Anger* is situated "on a theatrical fault line," but Demastes treats the transition differently. For him, there is a clear division between the dramatic conventions of modernist realism and postmodern multilinearity, and the play must be appropriately contextualized to be properly performed. Far from being what Hayman calls "the one-man play *par excellence*," *Look Back in Anger*, Demastes argues, effectively deconstructs its main character, who lacks both stable convictions and unified goals, and actors have yet to come to terms with the play's major characters and central relationship.

Worthy attempts by Kenneth Haigh and Richard Burton, the original interpreters of the role, to convert Jimmy Porter into a heroic figure, were, Demastes suggests, misguided attempts to offer the audience a figure of emulation in spite of the fact that Porter's views not only lacked general appeal but were, and are, unacceptable to many. For Demastes, "It is not entirely clear that a production needs to create a sympathetic Porter for this play to be successful." Indeed, the Jimmy Porter who "drifts without direction" is better regarded as "a catalyst awakening us to the issue of commitment," and the play then serves as an incitement to the audience to produce some thoughts of its own on issues of social change. In this context it is not Jimmy who becomes an exemplar of change but Alison, though her progress toward significant change falls short of providing a definitive conclusion to the issues the play raises. The two characters, in effect, confront each other across the gap between two different theatrical conventions, and the conflict between innovation and tradition impels the audience to generate some questions and answers of its own.

Luc Gilleman is less inclined to regard the play as one concerned with social analysis, and regards its failure to offer social insights or social alternatives not as an incitement to the audience to provide its own questions and answers about continuity and change but as an indication that the audience should look elsewhere for its interest. Noting Osborne's remark that "drama rests on the *dynamic* that is created *between* characters on the stage," Gilleman suggests that the play be approached not as a one-man show about Jimmy Porter's monologues but as a multi-voiced, dialogically structured example of "postwar language-oriented realism." His interest in Osborne's use of language, unlike Galef's, focusses less on the traditional problematics of language than on its complex possibilities for innovation and exploration. Such possibilities, in this play, remain embryonic rather than becoming actualized, and we need to understand the logic of that process.

The play's representation of reality, Gilleman argues, is based on a logic of communication rather than of character, a logic best clarified by a "systemic pragmatic analysis" that treats the language of the play less as a source of ideas than as a mode of interaction. In such a context, "one cannot not communicate," and the key issues are ones of vulnerability, strategy, and control. Jimmy and Alison find themselves caught up in a "self-perpetuating pattern of Alison's withdrawal and Jimmy's provocative behavior" that neither can alter because the potential move to metacommunication, to discussion of why they are trapped in the pattern, is resolutely blocked by both sides. This produces the constant feeling that both seem to want from each other things that neither of them can give.

The negative feedback mechanisms that block the path to metacommunication are, Gilleman argues, the family myth and paradox. The former sets the condition of possibility upon which a relationship stands and thus converts any explicit call for change into a threat rather than an opportunity. The latter, however, opens up paralogical possibilities as exemplified in the bear/squirrel game. In effect, this game allows the relationship to redefine itself in action so that new rules of mutual support for the relationship can emerge without being explicitly formulated. Such an approach clarifies the conflict between repetition and change in the play and explains its often puzzling bear/squirrel conclusion: "You'll keep those big eyes on my fur. . . . And I'll see that you keep that sleek, bushy tail glistening as it should. . . ."

Such an interactional approach to character, Gilleman argues, clarifies the relationship between fixity and change, distributes responsibility across all participants, and raises questions about political or feminist readings that divide classes or genders into us/them configurations. This does not necessarily render such approaches irrelevant but relocates the issues involved. Alison's return to Jimmy is not merely demeaning, because she recovers a mode of action and control along with a new mode of access to more positive aspects of Jimmy. Systemic pragmatic analysis, Gilleman suggests, seeking to move beyond conventions of response based upon character-oriented, issue-oriented, and plot-oriented realism, "draws a more intricate picture of lived and living reality that defies the arbitrarily drawn lines of political partisanship." It helps us recognize the ways in which the play demonstrates the responsibility of both men and women "for creating the interactional micro- and macro-environment of family and society that double-bind them in such a way that either protest or acquiescence only serve to strengthen their chains."

The essays on *Look Back in Anger* not only clarify, in their different ways, the innovative elements of Osborne's dramaturgy that coexist with its conventionality, but also suggest why they coexist. Osborne's dramatic experimentation seems to rely upon mixed forms not because Osborne is incapable of inventing the radically new but because the forms of social experience he is intent upon exploring seem so often to register the clash between inherited and emerging ways of configuring experience. In his discussion of *The Entertainer*, Robert Gordon argues that the play "stages a stylistic confrontation between the low-key naturalism of Terence Rattigan's *The Browning Version* (1948) and the overt theatricality of Noël Coward's *Red Peppers* (1936)." It also draws upon differing acting styles and contrasting speech modes as Osborne uses the music hall in which Archie Rice performs his act as a frame for the domestic action of the play. Past and present are cleverly interwoven as the scenes of contemporary domestic squabbling are presented as a series of items on the variety bill of a tawdry, debased music hall. This theatricalizing of everyday life is not a Pirandellian attempt to demonstrate that reality is always sustained by fiction, but an innovative means of suggesting that the England of this era has wilfully lost its ability to confront contemporary reality.

The play, Gordon argues, explores the price paid for survival in postwar England by a society unwilling to recognize that in some important sense it is not surviving at all. Archie's critique of the audience—"We're just as dead as each other"—links with the ambiguous demand he makes on his own family—"Be a little normal just for once, and pretend we're a happy, respectable, decent family"—to suggest that neither the apparently normal and happy nor the apparently abnormal and unhappy have managed to survive in a world constructed largely from cultural and national myths. As Gordon puts it, "The intercutting of different speech modes (naturalistic emotional outburst and music hall patter) expresses the contradiction between the image of a society inscribed in its cultural forms and the reality of an individual's lived experience of social existence." Refusing to depict the music hall as a site of recoverable authenticity but instead as one more instance of social degeneration, Osborne seeks to implicate the audience in the process of institutional decline and to use Billy Rice, the voice of an earlier era of individual dignity and social authenticity, as a challenge to the audience to establish a form of authenticity of its own. In pursuit of those feelings that the characters cannot express in the conventional rhetoric of the naturalistic play of domestic life, Osborne deploys and finds deficient a variety of "musical and theatrical forms."

This characteristic mingling of contrasting voices and competing theatrical forms is one of the reasons that Osborne's plays tend to lack definitive conclusions, and it leads logically enough to the episodic structure that David Graver locates in *Luther*. As a history play, however, *Luther* is oddly structured, and Graver notes the seeming disparity between an episodic structure and the linearity of historical thematic concerns. Though the play "traces the life of Martin Luther (1483–1546) from his youthful entry into an Augustinian monastery in 1506 to his settled, middle-aged family life in 1530," the play neither dramatizes the linear development of Luther's life nor chronicles the evolution of the historical issues upon which Luther's life impinged. Instead, it provides twelve separate tableaux of a character who seems to change very little. Once again, the relationship between fixity and change becomes problematic, and the structure of the play, Graver argues, is one of supplementation rather than development, with dramatic action giving way to theatrical display. Graver praises Osborne for the "rich and complex" nature of the spectacle created by "stylized tableaux, direct audience address, and images projected at the back of the scene," but wonders both about the theatrical effectiveness of an action whose episodic nature inclines it toward the static and about the historical efficacy of a history play that focusses more on one individual's personality than on his social relations and actions.

The issue of repetition, which earlier concerned Galef, now concerns Graver, who wonders whether for Osborne "history is essentially dead." Where Brecht employed episodic structures both to display a pattern of exploitation and to foreground the ideology that would otherwise disguise it, Osborne seems to want to dramatize the paradox of an historically important figure whose own experience is one of social isolation. As Graver points out, "The isolation of Osborne's individualist heroes has a special poignancy in *Luther* because it meshes well with the self-doubt under which Luther staggers." Consequently, "insofar as *Luther* is a meditation on the dynamics of alienation and self doubt, its lack of a well articulated socio-historical context and convincing dialogue is no handicap and even an advantage in some scenes." But if Osborne is unable to isolate the historical figure from the historical significance he invokes for the audience, the contrast between Brecht's attempts to make history material and Osborne's readiness to make it corporeal seems, to Graver, one that favors Brecht. The questions Graver raises relate directly to issues raised in other essays about the representative status not only of Jimmy Porter's idiosyncratic voice, but also of the defiant, despairing individualism of so many of Osborne's major characters.

The mixed modes of Osborne's dramatization that suggest to Graver a tension between static individualism and evolving history suggest something somewhat different to Mark Hawkins-Dady: a structural tension between fragmentation and intensification. In his essay on *Inadmissible Evidence* he notes, as others have noted, a mingling of theatrical conventions. The play moves, he argues, "from an opening dream sequence, through the apparent stage naturalism of office life, to moments of expressionistic vision." Hawkins-Dady relates these competing stage techniques to the contested forms of evidence implied by the play's title, which refers to attempts in courts of law to set aside evidence deemed as irrelevant or contrary to the rules of court. The play is deliberately structured, he argues, to make such rulings in legal/social/psychological domains inherently problematic: "The play's structure, as a case study of a man in his environment, purposely creates innumerable conflicts between strictly legal, causal, and rational motivations on the one hand, and the jumbled, inchoate, self-induced, and societal (the theoretically 'inadmissible') on the other, and challenges all who confront the play, from director to audience, to judge which are the more profoundly relevant." And relevance to Hawkins-Dady seems more dependent upon moral than legal judgment. But judgment of whatever kind is, in this world, inherently precarious.

The repetitive or reiterative depiction of the central character's decline hinges, Hawkins-Dady argues, on his inability to think things through in a world in which reality and recall seem inherently ambiguous. Bill Maitland's "exuberant solipsism" threatens both to absorb the world and to isolate him from it, and the failure of his various relationships resists satisfactory explanation as much as do those of his various clients. All find themselves struggling to reconcile the ambiguity and complexity of their marital relationships with the "polarised exaggerations of plaintiff and defendant" demanded by the legal system. Osborne thus manages to produce the strange effect of an increasingly isolated Bill Maitland interweaving his own memories and musings with the narratives of his clients. A tension is thus generated between the impression that Maitland's solipsism can absorb any material into itself and the impression that Maitland is discovering a strange fellowship with other alienated creatures who are likewise unable to articulate or address their own increasing vulnerability and despair.

This play, like other Osborne plays, treats social issues generationally, and Maitland is fascinated by his daughter Jane's ability to set aside as largely irrelevant the "responsibilities and anxious disabilities" that have rendered his life so traumatic. Though Maitland can address the generation of the liberated '60s, he can neither accept it for himself nor reject it for her, and Maitland's isolation, in characteristic Osborne fashion, seems to hover between competing possibilities, appearing at various times to be a solipsistic quirk, a generational disability, and an unavoidable aspect of the human condition.

Rather than answer the difficult questions posed by such a play, Hawkins-Dady sets out to clarify their complexity by comparing and contrasting two earlier productions (1964 and 1978) that starred Nicol Williamson with the most recent (1993) production in which Trevor Eve played the central role. He ultimately argues that "it was the strength and originality of Di Trevis's [1993] production that neither she nor Eve attempted to reproduce the volcanic Romantic disintegration characterising the Williamson productions, but went back to basics to rethink the balance of styles in Osborne's dramatic structure." Back to basics, in Osborne's dramaturgy, seems always to imply attempts to highlight and explain the balance between competing dramatic styles.

In his study of class and sexuality in *A Patriot for Me*, Robert Gross situates Osborne's play in the context of contemporary debate over politics and gender, but he is quick to historicize that debate by comparing the play to George Lillo's 1731 play, *The London Merchant*. To Gross, *A Patriot for Me* initially seems to take "the form of a coming out narrative. . . . that works by constituting its protagonist's homosexuality as a secret, and then disclosing it." But Osborne's inventive theatricality includes in this play an extravagant drag ball with costumes minutely described, a scene that constitutes, for Gross, "a vast and opulent display of a male homosexual culture, including a baron, a judge, and higher-ups in the military. . . . The size of this scene and the degree of spectacle in it gives the 'secret' homosexual culture of Vienna a theatrical impact far beyond any other culture presented in the play." Osborne thus situates the leading character, Alfred Redl, between the heterosexual and homophobic world of the first act and the exuberantly homosexual culture of the second act in such a way that he feels at home in neither. As Gross puts it, Redl moves from being "the isolated homosexual in a homophobic environment in Act I" to being "the isolated homophobe in a homosexual environment in Act II."

These changing forms of alienation raise questions about whether Redl's problems with his sexual orientation derive from external social forces or internal psychological ones. But the issue is further complicated by arguments from two of the characters that homosexuality is sooner or later physically visible and as such cannot be kept secret. Redl's desire to control his public image is thus already defeated and becomes, for Gross, an exemplification of the larger issue Osborne is exploring of the relationship between individuality and the social forces impinging upon it. If the two are not separable, then there is no self, and Redl's resort to espionage becomes a means of examining in another sphere whether a secret can be kept and whether an individual can stand apart from social pressures and public knowledge. In such a context, the army, as a self-proclaimed meritocracy, becomes a haven for individualism as it claims to judge individual soldiers solely in terms of their individual abilities rather than their origins or class. In neither case, however, is the issue as clear-cut as it seems at first glance, and Gross's argument here links with Bryden's interest in the relationship between the meritocracy and society in Osborne's work. Gross, too, remarks on the inherent conflict between aristocracy, meritocracy, and equality and, in the case of the Austro-Hungarian army, clarifies the cost to privacy of any meritocracy that can only make judgments about individuals by invading their privacy. Wherever Redl turns he seems to encounter forms of public surveillance that deny him any interior, private space. Neither the world of the army nor the world of espionage prove to be havens in this respect.

Exploring these complexities further in the context of spies, homosexuality, and class in postwar England, Osborne, Gross argues, makes strained attempts to relate differing stories and different dramatic forms. Ultimately, Gross argues, Osborne's treatment of homosexuality is inconsistent. He is sympathetic if the issue is seen as privacy versus public convention, but disdainful and even contemptuous if it is seen as a matter of effeminate Establishment decadence confronting public responsibility. Osborne's oscillation between the two perspectives eventually generates, for Gross, a structural tension in the play between presenting a coming out story and providing a story of the destruction of a promising young man by a corrupt status quo. In effect, Osborne "tries to unite a melodrama about blackmail with a satire about decadence, but the two dramatic impulses remain at odds with each other." "Despite its aesthetic confusion," however, Gross argues that the play remains "valuable as a cultural document" for it "registers the tension between two opposed constructions of homosexuality which . . . continues to this day."²

The contrasting perspectives that have emerged from Osborne's competing forms of stagecraft, from his characters' multiple viewpoints, and from Osborne's insistence upon the irreducibly multiple nature of individual and social experience achieved, for Sheila Stowell, a further consequence in his final play, *Déjàvu*. As she points out, the title alludes to a sensation of recall that is in fact illusory, for it is the sensation of recalling something that did not actually take place.

In effect, Stowell argues, "Osborne toys with audience expectations: what we are asked to witness in *Déjàvu* both is and is not—because we did not see 'rightly' the first time" when we attended *Look Back in Anger*. For Stowell, the retrospective impetus inspired by *Déjàvu* serves the earlier play better than the later, for *Look Back in Anger* successfully exploited the tension between the "angry outpourings" that characterize Jimmy's idiosyncratic perspectives and the various forms of constraint supplied by the play's structure, by the theatrical conventions of the time, and by the social conventions implied in the Lord Chamberlain's right to censor plays for public performance.

By contrast, *Déjàvu*, appearing at a time when almost anything is sayable, when the Lord Chamberlain has departed, and when J.P. is deprived of strong opposing voices, seems more of an exercise in self-indulgence than an effort to change people's minds. When unleashed, she argues, "The vituperative tongue of J.P. Senior points up the paradox that when everything is said nothing is." Stowell also takes issue with Osborne's attempts to give J.P. a Falstaffian lineage and with his retrospective attempts to redefine Jimmy Porter's role in *Look Back in Anger*. Reviewing published responses to the 1992 production, Stowell is ultimately inclined to regard the play as something of a docudrama whose subject is more John Osborne than J.P., but she notes that several respected critics regard the play more positively.

In his survey of current perceptions of Osborne's work, Kimball King also weighs the remarkable diversity of responses that continue to range, as they did initially, from extravagant praise to outright condemnation. Sifting through the various perceptions and misperceptions of Osborne's political, social, and aesthetic views, King argues that Osborne has always possessed the ability to shock audiences with his caustic, witty dialogue, while remaining steadfast in his indictment of class bias, social hypocrisy, and unethical behavior in personal and political spheres. As he puts it, "No doubt the Osborne of this decade is repelled by what he believes to be the self-righteous ardor of contemporary social activists. But he is not necessarily repelled by their particular causes, which can be used to distract followers from fundamental systemic changes." Osborne's characteristic mingling of perspectives generates a characteristically mixed response, and this makes it certain that his plays will continue "to enrage and delight audiences for decades to come."[3]

John Osborne died, while this volume was in preparation, on Christmas Eve 1994. Three English playwrights, John Mortimer, Arnold Wesker, and David Hare, responded in different contexts to Osborne's death, and their views on his remarkable life and career provide the conclusion to this work.

For Mortimer, Osborne's "singular achievement was to have created a total revolution in the British theatre." Though he was often "cantankerous, pugnacious, and unfair," his aggressiveness was rarely merely negative, and his "anger was in defense of old values of courage and honor." Indeed, he was, Mortimer argues, in his own way, "as English as Dr. Johnson or Chesterton."

Wesker, who saw a touring production of *Look Back in Anger* in April 1956, gratefully acknowledges, "It changed my life." But not in the direction of a fellowship of discontent. "There never was," he argues, "an 'Angry Young Man' nor any such group as 'The Angry Young Men.'" Indeed, Osborne's most famous play was "not about anger but about a love affair that fails because of the absence of generosity of spirit." Ironically, contemporary critical response to Osborne's work was often characterized, Wesker suggests, by just such lack of generosity, and the premature categorization that resulted often meant that the plays "were described before they were read *and were read that way!*"

Wesker notes that he saw Osborne for the last time at the Cadogan Hotel where Oscar Wilde was arrested. The setting provides an apt illustration of his argument that England's literary commentators do little to nurture the talents of the writers whose work they subsequently come to revere. There is, he suggests, much work still to be done before we can come properly to terms with Osborne's life and his plays.

In a eulogy delivered at a memorial service for John Osborne at St. Giles-in-the-Fields in Covent Garden on June 2, 1995, David Hare remarked that it took the author's sudden death "to wake his own country into some kind of just appreciation of what they had lost." For Hare, too, critical response has some way to go before it grasps the full complexities of Osborne's life and work. "Central to any understanding of John's extraordinary life," he suggests, "is the striking disparity between his popular reputation as a snarling malcontent . . . and the generous, free-spirited man that most of us in this church knew and loved." Those too ready to reduce his voice to one of rabid indignation have overlooked the fact that "his celebrated gift for analysing the shortcomings of others was as nothing to his forensic capacity for making comedy from his own failings."

Far from being single and schematic, Osborne's voice was characteristically varied and exploratory, for he "devoted his life to trying to forge some sort of connection between the acuteness of his mind and the exceptional power of his heart." If it is impossible, as many have discovered, "to speak of John without using the word 'England,'" it is because he had by the end of his life, in a manner characteristically both traditional and innovative, "in some sense, made the word his own."

Patricia D. Denison

NOTES

1. T.S. Eliot, "The Music of Poetry," *Selected Prose*, ed. John Hayward (London: Penguin, 1953) 60.

2. After Osborne's death, Anthony Creighton spoke about his relationship with Osborne. See Nicholas De Jongh, "The Secret Gay Love of John Osborne," *Evening Standard* 24 January 1995: 12, and see Lynda Lee-Potter, "He Made Me Realize That Loving Is The Best Way To Live," *Daily Mail* 27 January 1995: 20–21.

3. All essays in this volume other than Mortimer's, Wesker's, and Hare's were written before John Osborne died on 24 December 1994.

Kimball King, in his essay "Osborne Today, Summer 1993," concludes that "Osborne retains the capacity to break new ground and to enrage and delight audiences for decades to come." Helen Dawson Osborne, in an interview given a month after her husband died, confirmed that Osborne was indeed planning further work: "He had at least two more plays in him that won't now get written. I'm so sick about those plays. And he'd just signed the contract to produce his third volume of autobiography." Lynda Lee-Potter, "He Made Me Realize that Loving is the Best Way to Live," *Daily Mail* 27 January. 1995: 20. Arnold Wesker, in his essay in this volume, also mentions other ventures: Osborne's "commission to write for TV a play on Purcell and the Restoration" and forthcoming revivals—*Look Back in Anger* at the Royal Exchange Theatre, Manchester, and *A Patriot for Me* by the Royal Shakespeare Company.

Chronology

Patricia Denison

John Osborne

1929   Born John James Osborne, 12 December in Fulham, London, to Thomas Godfrey Osborne, a commercial artist, and Nellie Beatrice, born Grove, a barmaid.

1938   Family moved to Ewell.

1940   Death of father, Thomas Godfrey Osborne.

1943   Spent much of the war in South London suburbs with his mother and then sent to a boarding school, Belmont College, in Devon.

1945   Summer, left school. Expelled for hitting a teacher but was already set to leave.

1946   Worked briefly as a journalist for trade magazines such as *Gas World*, *Nursery World*, and *The Miller*.

1948   Acted for the first time as Mr. Burrells in *No Room at the Inn*, Empire Theatre, Sheffield. In a touring group, also assistant stage manager and tutor to the juvenile actors.

1949   *The Devil Inside Him* (written in collaboration with Stella Linden), staged at Theatre Royal, Huddersfield.

1950–54   Acted with repertory companies around England and Wales and the London area. Ran his own company on Hayling Island, where he played Hamlet.

1954	Tour of South Wales in *Pygmalion*.
1955	1 March, *Personal Enemy* (written in collaboration with Anthony Creighton), staged at Harrogate Opera House.
1956	April, joined the English Stage Company as an actor. 8 May, *Look Back in Anger*, the Royal Court Theatre, directed by Tony Richardson, with Kenneth Haigh as Jimmy Porter, Alan Bates as Cliff, Mary Ure as Alison, Helena Hughes as Helena, and John Welsh as Colonel Redfern. May, first appearance as an actor on the London stage, at the Royal Court as Antonio in *Don Juan in Hell*, and Lionel in *The Death of Satan*. June, appeared in *Cards of Identity*, the Royal Court. October, appeared as Lin To in *The Good Woman of Setzuan*, the Royal Court. *Evening Standard* Drama Award as Most Promising Playwright of the Year. 5 November, *Look Back in Anger* transferred to the Lyric Theatre, Hammersmith, with Richard Pasco as Jimmy, Doreen Aris as Alison, Vivien Drummond as Helena, and Kenneth Edwards as Colonel Redfern.
1957	10 April, *The Entertainer*, the Royal Court, directed by Tony Richardson, with Laurence Olivier as Archie Rice, Brenda de Banzie as Phoebe, George Relph as Billy, Dorothy Tutin as Jean, Richard Pasco as Frank, and Stanley Meadows as Graham. May, appeared as the commissionaire in *The Apollo de Bellac*, and in June as Donald Blake in *The Making of Moo*, the Royal Court. July, *Look Back in Anger*, World Youth Festival in Moscow. 12 August, revival of *Look Back in Anger*, the Royal Court, directed by Tony Richardson, with Richard Pasco as Jimmy. 1 October, New York production of *Look Back in Anger*, Lyceum Theatre, directed by Tony Richardson, with Kenneth Haigh as Jimmy, Mary Ure as Alison, and Alan Bates as Cliff, received the New York Drama Critics Circle Award for the Best Play of 1957. 28 October, revival of *Look Back in Anger*, the Royal Court, directed by John Dexter, with Alec McCowan as Jimmy and Clare Austin as Alison. Marriage to Pamela Lane dissolved. 8 November, married Mary Ure, actress.
1958	11 February, *Epitaph for George Dillon* (written in collaboration with Anthony Creighton), the Royal Court, directed by

William Gaskill, with Robert Stephens as George Dillon, Yvonne Mitchell as Ruth, Alison Leggatt as Mrs. Elliot, Toke Townley as Mr. Elliot. 12 February, New York production of *The Entertainer*, Royale Theatre, directed by Tony Richardson, with Laurence Olivier as Archie Rice. 4 November, New York production of *Epitaph for George Dillon*, John Golden Theatre, directed by William Gaskill, with Robert Stephens as George Dillon, Eileen Herlie as Ruth, Alison Leggatt as Mrs. Elliot, and Frank Finlay as Mr. Elliot. Founded Woodfall Films with Tony Richardson.

1959   14 April, *The World of Paul Slickey*, the Pavilion, Bournemouth, directed by John Osborne, with Dennis Lotis as Jack Oakham, Marie Lohr as Lady Mortlake, and Adrienne Corri as Lesley. 5 May, first London production of *The World of Paul Slickey*, Palace Theatre. Film of *Look Back in Anger*, directed by Tony Richardson, with Richard Burton as Jimmy, Mary Ure as Alison, Claire Bloom as Helena, and Gary Redmond as Cliff.

1960   6 November, *A Subject of Scandal and Concern*, a play for television, transmitted by the BBC, directed by Tony Richardson, with Richard Burton as George Holyoake, Rachel Roberts as Mrs. Holyoake, and George Devine as Mr. Justice Erskine. Film of *The Entertainer*, directed by Tony Richardson, with Laurence Olivier as Archie Rice, Brenda de Banzie as Phoebe, Joan Plowright as Jean, Roger Livesey as Billy. Script by John Osborne and Nigel Kneale.

1961   26 June, *Luther*, the Theatre Royal, Nottingham, directed by Tony Richardson, with Albert Finney as Luther, Bill Owen as Hans, John Moffatt as Cajetan, and Peter Bull as Tetzel. The play was also produced at theatre festivals in Paris, Holland, and Edinburgh and on 27 July, opened at the Royal Court. Member of the Committee of 100, for unilateral nuclear disarmament through civil disobedience; 17 September, Trafalgar Square sit-down, arrested and fined.

1962   19 July, *Plays for England: The Blood of the Bambergs*, the Royal Court, directed by John Dexter, with John Meillon as Russell and Vivian Pickles as Melanie, and *Under Plain Cover*, the Royal Court, directed by Jonathan Miller, with Anton Rodgers as Tim and Ann Beach as Jenny. 13 November, first stage production of *A Subject of Scandal and Concern*, Nottingham Playhouse.

1963   Marriage to Mary Ure dissolved. 24 May, married Penelope Gilliatt, novelist and journalist. 25 September, New York production of *Luther*, St. James's Theatre, directed by Tony Richardson, with Albert Finney as Luther, Kenneth J. Warren as Hans, and Peter Bull as Tetzel, received the New York Drama Critics Circle Award and the "Tony" Award for the Best Play of 1963. Wrote script for *Tom Jones*.

1964   9 September, *Inadmissible Evidence*, the Royal Court, directed by Anthony Page, with Nicol Williamson as Bill Maitland, Arthur Lowe as Hudson, and Sheila Allen as Liz. Received the American Academy Award (the Oscar) for the screenplay of *Tom Jones*, directed by Tony Richardson, with Albert Finney in the title role. October, appeared as Claude Hickett in the revival of *A Cuckoo in the Nest*, the Royal Court.

1965   24 February, daughter Nolan Kate born. May, directed Charles Wood's *Meals on Wheels*, the Royal Court. 30 June, *A Patriot for Me*, the Royal Court, directed by Anthony Page, with Maximilian Schell as Alfred Redl and Jill Bennett as the Countess. New York production of *Inadmissible Evidence*, Belasco Theatre, directed by Anthony Page, with Nicol Williamson as Bill Maitland.

1966   19 January, George Devine died. 7 March, New York production of *A Subject of Scandal and Concern*, New Theatre Workshop. 6 June, *A Bond Honoured* (adapted from Lope De Vega), the National Theatre at the Old Vic, directed by John Dexter, with Robert Stephens as Leonido and Maggie Smith as Marcela.

1968   Marriage to Penelope Gilliatt dissolved. Married Jill Bennett, actress. 23 May, *Time Present*, the Royal Court, directed by Anthony Page, with Jill Bennett as Pamela. 3 July, *The Hotel in Amsterdam*, directed by Anthony Page, the Royal Court, with Paul Scofield as Laurie, Judy Parfitt as Annie, and Isabel Dean as Margaret, Joss Ackland as Gus, David Burke as Dan, and

Susan Engel as Amy. 29 October, revival of *Look Back in Anger*, the Royal Court, directed by Anthony Page, with Victor Henry as Jimmy, Jane Asher as Alison, and Martin Shaw as Cliff. Film of *Inadmissible Evidence*, script by John Osborne, directed by Anthony Page, with Nicol Williamson as Bill Maitland, Peter Sallis as Hudson, Jill Bennett as Liz, and Eileen Atkins as Shirley. Acted in David Mercer's *The Parachute* on BBC TV. Worked on film script of *The Charge of the Light Brigade*, with Charles Wood.

1969 Acted in *The First Night of Pygmalion*, TV production, and as Maidanov in a film of Turgenev's *First Love*. 5 October, New York production of *A Patriot for Me*, Imperial Theatre, directed by Peter Glenville, with Maximilian Schell as Redl and Salome Jens as the Countess.

1970 2 October, *The Right Prospectus*, a play for television, transmitted by BBC-1, directed by Alan Cooke. Acted with Michael Caine in *Get Carter*, a film.

1971 14 March, ITV "Sunday Night Theatre" transmission of *The Hotel in Amsterdam*, with Paul Scofield as Laurie, Jill Bennett as Annie, and Isabel Dean as Margaret. 17 August, *West of Suez*, the Royal Court, directed by Anthony Page, with Ralph Richardson as Wyatt Gillman, Patricia Lawrence as Robin, Jill Bennett as Frederica, Sheila Ballantine as Evangie, Penelope Wilton as Mary, Geoffrey Palmer as Edward, and Nigel Hawthorne as Christopher.

1972 28 June, *Hedda Gabler* (adapted from Henrik Ibsen), the Royal Court, directed by Anthony Page, with Jill Bennett as Hedda, Ronald Hines as Tesman, Denholm Elliott as Brack, Barbara Ferris as Mrs. Elvsted, and Brian Cox as Lovborg. 4 December, *A Sense of Detachment*, the Royal Court, directed by Frank Dunlop, with Rachel Kempson as Older Lady, Nigel Hawthorne as Chairman, and John Standing as Chap.

1973 4 December, revival of *A Patriot for Me*, Watford Palace Theatre, directed by Stephen Hollis, with Michael Byrne as Redl and Marianne Faithful as the Countess. Film of *Luther*, script by

Edward Anhalt, directed by Guy Green, with Stacy Keach as Luther.

1974   11 September, *Jill and Jack*, transmitted by ITV, Yorkshire Television, directed by Mike Newell, with Jill Bennett as Jill and John Standing as Jack. 24 September, *The Gift of Friendship*, transmitted by ITV, Yorkshire Television, directed by Mike Newell, with Alec Guinness as Jocelyn, Michael Gough as Bill, and Sarah Badel as Madge. 28 November, revival of *The Entertainer*, Greenwich Theatre, directed by John Osborne, with Max Wall as Archie Rice, Constance Chapman as Phoebe, Angela Pleasence as Jean, and Kenneth Cranham as Frank.

1975   16 January, *The End of Me Old Cigar*, Greenwich Theatre, directed by Max Stafford-Clark, with Rachel Roberts as Lady Regine Frimley, Jill Bennett as Isobel Sands, and Keith Barron as Leonard Grimthorpe. 13 February, *The Picture of Dorian Gray*, Greenwich Theatre, directed by Clive Donner, with Michael Kitchen as Dorian Gray, Anton Rodgers as Lord Henry Wotton, and John McEnery as Basil. Death of former wife, Mary Ure.

1976   19 September, *The Picture of Dorian Gray*, transmitted by BBC-1, "Play of the Month," directed by Clive Donner, with Michael Kitchen as Dorian Gray, Anton Roberts as Lord Henry Wotton, and John McEnery as Basil. 24 February, *Watch It Come Down*, the Old Vic, directed by Bill Bryden, with Jill Bennett as Sally, Frank Finlay as Ben, Michael Feast as Raymond, Michael Gough as Glen, and Susan Fleetwood as Jo, transferred to the Lyttleton, the National Theatre, 20 March. 1 September, *Almost A Vision*, transmitted by ITV, Yorkshire Television, "Wednesday Special," with Jill Bennett and Keith Barron.

1977   Marriage to Jill Bennett dissolved. Acted in *Lady Charlotte*, TV production. 28 July, inaugural meeting of the British Playwrights' Mafia, included Rodney Ackland, John Arden, Alan Bennett, Robert Bolt, Bill Bryden, Edward Bond, Christopher Hampton, Peter Nichols, Arnold Wesker, and Charles Wood.

1978   Marriage to Helen Dawson, drama critic and journalist. Acted in *Tomorrow Never Comes*, a film. Revival of *Inadmissible Evi-*

dence, the Royal Court, directed by John Osborne, with Nicol Williamson as Bill Maitland, Clive Swift as Hudson, Elizabeth Bell as Liz, and Deborah Norton as Shirley.

1980　20 January, *You're Not Watching Me, Mummy* transmitted by ITV, Yorkshire Television, directed by James Ormerod, with Anna Massey as Jemima, Peter Sallis as Leslie, Gillian Martell as Mrs. Colbourne, and Suzanne Bertish as Lena. 13 February, *Very Like a Whale*, transmitted by ITV, Yorkshire Television, directed by Alan Bridges, with Alan Bates as Sir Jock and Gemma Jones as Lady Mellor. 19 June, New York revival of *Look Back in Anger*, Roundabout Theatre, directed by Ted Craig, with Malcolm McDowell as Jimmy.

1981　23 February, New York revival of *Inadmissible Evidence*, Roundabout Theatre, directed by Anthony Page, with Nicol Williamson as Bill Maitland. 3 March, *Hedda Gabler*, abridged, transmitted by ITV, Yorkshire Television, with Diana Rigg as Hedda, Denis Lill as Tesman, Alan Dobie as Brack, Elizabeth Bell as Mrs. Elvsted, and Philip Bond as Lovborg. 15 March, radio performance of *A Patriot for Me*. *A Better Class of Person*, an autobiography covering 1929–1956, published.

1983　20 January, New York revival of *The Entertainer*, Roundabout Theatre, directed by William Gaskill, with Nicol Williamson as Archie Rice and Frances Cuka as Phoebe. 12 May, revival of *A Patriot for Me*, directed by Ronald Eyre, Chichester Festival Theatre, with Alan Bates as Redl and Sheila Gish as the Countess. Death of mother, Nellie Beatrice Osborne.

1985　6 April, *God Rot Tunbridge Wells* (an account of George Frideric Handel), transmitted by Channel 4, directed by Tony Palmer, with Dave Griffiths as the young Handel and Trevor Howard as the old Handel. 1 July, "An Extract of Autobiography for Television" (*A Better Class of Person*), transmitted by ITV (Thames), directed by Frank Cvitanovich, with Eileen Atkins as Mrs. Osborne and Alan Howard as Mr. Osborne. 13 July, initial "Diary" column in *The Spectator*.

1986　28 May, *The Entertainer*, revival at Shaftsbury Theatre, directed by Robin LeFevre, with Peter Bowles as Archie Rice, Sylvia Syms as Phoebe, and Frank Middlemass as Billy. Moved with his wife, Helen Dawson, to their spacious 1812 home, The Hurst, on thirty acres in Shropshire, overlooking the Clun valley.

1988   *The Father* (adapted from Strindberg), directed by David Levaux, the Cottesloe, the National Theatre, with Alan Armstrong as the Captain.

1989   August, Renaissance Theatre Company revival of *Look Back in Anger*, Lyric Theatre, directed by Judi Dench, with Kenneth Branagh as Jimmy, Emma Thompson as Alison, Gerald Horan as Cliff, Siobhan Redmond as Helena, Edward Jewesbury as Colonel Redfern.

1990   6 October, former wife, Jill Bennett, committed suicide.

1991   *Almost A Gentleman*, an autobiography covering 1955–66, published. November, death of Tony Richardson.

1992   June, *Déjàvu*, Comedy Theatre, directed by Tony Palmer, with Peter Egan as Jimmy Porter, Alison Johnson as Alison, Gareth Thomas as Cliff, Eve Matheson as Helena.

1993   May, death of former wife, Penelope Gilliatt. June, revival of *Inadmissible Evidence*, the National Theatre, directed by Di Trevis, with Trevor Eve as Bill Maitland. Lifetime achievement award by the Writers' Guild of Great Britain.

1994   *Damn You England*, collected prose, published. After suffering from complications of diabetes, died on 24 December, in Shewsbury, of heart failure, with his wife at his bedside. Buried in St. George's Churchyard, Clun, Shropshire, on New Year's Eve.

1995   2 June, memorial service, St. Giles-in-the-Fields, Covent Garden, London, for John James Osborne, Playwright and Actor.

John Osborne

THE HOUSE THAT JIMMY BUILT

Ronald Bryden

The Protagonist of John Osborne's play *Déjàvu*, staged in London in 1992, is a sixtyish Englishman known as J.P. to his children (one girl, one boy) and friends (two, one unseen, deceased offstage in Act III). He lives in a country house with about fifteen rooms somewhere in the Midlands, the counties bordering the River Trent, traditional dividing line between northern and southern England. He appears to live alone, except for a dying dog (deceased offstage in Act I); twice married, he is divorced from both wives. He seems to be wealthy: his cellar is stocked with wines fifteen and twenty-five years old, and he keeps a choice of champagnes (Moët and Dom Perignon) permanently on ice. His clothes, casual but expensive, bear the marks of Jermyn Street, the place to go in London for handmade shoes, silver-backed hairbrushes, and Turnbull and Asher shirts. But the source of his wealth is a puzzle to his village neighbors and to us—our only clue is a fleeting reference to America being "very nice" to him. In some ways he seems to the manor born: he is scornful of the lower middle class and Australians, and clearly is accustomed to shooting and drawing game birds for his table. But at other times he is equally scathing about people who inherit money and privilege, and he displays the light, lordly obscenity that characterized the culture of the British theatre in the age of Noël Coward, Binkie Beaumont, and "the Oliviers." It is the manner, you might say, of a walking gentleman—not the real thing, but its theatrical equivalent.

Whatever he is, he seems to take it for granted he will be the last of his kind. The visiting friend whom he addresses jocosely as "Whittaker," evidently because that is not his name, calls him in the same spirit "Lord Sandy." For someone who grew up in the British Empire in the 1930s, the nickname brings to mind the Korda film of Edgar Wallace's *Sanders of the River*, in which Paul Robeson sonorously sang the praises of Leslie Banks's hardworking, idolized Nigerian district officer—Sandi the wise, Sandi the strong, hater of lies, righter of wrong, and "Lord Sandi" to the paddlers of his African canoe. And indeed, there are moments when J.P. appears to regard himself as the only white, civilized person for hundreds of miles, in the jungle of Britain's postwar immigrations and "junk culture," as he calls it.

The character seems a new departure for Osborne: a novel, arresting synthesis of the snobbish writer in the television play *The Gift of Friendship*, reminiscent of Evelyn Waugh in old age, and the scurrilous, burned-out music hall comedian Archie Rice in *The Entertainer*. But from time to time you feel intimations that you have been here before. Throughout the first act, J.P.'s daughter, whose name is Alison, averts herself stonily behind an ironing board in the kitchen from his attempts to amuse or provoke her. There is talk of a time when J.P. and "Whittaker," whose real name turns out to be Cliff Lewis, ran a sweetstall together in a Midland market town. Later, a friend of Alison's named Helena takes up the sexual gauntlet J.P. throws down before her, and is next discovered in Alison's place, ironing one of J.P.'s shirts. "I feel very Dayzhar Voo," says J.P. gloomily, sprawled beneath a pall of pipe smoke and boredom, Sunday newspapers scattered at his feet.

Yes, he is indeed the Jimmy Porter of *Look Back in Anger*, revisited thirty-five years later. But as he explains to Cliff in his familiar lama-to-pupil manner, the phrase *déjà vu* does not mean seeing again something seen before. On the contrary, it names the sensation of having experienced previously something you cannot have known before and are encountering for the first time. Evidently part of Osborne's intention is to confirm Heraclitus's maxim that you cannot step twice into the same river. The J.P. of *Déjàvu* is a very different person from the twenty-five-year-old Jimmy Porter. "Pusillanimous?" he exclaims at one point, forgetting one of his most memorable tirades in the earlier play. "How do I know what it means? It's not a word I'd ever use." He performs his arabesques of discontented raillery as far out on the anarchic right wing of British politics as Jimmy performed his on the anarchic left of 1956. In spite of his distaste for most things American, you can imagine him approving distantly the party-of-one politics of Ross Perot.

The young Jimmy Porter was enraged by the inequalities of the English class system. The old one is enraged by the inequalities of intelligence that, he seems to consider, make class an inescapable fact of life, foolish to rail against. The young Jimmy lamented the lack of "good, brave causes" to command the altruism of his generation. The old J.P. denounces altruism, especially when packaged with the labels "concern" or "caring," as "busybody's gin." Young Jimmy waged war on religion, while crying out for a world built on hope and charity. J.P. appears to have come to terms with faith—he keeps Cranmer's Prayer Book on his kitchen shelf, and actually flings wide his windows to let in the sound of church bells—but almost as sternly he derides charity: he warns his daughter, single, pregnant, and in obvious need of comfort, not to look to him for hope "that is in no one's gift." If he were more given to self-scrutiny, you might imagine him putting to himself the kind of question Lawrence of Arabia, in Terence Rattigan's play *Ross*, addresses to the persona with which he punishes himself for his celebrity: "Oh Ross, how did I become you?"

How did Jimmy Porter become J.P.? Part of the answer seems to be that, since 1956, his life has come to share more and more circumstances with that of his creator. For example, we learn that his first wife, the original Alison, left him eventually to become an actress. It is hard to imagine the fragile, deeply private young woman who played squirrel to Jimmy's bear having a life beyond the play's final curtain, let alone becoming a star of AIDS galas in the '90s: but it may be easier if you conflate her with the actress Mary Ure, who created the role and became Osborne's second wife, as well as with the other actress, Jill Bennett, who for some years was the fourth Mrs. Osborne. Similarly, J.P.'s description of his second wife, mother of young Alison and Jimmy Junior, reproduces details from Osborne's account in *Almost a Gentleman*, his second volume of autobiography, of life with his third wife, the writer Penelope Gilliatt. Like Ms. Gilliatt, the second Mrs. Porter is said to greet people with an intensity of concern that suggests they have suffered some bereavement, to divide the world into "first-class brains" and the rest, and to make clear to which camp she assigns her husband by calling him "muddle-headed Jimmy." Both ladies are described making sure of their places in the first category by discussing the morphology of Croatian verb endings with junior diplomats.

The rudest of the little songs with which J.P. tries to provoke or amuse his daughter is one that Osborne has recalled Laurence Olivier singing to cheer him after the chilly New York first night of *The Entertainer*. Most surprisingly of all, Jimmy's friend Hugh Tanner, who took off for China or beyond in quest of the Just Society shortly before the wet Sunday that opens *Look Back in Anger*, turns up in *Déjàvu* directing films in Hollywood. "A subject of interminable speculation and bafflement," reports Cliff. "He's very gifted, but no one is quite sure what the gift might be . . . the producer of fairly spectacular flops, he's a kind of fireball of intelligent tastelessness." The description fits the later years of Tony Richardson, director of Osborne's first three plays and the film *Tom Jones*, which made both their fortunes. To make sure that no reader of *Almost a Gentleman* misses their resemblance, Hugh is imagined speaking the mantra with which, according to

Osborne, Richardson used to greet all setbacks, disappointments, or triumphs of philistinism: "What did you *expect*?"

This is not to say that J.P. has been made into a self-portrait of the artist as an old malcontent. He is a dramatic creation, presented in the round: it is Osborne who makes us understand that not all J.P.'s pronouncements should be taken seriously, that he's someone who habitually climbs out on the frailest limbs of the unreasonable in order to discover who really loves him. Like Mark Twain, he regards a true friend as someone who will stand up for you when you are in the wrong— almost anyone will stand up for you when you are in the right. It is Osborne, too, who makes us see this as the cause of J.P.'s isolation: he has carried this strategy so far that he has alienated everyone he cares for most, with the exception of the loyal Cliff. But at the same time, it is clear that the playwright is playing demure theatrical games, hinting that J.P.'s reality is only that of a character in a play—a short-lived stage career and three decades of critical comment and speculation about his character, motives, and sexuality. "J. Porter, Esquire?" says Alison viciously at one point. "He doesn't exist. For any of us." "Perhaps he never did," replies Cliff, to which Alison, recognizably her father's child, rightly rejoins, "Don't be so bloody precious!"

Presumably the fleeting correspondences between J.P.'s past offstage life and Osborne's autobiographies are there to define their relationship and furnish audiences with a key to J.P.'s nature and function. Clearly he is to some extent a mouthpiece for his creator—it is easy to imagine his diatribes against postal codes, ballet, trendy churchmen, anti-smokers, European Union, and people who use the words "lifestyle" and "meaningful," as letters of the kind Osborne sometimes writes to the editors of the *Times* and London's other "posh papers," as Jimmy Porter first named them. At the same time, however, we are obviously meant to recognize them as letters that never got sent, that J.P. has turned instead into hearth rug party pieces, domestic vaudeville, topical comic monologues of a kind to make you wonder whether in his early life he was not only Jimmy Porter but also Archie Rice. Not a portrait of the artist, then, but a peculiarly complex emanation of him—a household clown who is allowed to make intimate family jokes, like Lear's Fool. Still, though one cannot identify dramatist and creation, it seems fair to subsume the question of how Jimmy Porter became J.P. within the larger one: how did the Osborne of *Look Back in Anger* become the Osborne of *Déjàvu*?

The usual cliché of Osborne criticism (Osborne mocks it scathingly in *Almost a Gentleman*) is to say that success turned the angry young revolutionary of 1956 into an irascible Tory squire by the end of the '60s. To say that is to misread not only Osborne but the social revolution Britain passed through in the postwar years and the special ways in which Jimmy Porter was an expression of it. The changes legislated by Britain's postwar Labour government were of three kinds, only one of which was of interest to Jimmy. There were the measures to establish the Welfare State—national health service, unemployment insurance, and national pension plan. There were the nationalizations of major industries—coal, steel, and railways—to build the infrastructure for a socialist state. And finally, of most importance to people who saw socialist politics and economics simply as instruments for bringing about social equality, there were the measures that implemented the Education Act of 1944, Labour's price for participating in Churchill's wartime coalition. These for the first time winnowed the brightest children from the public primary school system and channeled them by means of scholarships, at the age of eleven or thereabouts, into the grammar schools, hitherto inaccessible because of their fees, which prepared pupils for entrance to the older universities. For the first time it became possible in Britain, as in France, for the brilliant child of poor, working-class parents to gain an education that fitted him or her to compete with the products of the great private schools—Eton, Harrow, Winchester, Roedean—for places at Oxford and Cambridge. From these nurseries, historically, came Britain's ruling class—cabinet ministers, senior civil servants, leading capitalists, intellectuals, and makers of opinion. Now at last the doors stood open for a new aristocracy, based not on land or wealth but on intelligence, to find careers—the best in the country—suited to their talents.

Jimmy Porter dismisses the socialist rebuilding of postwar Britain as "the Brave-new-nothing-very-much-thank you." One can easily imagine him speaking the line, jotted for possible use in Osborne's 1954 notebook among many that found their way into the play, "The Welfare State: everyone moping about having to bear the burden of everyone else." He has nothing to say about nationalization. His interest and his bitterness are focused on the relation, or lack of it, between education, intellect, and power in British public life. He would rather sell candy than put the education he acquired in his "white tile" university at the service of advertising or journalism of the kind he has tried his hand at. Meanwhile, he has to watch his brother-in-law Nigel, "the chinless wonder from Sandhurst," drift effortlessly toward a political career that will probably lead to a seat in a Tory Cabinet. (In the event, we learn in *Déjàvu*, Nigel winds up with a seat in the European Parliament.) But while he goads his friend Cliff to better himself by reading more, he attacks his wife for looking down on Hugh Tanner's mother because she is ignorant. His attitude to education and what's happening to it in Britain in the 1950s is wary and ambivalent. Like Stendhal's heroes, he resents the society that has brought his talents to flower but plants them in a sunless garden. But at the same time, he mistrusts any career that might enroll him in the service of that society as it stands. He would rather pretend to plan a future with Cliff in the moribund British music hall than take any of the paths open to working-class university graduates that might lead to actual power in the state.

Not all of this can be blamed on Jimmy's tangled pride, diffidence, and perversity. Other people in Britain in the 1950s were looking doubtfully at the 1944 Education Act and the new society was beginning to shape. The best guide to the subject is sociologist Michael Young, who gave a name to the emerging ruling elite, and two faces, in his brilliant social-science fiction *The Rise of the Meritocracy*, published in 1958. This Swiftian fable begins as a utopia but ends by revealing Utopia to be a dystopia. It pretends to take the form of a background paper written in the '20s and '30s by a Whitehall mandarin for his political master, recalling the history of education policy and its consequences in Britain since 1944. The creation of a meritocracy, a governing elite of the best minds in the most important positions in public life, at first seems the birth of a new Golden Age for Britain. No longer is masterful intelligence or talent wasted in class warfare, no longer are the most vital political and economic decisions reserved for eldest sons whose only training was in the hunting field or playing fields of Eton. Politics became rational, industry and trade boom. But slowly the disadvantages of the new aristocracy-by-examination begin to appear. Compared with the old aristocracies of land and money, meritocracy is dangerously rigid. When all the highest IQs have been promoted to the top of society, what is to become of the others and their children? The intellectually disadvantaged must sink to the bottom, condemned with the inheritors of their genes to perpetual servitude as worker bees in a hive whose honey is all reserved for the best brains. Hence, the mandarin suggests as his historical survey nears its end, the recent rumblings of a new kind of revolution—the uprising of the dunces from the back of the class against the prize-winning swots who monopolize the front row. There have been riots in the streets, one is mustering in Trafalgar Square to march down Whitehall as the mandarin writes. It is drawing nearer . . . The writing ends abruptly, as blood drowns the page.

Young suggested another drawback to the meritocratic principle. It makes for a peculiarly nervous, unpleasantly competitive society. The landed aristocrat can feel safe in the knowledge that his family have held their estates for centuries. The plutocrat knows that this wealth is secure so long as he invests it judiciously. The meritocrat's only fortune is his brain: he lives, literally, by his wits. He has to fear not only the decay of his mind as age approaches but also the advance up the meritocratic greasy pole of every new child prodigy fresh out of Oxbridge. This can lead to a nastily combative style of social intercourse, in which meritocrats compete in displaying their culture and education as aristocrats once competed with elaborate wigs and tailoring, and plutocrats with the size of their carriages and the numbers of their footmen. Young had no need to develop this danger of meritocracy in detail. It had already been seized on wittily by the *Punch* humourist Stephen Potter in his books *Gamesmanship* and *Lifemanship*, with their sample tournaments of cultural ostentation—lessons in how to put yourself "one up" in any conversation about travel, art, literature, music, or philosophy.

Rereading *The Rise of the Meritocracy* thirty-six years later, it seems uncannily prophetic. Its main miscalculation was in supposing it might take sixty or seventy years for the backlash against meritocracy to manifest itself. One could argue that it took only the half-dozen years between the writing of the book and the rise of the Beatles in the early 1960s, demonstrating that there were paths to wealth and world fame that bypassed entirely the meritocratic ladder of homework, scholarships, grammar school, and university. In the same time span, the brilliant flowering of what seemed a Golden Age of talents risen from classes where talent had never been sought out before, particularly in the British theatre, turned into one of darkly sardonic comedy, almost Jacobean in its venom and disillusion, tilting at the society meritocracy had built. There are whole scenes by Harold Pinter and Joe Orton that might be sample dialogues of cultural warfare from the pages of Stephen Potter's *Lifemanship*. Meritocracy and its problems—the distance it sets between scholarship children and their working-class parents, between meritocratic husbands and the wives they married in their provincial youth, between meritocratic parents and the children who have never known any life before affluence—is the major, overwhelmingly rich subject matter of the postwar British theatre. In ways that have been insufficiently analyzed, I think, it is one of the major topics of John Osborne's drama. The principal obstacle to its analysis has been his ambivalence on the subject. He veers back and forth, now for, now against meritocracy, often in the same play.

In his zigzagging, Osborne is simply doing what he has always done best: reflecting the dividing mind and will of his country and generation. Without Michael Young's guide to the Britain of meritocracy, it would be hard to know whether to call Jimmy Porter meritocracy's first protagonist or antagonist. With Young's help, one can see that he is both. Obviously, Jimmy's is one of the first of the outstanding brains selected and advanced by the new Education Act. But once educated, his upward progress is checked by meritocrats of another kind—the intellectual aristocrats of the old class system. Instead of making room for him at the top, these old-style mandarins make it clear that no doors will open to him until he has turned himself into a docile replica of themselves: snobbish, allusive, tennis-playing, perpetually concerned to guard their shrines against any hint of the vulgar. To champion the new meritocracy, Jimmy has to fight a cultural war amazingly similar to those that now divide the campuses of the West—to redefine the syllabus that constitutes the minimum equipment of "an educated person." When he rails against the French phrases that pepper the Sunday arts pages, the scarcity of English classical music on the radio, he is demanding a meritocratic curriculum open to every English speaker, which awards no extra points for attending Swiss finishing schools or French crammers, or for taking the Grand Tour.

In this he sounds like a disciple, like so many of his contemporaries at British provincial universities, of the embattled Cambridge critic F.R. Leavis. At the heart of Leavis's aesthetic lay a Wordsworthian belief that the roots of morality intertwine with those of language. The Good Englishman, his criticism assumed, is the product of plain English living, preferably in a provincial home, furnished with the classics of plain English speech—Bunyan, Defoe, George Eliot, D.H. Lawrence. Alison's description of Jimmy Porter's first irruption into her life, with bicycle oil on his dinner jacket (presumably bought for his jazz gigs) and the glow of a day in the sun still in his hair, skin, and eyes, is reminiscent of Connie Chatterley's various epiphanies of her gamekeeper Mellors. Lawrence, in Leavis's critical pantheon, is the last of the great English novelists, a line whose role in history he treats as comparable with that of the prophets of the Old Testament Israel. This may account for the extent to which Jimmy sees himself as a prophet dishonoured in his own country for preaching the Laurentian virtues of honest feeling, classlessness, and unashamed sexuality. The fact that at the end of the play he has achieved only one disciple and one weeping convert feeds his sense of being a warrior in the long battle for a regenerated British culture.

On its surface, *The Entertainer* seems even more confused than *Look Back in Anger* in the stances it adopts toward meritocracy. Studied closely, however, it reveals the same complex but coherent pattern of attitudes, stated with somewhat greater exaggeration. Archie Rice, we learn, has turned his back on his private schooling as a gentleman to pursue at a defiantly shabby distance his father's career as a music hall entertainer. Such hope as he still allows himself he invests in his daughter Jean, a spirited young meritocrat of the postwar school system, determined to overthrow the old men responsible for Britain's humiliation at Suez. But insofar as he has an agenda of his own, it is even more radical than Jimmy Porter's. He would replace the curriculum of Britain's discredited educated classes with a culture even more down to earth than that of Bunyan, Wordsworth, and Lawrence. If he were given the task of rebuilding Jerusalem in England's green and pleasant land, his foundation for it would be the memory of the Edwardian music hall.

The idea was not so farfetched in its '50s context as it may seem now. During the summer of 1956, while gestating *The Entertainer*, Osborne may well have listened to a series of BBC radio programs of music from the halls titled "The Boy in the Gallery," after the Marie Lloyd song that Phoebe Rice sings with sad sweetness in the play's central scene. Produced by Charles Chilton, who later devised a sequel to it in Joan Littlewood's macabre Great War concert party *Oh, What a Lovely War!*, the series was mostly written by the novelist Colin MacInnes, who subsequently expanded his commentary into a book called *Sweet Saturday Night*. The thesis of the book and programs was that the music hall, its songs and jokes, expressed a whole urban working-class culture, the only authentic one Britain has known, with its own indigenous attitudes to marriage, sex, leisure, money, mothers-in-law, politics, and the Empire, rooted in working life and owing no debt to the working man's masters. In the early postwar years, it had become fashionable for British intellectuals, particularly those of the Left, to argue that American jazz was as essential a part of the educated person's culture as Mozart or Brahms had been to earlier generations. Jimmy Porter's enthusiasm for it was one he shared with Philip Larkin, Kingsley Amis, and the historian Eric Hobsbawm, whose jazz columns he presumably read in the *New Statesman*. After 1956, and even more after *Oh, What a Lovely War!*, many British intellectuals would have argued a similar necessity to include the songs of the music halls, and their successors and parodies in the Flanders trenches, in the official culture of the British people. By the time Richard Attenborough filmed *Oh, What a Lovely War!* in 1970, he was able to cast it with most of the knights and dames of the British theatre and to invest Joan Littlewood's savage political cabaret with all the national solemnity of a royal funeral or Armistice Day parade. The fight to install the music hall in the history of British culture needs to be seen as part of the postwar upheaval in the writing of British history, led by Christopher Hill, E.P. Thompson, and Hobsbawm in the steps of the French school of Annalistes. Its object was to rewrite the history of Britain from the point of view of its common folk, the "people of England" in Chesterton's poem "who have not spoken yet." Archie Rice's lament for the halls his father played was Osborne's contribution to the new historiography and its efforts to redefine the syllabus of the "educated person" in Britain's new meritocracy.

But by the time Osborne wrote *Inadmissible Evidence* in 1964, meritocracy had taken on a new meaning in the British mind. Bill Maitland, the foundering lawyer whose implosion on himself is the action of the play, mocks sneeringly at the rhetoric of Harold Wilson, recently installed as Labour prime minister, promising the salvation of Britain by crack commandos of scientists, technologists, and administrative wizards. Bill lumps these new age meritocrats along with such phenomena as minicars, television dons, property developers, and the inventors of Swinging London, as bread-and-circus diversions from the real sickness of Britain: the loss of the nation's sense of itself and its place in the world. What Bill wants is what he sees Britain needing: to be whole, to be certain, to be able to cope with reality, to be himself again as he remembers being when young. Maitland embodies his country's sense of loss and impotence, of being the outcast inheritor of a shrunken estate, robbed of great expectations. The only help meritocracy could give him in his predicament would be the comprehension of a great artistic intelligence: a talent large enough to understand him and portray him to himself. That, of course, is what Osborne does in the play, never likely to be his most popular but arguably his best. But the dramatist has no representative within the play to bring comfort to his contemporary Everyman, forsaken by Knowledge, Wit, Discretion, Beauty, Fellowship, and the rest.

It is understandable why after *Inadmissible Evidence* Osborne's attention to the meritocratic idea shrinks to depictions of the new class within the arts. In *Time Present* (1968), the actress Pamela Orme moves in with her friend Constance, a member of Parliament soon expected to be offered a seat in the Cabinet. Constance is all affection and kindness to Pamela, but Pamela clearly finds her friend fretting in some way to her nerves. Her political intelligence, her shelves of blue books, have led her to a language of social-science generalizations and approximations irksome to someone whose profession is to handle words with knife-edge precision. "Like so many people, you don't understand the content of tone of voice," Pamela complains. "You're like an American, you have no ear." Because of her fuzzy use of language, Pamela finds Constance sentimental, insufficiently discriminating, dishonest with herself—long before Constance knows it herself, Pamela is aware that her friend's feelings for her are more than those of a friend or hostess. Constance is a meritocrat's meritocrat, a fine brain in exactly the right job for it. But beside her, Pamela is seen as the practitioner of a higher calling: one of the few who can make language an instrument for distilling truth.

Increasingly, an Orwellian perception of the science of words underlying politics, social justice, and all the other arts of living becomes central to Osborne's later plays. The climax of *The Hotel in Amsterdam*, written as a companion "Play for the Mean Time" to *Time Present* in 1968, is a declaration of love by a film writer to his best friend's wife. He declares it by proffering to her, as carefully and slowly as emeralds from a jeweler's tray, ten adjectives that he says describe her for him. The fact that his selection includes a couple of embarrassing duds, revealing both him and Osborne as something less than the imperial wordsmiths of Yeats's Byzantium that the moment hopes for, does not alter its dramatic statement. It gathers all the play's implied values into a demonstration that love and truth are the hardest, most precious, and important of human activities, and inseparable. The only meritocrat who matters is the master of language.

This conclusion, worked out gradually in Osborne's plays of the 1960s, moves front and centre in his two major plays of the '70s, *West of Suez* (1971) and *Watch It Come Down* (1975). It may account for their exaggerated, almost paranoid dramatization of the danger to civilization contained in the backlash against meritocracy. The educated characters in these plays—uneven and clunky trays of emeralds in both cases, but represented as of unquestionable value—are seen as beleaguered garrisons of late Romans, guarding the last flickering lamps of humanism against encircling hordes of uncomprehending but jealous barbarians. In *West of Suez*, they are the family of a self-concealing old English novelist, Wyatt Gillman, who combines traits of Robert Graves, J.B. Priestley, and Somerset Maugham, holidaying at the Caribbean villa of one of Gillman's daughters. In an unwary interview with an island journalist, Gillman is stung into saying pejorative things about the islanders and the decline of public order among them since they became independent, which bring violent reprisal. An American radical who has been preaching revolution on the island arrives as its herald.

> Believe me, babies, old failing babies, words, yes I mean words, even what I'm saying to you now, is going to be the first to go . . . Do you understand one word, those old words you love so much, what I mean? No. And you won't. If it ain't written down, you don't believe it . . . There's only one word left and you know what it is. It's fuck, man. Fuck . . . That's the last of the English for you babies.

Armed islanders step out of the darkness and shoot Gillman down. "My God," says one of his sons-in-law, "they've shot the fox." He seems to mean not only that they've done the unspeakable, in hunting society terms, but that they've killed their own quarry and pacemaker. With Reynard gone, there will be no one to lead the field.

In *Watch It Come Down*, the barbarians are now within the gates, carrying fire and the sword, like the Danes of the Dark Ages, through the English countryside. A group of meritocratic bohemians—a film director, his wife, a writer, a painter, and assorted lovers and hangers-on—share a disused railway station as a country hideaway. At the end of the play, with no preparation to speak of, rural hooligans surround the station and shoot it up, breaking its windows and apparently killing the director. The only implied explanation is that the bohemians have made themselves unpopular by their alien wealth and city behaviour—by comporting themselves, in the villagers' view, as if they held themselves superior but behaving much worse. By withholding any more circumstantial motivation, Osborne makes their enmity primal—the barbarian's hatred of the civilized, the brute's detestation of brains. The nightmare of Michael Young's mandarin in *The Rise of the Meritocracy* has arrived. The dunces have risen in rebellion against the swots.

Is Osborne to be classed with the mandarin's blind masters, then, who could see no flaw or built-in dangers in the meritocratic system? Only up to a point, surely. It is important to recall once more that meritocracy never had anything to do with equality. It simply proposed a redistribution of society's rewards in such a way as to recruit a new kind of elite based on a new set of values. Jimmy Porter's pirate raids into the semi-stately homes of Alison's acquaintances indicate that it is not the incumbent ruling class's prerequisites that he disapproves of, only the people currently in receipt of them. But to equate Jimmy's creator with the masters of Michael Young's imaginary mandarin is to overlook the extent to which his discussion of meritocracy focusses on redefining the old syllabus of British education. If Osborne has a utopia, it is the one sketched in his entertainment *A Sense of Detachment*, a dramatic occasion that comes close to what the nineteenth century called an "At Home," in the course of which actors tell jokes, sing music hall songs, talk dirty, and read favourite examples of cavalier love poetry and erotica. It is as if the Earl of Rochester had taken over the bar parlour of the old Bull and Bush for an evening with friends. *A Sense of Detachment* appeared in London a year or so after Kenneth Tynan's revue *Oh, Calcutta!* and was clearly in some sense a rejoinder to it. It baffled and repelled audiences, while *Oh, Calcutta!* packed them in. But in many ways it was the warmer and more audience-friendly of the two shows, with a wider, more generous sense of the kind of audience the master of the evening wished to attract. Tynan aimed at the class not yet identified as "yuppies." Osborne was clearly aiming at rakes of all classes.

But in any case, before taking the endings of *West of Suez* and *Watch It Come Down* literally as Osborne's declaration of allegiance on the side of meritocracy in its war with the rest of the world, one needs to consider the extent to which both scenes are coloured with the dyes of Osborne's insufficiently recognized gift for phantasmagoria. The role that phantasmagoria plays in *Inadmissible Evidence*, of course, is too central to have been overlooked: almost all of Bill Maitland's contacts with reality appear to him as nightmarish figments of his own fears and guilt. But few critics have paid attention to the way in which the collision of private worlds with public ones in Osborne's work call up an element of distortion and fantasy in his writing, as if the private truth of the individual—Archie Rice, Luther, Maitland, Alfred Redl, Coriolanus, Dorian Grey—were being confronted by a phantom realm of clichés, impostures, abstractions, masks, and Kafkaesque functions: a world of lies, to which the Devil is father.

The confrontation of the meritocrats in *West of Suez* and *Watch It Come Down* with phantasmagorias of hostile barbarism brings together overtly the two main themes in Osborne's writing. But from the beginning it is implicit in his depictions of the new meritocratic class that their main purpose must be the dismantling of the phantom empire of falsehood that in his view Britain has become. Deeper than all the other grounds of Jimmy Porter's anger with his country and countrymen is his sense of having been lied to, of having been fobbed off with an inauthentic inheritance. It seems unlikely that criticism will ever be able to disentangle Osborne's quality as a dramatist entirely from his role as pacemaker and leader of the field in the long, slow revolution in the British people's national consciousness in the years after the Second World War.

Obviously, in talking of a whole nation's mindset altering, one is on dangerously general ground. For that reason, historians prefer to consider major historical changes in the light of altering technologies, economies, or military preparedness. And yet it is obvious that the most momentous historical changes of our century have been the simple results of great masses of people changing their minds, exchanging one system of beliefs for another, in Russia, in China, in Germany in the 1930s, in the United States during the Vietnam War. Because there is no generalization one can make confidently about the beliefs of all British people at any time in the past half-century, the British themselves have been chary of talking in such sweeping terms about their own postwar transition— chary, indeed, of talking about national belief as if it could be compared to religious faith. Yet it is perfectly obvious that the principal conviction shared by Osborne and the British playwrights who followed him was that Britain's sense of itself had become a monstrous self-deception, and that their main task as artists and meritocrats was to redefine the nation's articles of belief. Equally obviously, it is impossible to talk about their works without discussing them as calculated excursions in national blasphemy.

It is probably impossible for anyone who did not live through the 1950s in Britain to conceive how sacrosanct the memories of Britain's recent history were then. To question Britain's place in the world, the virtues of the royal family, the heroism of Winston Churchill, Britain's Finest Hour and the Few who saved her during it, was tantamount to treason. I can still remember the shock with which I read a 1958 novel, John Rae's *The Custard Boys*, which dared to suggest that a home front life of wartime propaganda and legends of commando exploits was a brutalizing rather than an ennobling experience for British children, raising a generation ready to welcome James Bond. As late as 1961, the clever young meritocrats who devised *Beyond the Fringe* found themselves compelled to assure the press that their sketch "Aftermyth of War," in which an RAF pilot is told to get lost over Germany ("We need a meaningless sacrifice at this point. It will raise the whole tone of the war.") was directed at the braggadocio of Arthur Rank's war films, not at the RAF. Probably the most vivid record of the period's hypersensitivity is the extraordinary list of censorship cuts demanded by postwar Lords Chamberlain in plays offered by the English Stage Company at the Royal Court Theatre. Possibly because the most imposing statements of Britain's continuing greatness and splendour were made by the public theatre of royal occasions, the theatre was the first of the arts to reflect how much of Britain's postwar projection of itself was histrionic and artificial in its nature.

Osborne captained that enterprise. The uproar provoked by *Look Back in Anger*, incomprehensible today, was about its breaking, for the first time on the British stage, most of these loyal British taboos. In his first volume of autobiography, *A Better Class of Person*, Osborne makes it clear that, even before the war ended, he had begun to feel trapped in a world of inauthenticity: of imitations, hand-me-downs, tinny ersatz replicas of the things he had been told made Britain great. The newspapers favoured by his family, he mentions, were the *Daily Express* and *Daily Mail*, populist Tory journals that had grown rich selling the imperial adventure. In its decline, they marketed denial, trumpeting that all continued well with throne and empire with a brassy assertion whose overstatement rang hollow. Osborne went to a private boarding school, paid for by his father's Benevolent Society, which in his description is an Evelyn Waugh parody of Eton or Harrow. In the provincial repertory theatres that were his universities, he performed replicas of West End hits for audiences seeking a surrogate for life, interspersed with simulacra of love affairs in lodging-house imitations of home comfort, mostly reproduction furniture and pinchbeck ornaments. *Look Back in Anger* was his cry for something authentic to care for in an England of pretense and shams, a phantasmagoria of falsehoods denying the loss of an England that had once been true. J.P. sees things in *Déjàvu* more clearly than his younger self. "Anger is not *about* . . . It is mourning the unknown, the loss of what went before you . . . the deprivation of what, even as a child, seemed to be irrevocably your own, your country, your birthplace . . ."

Obviously *Look Back in Anger* could not have created the sensation it did without some answering feeling in its audience with which it struck a chord. Of course there had been literary works implying a resemblance between postwar Britain and the garden run to seed where Richard II's queen, in Shakespeare's play, overhears the royal gardeners lamenting the state of the kingdom. But most of these had implied their blasphemous thought delicately, through the medium of symbolism, in the form of fiction. Students of the British novel in the decade or so after 1945 will notice a rise in the number of stately or modestly upper-class homes falling to decay because of some guilty secret or family skeleton hidden in the cupboard. In *Brideshead Revisited* it is Lord Marchmain's falling away from the family's old faith that has darkened the sanctuary lamp in the chapel. In Angus Wilson's *Anglo-Saxon Attitudes* it is an archaeological fraud that brings down the house of the Portways, Melpham Hall. In L.P. Hartley's *The Go-Between* it is the secret of a pre-1914 affair between the daughter of the house and a tenant farmer. In Elizabeth Bowen's *The Heat of the Day* it is the treasonous spying for the Germans of Robert Kelway. But in all of them the dominant impression left is of a noble facade beginning to betray by signs of neglect and dilapidation a decay from within whose root is falsehood or moral failure. Tacitly, critics avoided calling them novels about the state of England, but all their readers recognized that this was what they were.

Osborne's early plays take over the symbol of a crumbling edifice or facade, with much more overt meanings. In *The Entertainer*, Archie Rice warns the audience sardonically not to clap too hard, "we're all in a very old building." In *Luther*, we are made aware in the climactic scene at the Diet of Worms that the theatre's roof has become that of the great hall where Luther defends his theses before Emperor Charles V, and by extension the tottering roof of Christendom itself. In *A Patriot for Me*, constant references remind us of the offstage presence of the Hofburg, black anthill of the

Hapsburgs and their bureaucracy, representing the empire that Alfred Redl will help to bring down. Even in *Look Back in Anger*, sufficient weight is given in the dialogue to Alison's home and family that it is easy to imagine an alternative version of the play set *chez* Redfern, with Jimmy the freebooter invading a slumberous palace of Benares brasses and cashmere shawls to wake and carry off its sleeping princess. Like those in the novels referred to, Osborne's overarching edifices are treated as derelict, ripe for demolition, because too far gone in lies and fantasy to be regenerated. In all four, analogies between the buildings, the empires they represent emblematically, and contemporary Britain are ready to hand.

Having made this observation, it is interesting to notice that in Osborne's next five "condition of England" plays, large buildings and places people could call home are conspicuous by their absence. Bill Maitland in *Inadmissible Evidence* sleeps in his office rather than go home to his wife or to his mistress's flat. Both places, it seems, are such morasses of falsehood and bad faith in his mind that only by walling himself away in his office, alone with the army of his guilts and fears, can he still feel some hold on reality. Pamela in *Time Present* moves in with Constance to avoid staying in her own apartment, where a long-standing affair has wound down to its end. Truth obviously suffered too many wounds there for it to feel like a real home. When she leaves Constance, she moves in temporarily with her gay agent, who is helping her find an abortionist. He knows the truth about her, Constance will never face it, and clearly there is no true home for her anywhere since the death of her father, the old matinee idol who taught her his actor's code of vagrant honour.

The six friends who fly to Holland for a weekend in *The Hotel in Amsterdam* do so to escape the film producer they all work for. (Vanessa Redgrave has described him as a malicious portrait of Tony Richardson.) Their object is to be themselves, without effort or pretense, something apparently impossible at home where he can reach them day or night by telephone. For the writer Laurie, there is also the hidden objective of confessing his love to Annie, wife of his friend Gus. Away from home, in a holiday from their real lives, he seems to feel, there is less bad faith and deceit in his confession than there would be in London. Home is where the truth cannot be told, which is why he needed to get away from it.

Wyatt Gillman and his daughters in *West of Suez* gather in a holiday house in the Caribbean because there is no longer—has not been since their childhood—anything they could call a family home. Their memory of home is a litany of objects their grandfather, a colonial administrator, kept in his study wherever he was stationed: joss sticks, saddle oil, Burmese guns, an

Urdu handbook, brass iguanas, dried python skins, and yellow photographs of polo teams, tennis parties, garrison clubs, and amateur theatricals in Indian hill stations. Reciting the list, they clearly speak from deep within their true selves—these were the furnishings of their true lives. By implication, everything they have known since then has been less true, the compromises imposed by exile. Home, it seems, is only home when it is where truth is spoken. For the Gillmans, truth lies in the past, lost with the Empire. Which may be why Wyatt, suddenly and rashly, tells the local journalist what he really thinks about her island and fellow islanders. He was once a real writer. Truth was once his business.

The same sense of homelessness hangs over the characters in *Watch It Come Down*. Sam Prosser, a film director, has bought a disused railway station because it is the sort of thing Sunday supplements have recommended as chic to meritocrats with no roots of their own in the countryside. He gathers there the people he cares for most: his wife, an old homosexual writer named Glen, and Jo, the young woman who looks after Glen as Carrington looked after the dying Lytton Strachey. But from the first scene it is clear that no one is at home here. The place is only a way station on their various journeys toward death—for Glen the last, like the station where Tolstoy died. Their community is built on a falsehood, Ben's marriage to Sally, gone violently sour. To help her decide whether to leave, Sally spreads the rumor that they mean to separate, in order to see how the others react. Some truths get spoken, but too late to save either marriage or community from the phantasmagoric Britain surrounding them, whose wild imaginings bring down their way station around them as if it had tried to be a tiny empire of truthfulness. Reread today, the play seems a disjointed prophecy of the coming age of Thatcherism, in which the phantom of the old Empire would be reassembled, tied on its horse and whipped into battle like the dead Cid. No meritocratic attempts to found livable utopias in opposition to it would be tolerated.

After this survey of the housing arrangements in Osborne's major plays, those in *Déjàvu* appear in a somewhat different light. It is impossible not to take pleasure in the fact that J.P. has found a roof to put over his head, even if there is fifteen times as much of it as one man needs. And while he rewards himself somewhat disproportionately for his career as a meritocrat, it is obvious that he has been more punished than rewarded by his countrymen. On the whole, he can claim that he has made a home, a place where truth is spoken, even if his truths have driven away the children he evidently made it for. Like the young Jimmy, of course, he fantasizes extravagantly, but one can see that these fantasies are the forces he musters to meet the phantasmagoric world of lies, pomps, pretensions, and vanities that billows against his door. He makes clear enough that he and Cliff recognize the most important truth distilled by a writer in English in 1956, and have made it their own. Like Vladimir and Estragon in *Waiting for Godot*, they bicker, joke, make up, complain of sore feet, but wait patiently and with some courage for the phantasmagoria of life to pass on to its end.

Beyond Anger

Osborne's Wrestle with Language and Meaning

David Galef

When a character in an Osborne play tries to communicate to the audience that he cannot communicate—and this happens fairly regularly—it is generally assumed that he is on the wrong side of the cultural divide. The British Mass Education Act of 1944 produced an entire generation of graduates too educated for the working classes, yet not aristocratic enough for the upper crust: the Jimmy Porters, Jim Dixons, and Charles Lumleys of this era. But as Angela Hague has pointed out in "The Angry Young Novel" (209), not every voice from that era fits the stereotype, and many of the concerns are more philosophical and further-reaching. If T.S. Eliot in the 1940s complained of "the intolerable wrestle / With words and meanings," the generation of British writers in the '50s felt the dislocation even more keenly. As Osborne describes himself circa 1948 in his autobiography: "Existentialism was the macro-biotic food of the day and Mickey Wall and I were 'into' the impenetrable brown rice of Heidegger, Kierkegaard, Jaspers and, of course, Sartre" (171). Wittgenstein and Beckett were also publishing some of their most important work, taking the categories of semantics and epistemology and dismantling them beyond recovery. Rebellion against language was part of the *Zeitgeist*.

The arc of Wittgenstein's own career suggests a rebellious turn. Having taken the limits of language as far as they would go in the *Tractatus*, he ended on a note of silence and began to regroup in what would eventually result in his *Philosophical Investigations*. In the *Tractatus*, he states, "*The limits of my language* mean the limit of my world" (149). But as Allen Thiher has noted in his work on Beckett and Wittgenstein, "Much of modern language theory is concerned with setting the bounds of the sayable," while many postmodern writers such as Beckett are simultaneously exploring and denying those bounds (80). Osborne, with his protagonists continually trying to say what they mean, closely fits this pattern.

In the *Investigations* and work published posthumously, Wittgenstein posits three steps in the unraveling of language. The first involves recognizing the arbitrariness of ordinary meaning: "When we say: 'Every word in language signifies something' we have so far said *nothing whatever* . . ." (*Invest.* 7). The second is questioning whether one can share meaning with others, in Wittgenstein's arguments about private language and experience: "The essential thing about private experience is really not that each person possesses his own exemplar, but that nobody knows whether other people also have *this* or something else" (95). The third and final step is wondering whether even one's own meanings can remain consistent to oneself: "Imagine a person whose memory could not retain *what* the word 'pain' meant—so that he constantly called different things by that name—but nevertheless used the word in a way fitting in with the usual symptoms and presuppositions of 'pain'—in short he uses it as we all do" (95). While some of Osborne's characters remain occupied with the first step of deconstructing meaning, the majority are painfully involved in trying to communicate the meaning of their experience, and a rare few break through to the final uncertainty of meaning in themselves. The plays, as Georg Henrik von Wright said of Wittgenstein's writings, are a "*Form der Batruchtung*" (216).[1]

So many of the situations in Osborne's plays reflect a semantic gap. The opening of *Look Back in Anger*, significantly, shows a jungle of newspapers and weeklies, a cover of ostensible meaning, hiding two characters. For Jimmy Porter, the senseless conflation of meaning in society has become a point of contention. As he remarks of what he is reading, "Different books—same reviews," and the clergyman's address he looks at next amounts to "Dumdidumdidumdidum" (10, 13). Concomitantly, words in themselves become objects of curiosity, such as *pusillanimous*: "one of those words I've never been quite sure of, but always thought I knew" (21).

Spurning conventional meaning, Jimmy is naturally prey to worries about communicating. Helena's father, Colonel Redfern, oddly sympathetic, remarks, "As for Jimmy, he just speaks a different language from any of us" (64). Or, as Alison earlier says to Jimmy about his acquaintance Webster: "I thought you said he was the only person who spoke your language"—with an unintentional pun on the Webster of lexicography. Jimmy's reply, "So he is. Different dialect but same language" (18), does not conceal the real gap between them, and he eventually admits that Webster does not get along with him. In fact, Jimmy speaks in what Wittgenstein termed private language: "The individual words of this language are to refer to what can only be known to the person speaking; to his immediate private sensations. So another person cannot understand the language" (*Invest.* 88–89). The alienation effect, in other words, is far more than a cultural phenomenon; it is intrinsic to the individual.

Osborne has said that he does not consider himself a social critic. He maintains that his primary concern is "how people relate to each other and to themselves" (Wager 84, 75)—which in Osborne's work means how they fail to relate. Peculiarly Wittgensteinian or, to coin a term, Osbornean, is the extension of noncommunication back into the individual: a whole that finds it doesn't agree even with itself. On the simplest level, this is simply a contrariety of parts, as with Jimmy's "disconcerting mixture" of personality traits (10). But the disjunctions go deeper, part of a real epistemological fissure. As Cliff says of Jimmy: "Don't think he knows himself half the time" (78). Critics have for so long seen Jimmy as a creature of intense conviction that this uncertainty may come as a surprise.[2] The unsureness again reflects a universal rather than idiosyncratic tendency, as Wittgenstein proposes in a paradigm that has become famous: every time one feels a certain sensation, one jots down an "E" to record it, but how can one ever be sure that one "E" is the same as another? (*Invest.* 92–93).

The struggle with the self can be maddening. No wonder Jimmy questions whether he or Alison is crazy, exclaiming, "Is it me, standing here like an hysterical girl, hardly able to get my words out?" (59).[3] This is not just impotent rage but also a difficulty in thinking univocally. As Wittgenstein remarks wistfully, "I never more than half succeed in expressing what I want to express" (*Culture* 18). Intention and expectation are also problematic in their attempts to connect thought and reality (see *Zettel* 10–12). The problem is inextricably bound up with the unreliable self. Similarly, when Jimmy tells Helena that he may write a book about his suffering "Written in flames a mile high," he claims, "It's all here" and slaps his forehead (54). The wrestle with meaning, to put something into words, begins—and sometimes dies—in the mind.[4]

In his study of Osborne, Simon Trussler has noted that Jimmy is neither adjusted to his era nor a spokesman for it (11). The angry young voice rants against language while using the selfsame tool of expression to do so. This is Beckett's territory, as Thiher has observed: the postmodern protest against a self limited by language, a voice that ironically affirms what it speaks against (90). Though one should take care not to conflate Osborne and his protagonist, Jimmy's concerns about language seem as much the playwright's as the Unnamable echoes Beckett's frustrations. Curiously, there is no solution suggested, no program for relief. As von Wright described Wittgenstein, his attitude toward language was fighting but not reformist (208), and this description seems to fit Osborne as well.

The plays immediately following *Look Back in Anger* continue this theme *passim*, specifically the impossibility of shared meaning. In *The Entertainer*, Archie Rice and his family are astride a generational divide, but the rift at times seems more universal, tracing the limits of what one can know about others' experience. One of Wittgenstein's most noted examples is that of a person suffering from a toothache—how can it be compared to the sensation of someone else's toothache? (*Lectures* 17). Similarly, as Archie claims, he can connect with no other's experience "Simply because we're not like anybody who ever lived" (54). Of his daughter Jean's mother, he says, "I was in love with her, whatever that may mean. I don't know" (70). Jean herself is a good deal more vocal on the subject, having just broken up with her boyfriend Graham:

> You know, I hadn't realized—it just hadn't occurred to me that you could love somebody, that you could want them twenty-four hours of the day and then suddenly find that you're neither of you even living in the same world. I don't understand that. I just don't understand that. I wish I could understand that. It's frightening. (29)

One simply (or complexly) cannot know what another is feeling: we live in a world where such presumed connection has been proven to be an illusion. Osborne is all too aware of this, writing in his notebook for 1955: "He suffers the realization: *that there is no real communication with those we love most*" (*Better Class* 272). In a more general vein, Archie tells Jean, "My dear, nobody can tell you what they mean" (51).

If these problems in meaning were simply Osborne's perception of post–World War II England, his history plays should preclude these concerns. But semantic slippage and faulty communication are, for Osborne, part of the human condition, and so the past is simply a paradigm for the present and the future. In *Luther*, for example, Martin Luther lives along the same isolating continuum as Jimmy Porter. He begins with the same questioning of accepted vocabulary and ritual, in this era specifically religious. Quibbling with Brother Weinand over confession, he continually nudges: "What do you mean?" "How do you know?" "Tell me what you meant" (26). His precarious state of mind stems partly from trying to pin down the interpretation of a verse from Proverbs: "It's the single words that trouble me" (27). He is approaching apodictic doubt. As Wittgenstein writes: "If you are not certain of any fact, you cannot be certain of the meaning of your words either" (*Certainty* 17).

Cardinal Cajetan says that Martin's sermons imply "a man struggling for certainty, struggling insanely like a man in a fit, an animal trapped to the bone with doubt" (73). But, as one individual cannot exactly interpret another's experience, Cajetan has misconstrued Martin's doctrinal doubt as spiritual doubt. Martin's quarrel is not so much with the Word as with words.[5] He tells Vicar General Staupitz: "only *you* could live *your* life" (58). Unable to communicate his experience, Martin turns inward and there finds his own instability. As he says to Staupitz later, "They're trying to turn me into a fixed star, father, but I'm a shifting planet" (99). This is akin to the most unsettling prospect of Wittgenstein's tenets taken to its logical conclusion: that man is an unstable amalgam. Martin begins with the statement "I am alone. I am alone and against myself" (20). By the end of the play, despite his doctrinal victories, he has mostly confirmed this status.

In *A Subject of Scandal and Concern*, Osborne shifts from sixteenth-century Germany to nineteenth-century England. Concerning the last man in England to be jailed for blasphemy, in 1842, the play is naturally concerned with the slippery implications of words and their consequences. The protagonist, Holyoake, attacked ceaselessly for his beliefs when the quibble is really about the words he said, finally answers the magistrate: "I don't know, sir. I did not know before and I do not know now. But I do think that I am alone in this matter and will remain so" (24). The protest is similar to that of Osborne's Martin Luther: both have questioned established meaning only to find that the questioning does not simply stop there.

Is the zetetic enterprise fulfilling? It leads inevitably to disquieting conclusions. It is even somewhat teleological, since the search for meaningful distinctions eventually distinguishes oneself in a meaningful way, not shared by others. As Katharine J. Worth notes in "The Angry Young Men": "Imaginative suffering is a profoundly solitary experience" (Taylor 105). In Osborne's *A Patriot for Me*, Alfred Redl's alienation eventually leads him to become a double agent and sexual adventurer extraordinaire. But as the Countess Sophia presciently tells him, "You'll always be alone" (60). Speaking more *ex cathedra*, Osborne himself has broadened this statement to apply to everyone, including as the audience: "The inexorable process of fragmentation is inimical to all public assumptions or indeed ultimately to anything shared at all. A theatre audience is no longer linked by anything but the climate of disassociation in which it tries to live out its baffled lives" ("Thesis" 20). This is partly a legacy from modernist alienation—T.S. Eliot's *Waste Land* fragments—intensified by postmodern currents washing even those shards away.

All of these concerns come to a head in what is perhaps Osborne's most tortured play, *Inadmissible Evidence*. In making the main character,

Bill Maitland, a solicitor, Osborne has shifted significantly from those who question the law to those who oversee it on a daily basis. But as a philandering lawyer who handles adultery cases, Bill has sadly, ironically, become involved in the very situations he prosecutes. As his private experience subsumes his professional public life, he becomes a character whose semantic and epistemological distinctions are caving in on him.

From the outset, Bill has the dimensions of a Beckettian figure, down to the rambling "can't go on" diction of the unnamable: "Still, I'm pretty strong. I must be. Otherwise, I couldn't take it. That is, if I *can* take it. I can't, I'm sorry, I can't find my pills" (14). Meaning has begun to disintegrate on a double level, since the *lexis* of words is related to the *lex* of law. When the judge in the opening dream scene questions the use of the word *objects*, Bill answers, "I think that's what I meant to be saying" (11). He tells the judge twice, "I seem to have lost my drift" (17, 18). As semantic clarity eludes him, so do thought and reality itself. He complains continually that he wishes he could see more clearly (11, 93, 115). Again and again, he confesses, "I don't know" (44, 46, 93). On the phone with his wife, he claims: "I don't know yet. . . . I simply don't know. . . . I don't know now. . . ." (43). These statements do not show ignorance or elusiveness so much as an epistemological slippage.[6]

At the center of Bill's misery is the Wittgensteinian realization that he cannot share what is happening to him any more than he can share the headaches that now plague him. All that he experiences is, in effect, inadmissible evidence. "If you knew me, if you knew me . . ." (15), he tells the judge in his dream. If the judge functions as a superego, a common oneiric metaphor, then Bill does not even know himself: the third Wittgensteinian disjunction. His chief clerk Hudson offers the consolation, "Well, we all have our different methods, as I say. Different ways of looking at things" (26). As a descriptive statement of affairs, this may be more isolating than comforting. In any event, just as Martin Luther and Archie Rice with both pride and pain claim the uniqueness of their lives, Bill tells Hudson, "I don't want to live anyone's life, not anyone's" (31).

As the play progresses, Bill moves toward what Wittgenstein terms "disintegration of the sense" (*Invest.* 175). Since Bill cannot be sure of which words have what emotional affects, he does not properly feel; since he does not recall much, he cannot correlate his experiences with others' or even his own. In such a situation, chance comments acquire an echolaliac resonance. He complains repeatedly that he seems to retain very little (18, 40–41, 92). When his mistress Liz jokingly calls him catatonic, Bill explains to his secretary Joy, "That's her way of saying I don't seem to be able to hold on, on to, to anything" (109). Throughout the play, the stage directions themselves collude with the blurring of memory, meaning, and acquired fact; and the isolation that accompanies it: Osborne mentions "*the ambiguity of reality*" (63) and "*a feeling of doubt as to whether there is anyone to speak to at all*" (59).

In such a blurred situation, references meant for the law segue into a deeper philosophical absence of rule. Trying to procure a witness, Bill claims, "All we want is one reliable person" (75). He even counsels a client to plead guilty because, as he says, "It has the advantage of certainty" (97). But there is no way out from this descent into solipsism because meaning is hermetic and words are arbitrary. Like Beckett's *Waiting for Godot*, the play ends where it has begun, with a repetition that precludes action: "I think I'll stay here. . . . I think I'll just stay here. . . . Goodbye" (115). The final word may be taken as the close of a phone conversation or a valediction.

In his later plays of the '60s, Osborne continues writing about these kinds of breakdowns, but with a different slant and lessened intensity. This is partly because he is now analyzing groups of individuals rather than focusing on the etiology of one mind thinking. *The Hotel in Amsterdam*, for instance, is not so taken up with the slide into semantic confusion as it is preoccupied with the private experience of emotions. The action is nonetheless mostly conversation among the three couples staying together at the hotel, with the scriptwriter Laurie as the Wittgensteinian self-reflexive type that questions the very questions he sets up. Ruminating on the wordage he manufactures out of chaos for his boss, K.L., he wonders whether it can be any good. "Should it not be, I ask myself? What do I ask myself, perhaps I shouldn't be rhetorical and clutter conversations with what-do-I-ask-myselfs?" (275). There is a shifting ground below what Laurie says, to the point where he gives accounts "with two versions to every story, one tragic and one comic, the tragic one always being comic and the comic one always tragic" (298). As it happens, this apposition neatly describes the situation among the six characters onstage and the one offstage. While the three couples are on holiday in Amsterdam in an escape from the magnate K.L., K.L., back in London, commits suicide. The relationship is somewhat like that of Beckett's underlings discussing Godot, or the sextet in Woolf's *The Waves* describing the absent Percival, but with a heavy degree of scorn.

As the character whose daily business is with words, Laurie should be surest of what he means, but there can be no such precision without accurate recollection. Like Osborne's earlier forgetful character Bill Maitland, he is enmeshed in a series of shifting affections: Margaret, his second wife; his new romantic interest, Gus's wife Annie; and the memory of his first wife.

When Laurie and Annie talk about his previous marriage, the exchange shows the blurring of experience through repetition of relationships:

> Laurie: I don't think she likes me.
> Annie: Why not?
> Laurie: I imagine I wasn't very kind to her.
> Annie: Weren't you?
> Laurie: I don't know. I wish I could really remember. I try to. I hope not. But I'm sure I was. (305)

The unreliability of semantic meaning has escalated to the complexities of human relationships, though the two remain connected through a solipsism that is a part of the human condition. After Laurie apologizes for bad-mouthing his pregnant wife Margaret, Dan the artist says, "Not your fault," and Gus the film editor adds, "Not anybody's fault" (301). Unreliable recall steps in for Laurie's capper to the exchange: "As Beaudelaire [sic] said: can't remember now" (301). By the end of the play, when Dan wonders out loud if they'll ever come there again, Laurie answers: "I shouldn't think so. But I expect we might go somewhere else . . ." (311). The suggested shift in locale does little to mask the inevitable sameness and repetition, the source of both confusion and acedia.

This is not the first time Osborne has used a writer as a main character; in his early collaboration with Anthony Creighton, *Epitaph for George Dillon*, the protagonist is a budding playwright who calls the truth a caricature and gets as his comeuppance a caricature of an existence. But Osborne's protagonists seem to age along with him, and, in *The Hotel in Amsterdam*, the writer figure has become entangled and embittered. By the time of *West of Suez*, the writer is an older man named Wyatt Gillman, a patriarch more resigned to his fate.[7] At the island villa of one of his four daughters, he is a cross between Prospero and Lear.

Significantly, much of the responsibility for any dialogue questioning semantics and epistemology has passed on to the younger generation, Wyatt's daughter Frederica and her pathologist husband Edward. Frederica banters with Edward in an almost Beckettian sequence, discarding semantic alternatives:

> Frederica: Don't spar with me.
> Edward: I wouldn't dream of it. I haven't the equipment.
> Frederica: You haven't.
> Edward: Or inclination.

Frederica: Or energy.
Edward: Or stamina.
Frederica: Or interest.
Edward: That either. (11)

The two complete each other verbally as well as in personality: Osborne's probing of individual meaning has led to what individuals mean to each other. The philosophical problem of slippage in meaning has infected personal relations.

As in *The Hotel in Amsterdam*, talk is action, but of an evasive sort. "All art is organized evasion" as Osborne writes in "They Call It Cricket" (*Declaration* 69). What Edward and Frederica do is feint back and forth. When Edward starts off, "We can't be," Frederica finishes, "Responsible for others" (14). On a surface level, she is simply being flip, but the words also suggest a minor paradox: Frederica is obviously taking responsibility for Edward's intended meaning, though the way she has completed his sentence suggests that no one can do this. In fact, as Edward states a moment later, "If I am unhappy, it is my own responsibility" (14). When Edward changes tack and tries to persuade Frederica that she produces effects in others "As if you were them. Or me," she replies, "I'm afraid I don't understand that. And I shouldn't think you can" (19). Here is Wittgenstein's language and sensation argument personalized: no one can appreciate another's pain; no one can put him or herself in another's place. The argument is incontrovertible, and Edward is forced to agree: "No. Sometimes I don't feel I can understand a word of anything anyone says to me. As if they were as unclear as I am . . ." (19). The problem has reverted to the crux of language again.

Wyatt, the presumed master of language, is a nostalgist at heart. When Mrs. James, the interviewer from the local paper, asks him whether he believes words have any meaning, value, or validity, he replies, "I still cling pathetically to the old bardic belief that 'words alone are certain good'" (61). But as Edward notes, "Those who make an ethic out of truthfulness do not incline to rhetoric" (10). Perhaps this is why Jed, an outraged American tourist, shouts at Wyatt, "—words, yes I mean words, even what I'm saying to you now, is going to be the first to go" (69). Wyatt the solipsist has retreated to an island, but his verbal edifice cannot defend him. In the end, Wyatt is shot by the anticolonial islanders, who have no use for his language.

In her essay "Verdict on Osborne," Mary McCarthy notes: "Reiteration is the basic mode of the Osborne harangue, and repetition is the basic plot of the Osborne plays" (17). Osborne's repetition is in fact part of his message: that the same situations recur with dismal frequency because of universal states of affairs. Still, one cannot pound this sort of drum too long without growing sick of the same noise or else slightly deaf. Osborne's plays in the early '70s are mostly repetitions, amplifications of the earlier works.

In *Very Like a Whale*, whose title suggests the isolated perceptions of a Hamlet, Jock and Lady Mellor pursue the by now familiar conundrum of meaning, experience, and isolation. When Lady Mellor concludes a discussion of money with "If you know what I mean," Jock replies, "No. I don't. I don't think *you* do. I think I know what perhaps you ought to mean." She answers, "Complicated . . . I feel so alone . . .," and Jock concludes, "One always does" (13). This is ground covered by Frederica and Edward in *West of Suez*, along with other couples in other Osborne plays. To some extent, it is the sheer audacity of presuming to know what another means that sets off Osborne's characters. When a lady journalist interviewing Jock happens to say, "You know what I mean," Jock is savage: "I don't know what you mean. I don't know you for a start and I know less and less what anybody means" (16). This is retreatism without a sufficient struggle, and Jock's death and its aftermath reflect this fact. As his father watches the televised account of Jock's death, he responds about as much as the dog beside him.

A Sense of Detachment goes beyond even the attempt to make sense. Its aim seems to be to impose chaos on order, as the character simply listed as "Chap" declares (19). Osborne's earlier borrowings from Beckett are acknowledged yet derided with a chorus that includes the line, "Old Uncle Sammy Beckett and all" (25). The references to Arnold Wesker, David Storey, Edward Albee, and Edna O'Brien are equally gratuitous. Perhaps the most telling reference comes from the Interrupter, who mentions the Theatre Workshop and its improvisational experiments in the late '50s: "Joan Littlewood did this years ago" (28). The painful project of making sense is haplessly divided among a polyglot multitude. As the character called Girl says, "We are not language. We are lingua. . . . Oh yes: we talk. We have words, rather . . ." (58). The sense of detachment alluded to in the title is entirely deserved. Admittedly, some of the impatience with public meaning follows Osborne's political career from liberal to conservative, along with such contemporaries as Kingsley Amis and John Wain. The counter-argument Amis advances, with some validity, is that they haven't changed at all; society has (207–10).

The last play worth mentioning here is *The End of Me Old Cigar* because it suggests a specific qualification of the mind-language problem. As the two characters Len and Isobel lie fully clothed together on the bed, he says of his sex, "*We* are uncertain, undefined, perhaps unnecessary . . ."

(42) and "I mean a chap must be utterly chaotic inside?" (48). Here is the muddle of meaning narrowed to the gender gap. In one way or another, Osborne has used this theme since Alison and Jimmy, who, for all his ranting, is surprisingly incommunicative at times. Perhaps for this reason the journalist Stella Shrift in *The End of Me Old Cigar* says of men, "*They* like the language of concealment. Not us" (25). This suggests an etiology that ought to be pursued further. Unfortunately, Osborne's misogyny undercuts most of the lines, so that the most one can say here is that Osborne, despite himself, occasionally registers a truly provocative observation instead of a merely provoking one.

There is, in fact, a quotation from Wittgenstein by Isobel in the second act (48): a translation of the famous last line from the *Tractatus*, "Whereof one cannot speak, / Thereof one must be silent." A comic response to Len's complaints about impotence, it nonetheless functions in much the same way as so many other of Osborne's shrugs over language and the inability to share experience. Impotence can apply to far more than just sexual expression. Whether this suggests a collective plan of action is another matter. Even if there exist hundreds of Lens—or Jimmy Porters—each is uniquely problematic, with a way of meaning that is no one else's. The most significant comment in this connection comes from Len, who says to Isobel, "The thing is to use *your* language and not someone else's" (49). The sense of this suggests a parallel with Sartre's existentialism, wherein the courageous gesture in the face of meaninglessness is to continue to mean something to oneself. Perseverance itself, on one's own terms, is a triumph of sorts.

More than twenty years ago, Osborne stated, "I have a great allegiance to words," while all too aware of the "verbal breakdown" around him ("Osborne" interview 21). In other words, his view is Beckettian: language is a defective means of communication but the best we have. The difference between Beckett and Osborne is that Osborne's plays are more social documents, tied to a given era, but the underlying philosophies are akin. For Osborne, epistemology is a solitary pursuit. As the Narrator in *A Subject for Scandal and Concern* notes: "If it is meaning you are looking for, then you must start collecting for yourself" (46). In the end, Osborne's crippled heroes emerge with a pyrrhic victory, convictions that are bitter because they cannot be shared. Or, as Wittgenstein notes late in his career: "I act with *complete* certainty. But this certainty is my own" (*Certainty* 71).

NOTES

1. This deconstruction of meaning as an end in itself is amplified at far greater length by Harry Staten in *Wittgenstein and Derrida*.

2. See, for example, the traditional responses in John Russell Taylors's *John Osborne: "Look Back in Anger," A Casebook*. Herbert Goldstone's *Coping with Vulnerability: The Achievement of John Osborne* is more to the point regarding ineffability, but deals mostly with emotional barriers.

3. Significantly, the women often suffer the effects. While Jimmy is noisily wrestling with meaning, Alison and Helena cry out the identical line: "I can't think!" (11, 91).

4. As Osborne writes of Tennessee Williams's work: "These are plays about failure. That is what makes human beings interesting" ("Sex and Failure" 317).

5. It is worth noting that Wittgenstein did not at all deny spirituality. He did believe in something numinous, whose ineffability neatly fit in with his own philosophy. "Only the supernatural can express the Supernatural" (*Culture* 3).

6. Despite the sheer repetition of words in Bill's speeches, one must take into account a subtle Wittgensteinian point, that repetition is never the same as the first time, if only because it is in relation to what has come before it. (See *Invest.* 86.)

7. Osborne again uses a writer, the dying Jocelyn Broome, as the main character in *The Gift of Friendship*. The moribund progression seems to stop here.

Works Cited

Amis, Kingsley. "Why Lucky Jim Turned Right." *What Became of Jane Austen? And Other Questions*. New York: Harcourt Brace Jovanovich, 1971. 200–211.
Carter, Alan. *John Osborne*. 2nd ed. New York: Harper & Row, 1973.
Goldstone, Herbert. *Coping with Vulnerability: The Achievement of John Osborne*. Washington, DC: UP of America, 1982.
Hague, Angela. "Picaresque Structure and the Angry Young Novel." *Twentieth Century Literature* 32.2 (1986): 209–20.
McCarthy, Mary. "Verdict on Osborne." *The Observer* [London] 4 July 1965: 17.
Osborne, John. *A Better Class of Person: An Autobiography*. New York: Dutton, 1981.
———. *A Better Class of Person* and *God Rot Tunbridge Wells*. London: Faber and Faber, 1985.
———. *The End of Me Old Cigar* and *Jill and Jack*. London: Faber and Faber, 1975.
———. *The Entertainer*. London: Faber and Faber, 1957.
———. *Epitaph for George Dillon* [In collaboration with Anthony Creighton]. With Arnold Wesker, *The Kitchen*; and Bernard Kops, *The Hamlet of Stepney Green*. Harmondsworth: Penguin, 1964.
———. *Four Plays: West of Suez; A Patriot for Me; Time Present; The Hotel in Amsterdam*. New York: Dodd, Mead, 1973.
———. *The Gift of Friendship*. London: Faber and Faber, 1972.
———. *Inadmissible Evidence*. New York: Grove Press, 1965.
———. *Look Back in Anger*. 1957. Harmondsworth: Penguin, 1982.
———. *Luther*. London: Faber and Faber, 1961.
———. "On the Thesis Business and the Seekers after the Bare Approximate. . . ." *The Times* [London] 14 October 1967: 20.
———. "Osborne," Interview with Kenneth Tynan. *The Observer* [London] 7 July 1968: 21.
———. *A Patriot for Me*. London: Faber and Faber, 1966.
———. *A Sense of Detachment*. London: Faber and Faber, 1973.
———. "Sex and Failure." *The Beat Generation and the Angry Young Men*. Eds. Gene Feldman and Max Gartenberg. New York: Citadel P, 1958. 316–19.
———. *A Subject for Scandal and Concern*. London: Faber and Faber, 1961.
———. "They Call It Cricket." *Declaration*. Ed. Tom Maschler. London: MacGibbon and Kee, 1959. 61–84.
———. *Very Like a Whale*. London: Faber and Faber, 1971.
Staten, Harry. *Wittgenstein and Derrida*. Lincoln: U of Nebraska P, 1984.
Taylor, John Russell, ed. *John Osborne: "Look Back in Anger," A Casebook*. 1968. London: Macmillan, 1987.

Thiher, Allen. "Wittgenstein, Heidegger, *The Unnamable*, and Some Thoughts on the Status of Voice in Fiction." *Samuel Beckett: Humanistic Perspectives*. Eds. Morris Beja, S.E. Gontarski, and Pierre Astier. Ohio: Ohio State UP, 1983. 80–90.

Trussler, Simon. *John Osborne*. Writers and Their Work: no. 213. Essex: Longmans, Green, 1969.

Wager, Walter, ed. "John Osborne." *The Playwrights Speak*. London: Longmans, Green, 1967. 71–86.

Wittgenstein, Ludwig. *Culture and Value*. 2nd ed. Trans. Peter Winch. Eds. G.H. von Wright and Heikki Nyman. Chicago: U of Chicago P, 1980.

———. *Wittgenstein's Lectures, Cambridge, 1932-1935*. Ed. Alice Ambrose. Chicago: U of Chicago P, 1982.

———. *On Certainty*. Trans. Denis Paul and G.E.M. Anscombe. Eds. G.E.M. Anscombe and G.H. von Wright. 1969. New York: Harper, 1972.

———. *Philosophical Investigations*. Trans. G.E.M. Anscombe. New York: Macmillan, 1953.

———. *Tractatus Logico-Philosophicus*. Trans. C.K. Ogden. London: Kegan Paul, Trench, Trubner, 1933.

———. *Zettel*. Trans. G.E.M. Anscombe. Eds. G.E.M. Anscombe and G.H. von Wright. Berkeley: U of California P, 1967.

Wright, Georg Henrik von. *Wittgenstein*. Minneapolis: U of Minneapolis P, 1982.

The Personal, the Political, and the Postmodern in Osborne's *Look Back in Anger* and *Déjàvu*

Austin E. Quigley

Forty years after it made its historic appearance on the London stage, *Look Back in Anger* is widely regarded as a very important but not very good play. A generation of British playwrights, including Brenton, Stoppard, and Hare, have acknowledged its importance to their subsequent careers, but most, including Osborne, who later described it as a "rather old-fashioned play,"[1] now see its weaknesses as clearly as its strengths. Hare's recent praise of the play is characteristically qualified:

> I think that all of us, people who write, we all want to write a play after which things will be seen differently. . . . And most of us are very jealous of Osborne because he pulled it off. . . . Whether you think it's a good play or a bad play, it was a rallying point.[2]

This apparent disjunction between the quality of the play and the scope of its impact remains something of a puzzle, but one whose nature becomes clearer in the light of the sequel, *Déjàvu*, that Osborne wrote in 1991.

Structurally, of course, *Look Back in Anger* does indeed seem a rather old-fashioned play, tracing the separation and reconciliation of Jimmy Porter and his wife, Alison, through a stagey three-act format that hinges on Alison's pregnancy and Jimmy's wrath. To describe the pattern of events in that way, however, is to draw attention to the fact that Jimmy's wrath has little to do with Alison's pregnancy and that the old-fashioned plot line of separation and reconciliation contributes more to the scaffolding than to the substance of the play. The difficulties that emerge between Jimmy and Alison are symptomatic of much wider problems that are neither fully summarized in nor adequately exemplified by the strains and stresses of that particular relationship. Indeed, one of the oddities of a play that focuses upon a single major relationship is that so many other characters who never appear are, in one way or another, caught up in the action. Besides Cliff, Helena, and Colonel Redfern, who appear in minor roles, the following never appear at all: Jimmy's best friend Hugh and his mother, Mrs. Tanner; Jimmy's ex-girlfriend, Madeline; his dying father and his disapproving mother; Alison's brother, Nigel; their ferocious mother; their outraged family friends; a gay radical; a rabid bishop; and sundry other people who earn a name but not a place in the story. As the action of the play demonstrates, however, neither a name nor a place in the story suffice to gain characters an influential voice, for Jimmy's voice dominates everyone else's throughout, and this serves to make even more visible the disjunction between the scope of the issues raised and the restricted nature of the central relationship within which they are dramatically explored.

The evident imbalance between Jimmy's role and everyone else's is widely regarded as the major structural fault of a play to which many other faults are attributed. The ending, with Jimmy and Alison playing at squirrels and bears, seems to lack the weight of an achieved conclusion; the death of their baby seems conventionally contrived and a fortuitous rather than organic means of reconciling the estranged couple; the readiness of Helena to oscillate between love and hate for Jimmy to suit the movement of the plot seems likewise rather contrived; and the central character, Jimmy himself, exhibits an unappealing mixture of cloying self pity, deep-seated prejudice, radical insensitivity, and rampant inconsistency. So widespread are these faults that it becomes evident why so many find it difficult to reconcile the play's structural limitations with its remarkable historical impact. But if we are to come to terms with the play, it must be by understanding the peculiar power of its odd structure, not by explaining its problems away. Indeed, there are few more remarkable things about this remarkable play than the famous description that Osborne offers in his initial stage directions of the limitations of the character who is, in effect, to carry the action of the whole play:

> *[Jimmy] is a disconcerting mixture of sincerity and cheerful malice, of tenderness and freebooting cruelty; restless, importunate, full of pride, a combination which alienates the sensitive and insensitive alike. Blistering honesty, or apparent honesty, like his, makes few friends. To many he may seem sensitive to the point of vulgarity. To others, he is simply a loudmouth. To be as vehement as he is is to be almost non-committal.*[3]

The "disconcerting mixture" of traits exemplified by the play's central character is thus no accident, and Osborne anticipates the variety of responses

Jimmy's behavior will provoke. His final sentence summarizes, in effect, a problem that seems central both to the character and to the play. Jimmy's aggressive rhetoric, which constitutes so much of the play's action, exhibits a savagery so widely deployed that it threatens to rob Jimmy of any clear point and the play of any clear goal.

To begin to make any sense of so peculiarly structured a play we need to come to terms not only with Jimmy's prominence and peculiarities but also with a further dimension of structural and tonal diversity: the one that generates Osborne's recurring insistence on the humor of a play that seems to have little to be humorous about. Jimmy's most famous remark, for example, that "There aren't any good, brave causes left" for his generation, is delivered not bitterly, as many might expect, but "*In [Jimmy's] familiar, semi-serious mood*" (104). Jimmy's humor and the "*cheerful malice*" that Osborne refers to at the outset are interwoven with his anger and aggressiveness throughout the action, baffling everyone at one time or another, but particularly Helena during their brief romance:

> Jimmy: Do I detect a growing, satanic glint in her eyes lately? Do you think it's living in sin with me that does it? (*To Helena.*) Do you feel very sinful my dear? Well? Do you?
> *She can hardly believe that this is an attack, and she can only look at him, uncertain of herself.*
> Do you feel sin crawling out of your ears, like stored up wax or something? Are you wondering whether I'm joking or not? Perhaps I ought to wear a red nose and a funny hat. I'm just curious, that's all.
> *She is shaken by the sudden coldness in his eyes, but before she has time to fully realise how hurt she is, he is smiling at her, and shouting cheerfully at Cliff.* (97)

These oscillations between humor and seriousness in Jimmy's behavior are exemplified most clearly in the newspaper rituals and music hall routines into which the characters are likely to lapse at any moment, but the humor has larger consequences than that of simply amusing the audience. The humor is characteristically an ironic humor that serves several purposes, not the least of which is that of saving the play from collapsing under the weight of Jimmy's self-pity and self-concern. Ironic humor provides distance, both for the audience from Jimmy and for Jimmy from his obsessive concerns. And this is of major importance in a play that is in many ways about the recurring problem the characters confront of relating their private lives to the urgent social issues Jimmy repeatedly raises. As Helena at one point exclaims in exasperation, "Jimmy, can we have one day, just one day, without tumbling over religion or politics?" (98). Jimmy's humor at his own, as well as everyone else's, expense prevents him from coming across as either an obsessive narcissist or an ideological fanatic. The humor serves, in effect, both to complicate his perspective and to establish a connection between the diverse issues that alternately command his attention. And this process of connecting diversity rather than converting it to uniformity is of both structural and thematic significance to a play that exhibits an innovative approach to some aggressively challenged conventions. But it is the nature of those conventions and the room they leave for establishing alternatives that helps us recognize what Osborne was trying to achieve by mixing rather than merging attitudes, aims, and anxieties.

When Alison abandons Jimmy midway through the play, she leaves him a note that concludes with "I shall always have a deep, loving need of you—Alison" (90). The rhetoric of the letter, as much as the decision to leave, makes Jimmy furious, and he denounces its civilized sentimentality as characteristic of a homogenizing way of life and of writing plays for which he has complete contempt. "Deep, loving need! I never thought she was capable of being as phoney as that! [*To Helena.*] What is that—a line from one of those plays you've been in?" (90). Jimmy would have much preferred, had Alison been intent on leaving, that she emphasize, rather than diminish, their differences by denouncing him as she feels he deserves: "Deep loving need! That makes me puke! . . . She couldn't say 'You rotten bastard! I hate your guts, I'm clearing out, and I hope you rot!' No, she has to make a polite, emotional mess out of it!" (90).

It is, of course, the kind of play that presents "a polite, emotional mess" that Osborne is trying very hard not to write. Both Jimmy's biting savagery and his ironic humor give this play a tonal range, and with it a range of implication, that lies beyond that characteristic of plays, particularly Rattigan's plays, that immediately preceded Osborne's on the London stage. The genteel delicacy and reserved nostalgia of the characters in Rattigan's *Separate Tables* (1954), for example, provide an illuminating contrast with what Osborne was trying to achieve with his oddly structured play. Whatever the virtues of Rattigan's plays (and there were many that Osborne overlooked), they often depicted characters whose determination to cope in difficult circumstances exemplified the civic virtues characteristic of a widely unified and steadily expanding country in which everyone was expected to do his/her social duty for the greater good of all. However, once English society, after World War II, began to lose both its sense of external destiny and its sense of internal unity, well-mannered acceptance of one's diminished lot seemed, to Jimmy, as to Osborne, a betrayal of social responsibility rather than a salutary example of it. The cheerful malice and savage humor of Jimmy Porter are thus Osborne's ways of widening the range of response of a country in increasing trouble and unable or unwilling to confront it. But this widening of the range of awareness of an increasingly divided society brings with it structural problems, not the least of which are those of focus and direction, that have left their mark on the play in general and upon Jimmy in particular.

One cannot, of course, deal with the structural imbalances of *Look Back in Anger* without relating them to the widespread acknowledgement that Osborne's plays are often "state of England" plays. While the thematic implications of that concern have been widely recognized, the structural implications have received much less attention. Yet Osborne's determination to grapple with the difficulties of writing a play about England at a time of radical national change is precisely what has precipitated the odd disjunction between the play's historical importance and its apparent structural infelicities. The key difficulty such a play confronts is that of preparing a canvas large enough to deal with the diversity of national themes without thereby losing the dramatic intensity generated by detailed attention to particular characters. The difficulty of reconciling individual and social concerns is thus an awkward issue both for characters seeking to impose some shape on their lives and for the author trying to establish an appropriate shape for the play. And it is only if we recognize the structural complexity of the situation Osborne was exploring that we will be able to make sense of the mixed moods, shifting contexts, and inconsistent arguments of a play that seeks to deal with a national situation by focussing the action primarily upon an idiosyncratic character whose voice is clearly not meant to function as a representative one.

To clarify the peculiar structural role of Jimmy in the play, we might consider again the structure of Rattigan's *Separate Tables*. In that double bill of one-act plays, Rattigan locates his characters in a state of England context by placing them in a residential hotel in the seaside resort of Bournemouth. The hotel location provides a convenient site of intersection for the lives and experiences of a variety of English people whose current interaction reveals both the diversity of their pasts and the common rules of social exchange that English society has taught them to observe. The key tensions in the two plays are generated directly from the gaps that open between the competing claims of the public and the private, the social and the individual, and the past and the present in a postwar England no longer able to sustain a narrative of national destiny that would serve to bridge its various social divisions.

Within the framework provided by a community rhetoric of "deep, loving need" and a shared set of rules for public decorum, the plays are beautifully structured, and they provide a painfully revealing exploration of the necessity for and inadequacy of self-sacrifice in a world in imminent decline. But, for Osborne, the plays lack the range and intensity of feeling that are needed to deal with an England whose decline should not be sadly recognized and nobly accepted but be angrily resisted with a range and intensity of response commensurate with the impending loss. And the outraged voice of protest is to be a means of registering not just a sense of personal deprivation, but also a sense of what becomes central to the play: intergenerational responsibility and betrayal.

When Jimmy looks back in anger, he is generationally situated as a voice of contemporary youth even as he is personally agonizing over the deaths of his father and his best friend's mother, struggling to come to terms with the hostility of his wife's father and mother, and grappling unsuccessfully with the implications of his and Alison's own imminent and aborted parenthood. To pursue the thematic implications of this generational approach to the state of England issue, we need to recognize how Osborne decided to deal with it structurally. Clearly it would have been possible for Osborne to follow Rattigan (and even Brecht) and widen the social canvas to give more time to opposing points of view and to include characters from a broader range of society. The danger would immediately be that the more characters and the more widely representative the characters the less room there would be for detailed presentation, in-depth exploration, and convincing dramatization of the complex authenticity of any individual character's response to England's changing world. What Osborne does instead, at great risk to the structure of his play, is to establish not one hotel room but one sensibility, that of Jimmy Porter, as the site upon which the generational crosscurrents of declining English society would be tracked. The gains would be the intensity of a detailed and lengthy personal response. The potential losses would be those of balance, representativeness, and persuasiveness. And it is precisely in terms of those apparent strengths and weaknesses that the play has widely been received. But if we are to do the play justice, we need to see clearly what Osborne managed to achieve by establishing a single idiosyncratic sensibility as his site of dramatic engagement with England's assorted and accumulating ills.

As we have noted, we will understand little of Jimmy's erratic and explosive behavior if we do not begin with a recognition that when critiquing the lives of other characters as well as himself, he is engaged as much with a national situation as with personal relationships. But he is no allegorical figure, and the play is not one of abstract analysis or general illustration. Osborne's effort throughout is to make Jimmy's response to the England invoked both idiosyncratically excessive and generally revealing. Jimmy functions in the play not by being balanced, authoritative, and right, but by raising in inflammatory ways questions that remain troubling even when the idiosyncracy of their formulation has been acknowledged. And this is, of course, the source of Jimmy's appeal even to those characters and members of the audience who are likely to find him the most objectionable.

Alison, Colonel Redfern, and Helena, in turn, acknowledge not that Jimmy is right but that some of his concerns should also be their concerns. In a manner doubtless calculated to outrage an audience, they all acknowledge, grudgingly or otherwise, that they have learnt something from him. Jimmy, however, is neither ideologue nor prophet. His generational claims to attention are that he is English and young, at a time when being young in England had acquired an historical and cultural resonance whose significance becomes clearer with each passing year. What was already evident in the '50s was that the naturally expanding contexts of youth were confronting the rapidly narrowing contexts of a country in decline.[4] The general tendency for the ambitions of youth to exceed its grasp was thus given particular historical resonance by recurring reminders that, for many members of an earlier generation, England provided a much more advantageous situation in which to grow up. And the odd mixture of sympathy and savagery that characterizes Jimmy's attitude to Alison's father captures an ambivalence about intergenerational perspectives that becomes central to the play:

> I hate to admit it, but I think I can understand how her Daddy must have felt when he came back from India, after all those years away. The old Edwardian brigade do make their brief little world look pretty tempting. All homemade cakes and croquet, bright ideas, bright uniforms. Always the same picture: high summer, the long days in the sun, slim volumes of verse, crisp linen, the smell of starch. What a romantic picture. Phoney too, of course. It must have rained sometimes. Still, even I regret it somehow, phoney or not. If you've no world of your own, it's rather pleasant to regret the passing of someone else's. I must be getting sentimental. But I must say it's pretty dreary living in the American Age—unless you're an American of course. Perhaps all our children will be Americans. That's a thought isn't it? (11)

It is only Jimmy's sustained irony that enables him to share the colonists' sense of loss without sharing their views on colonization, to sustain that sense of loss while suggesting that much of what was lost wasn't real in the first place, and to strike an international chord of disapproval of America's increasing prominence that continues to echo even as the envy generated by an England in decline is openly confessed. But the complex ironies that provide a degree of credibility to his vehement intergenerational judgments also serve to open a gap between Jimmy's passions and his actions that bears directly upon his odd role in the play.

Though Jimmy establishes the note of generational responsibility and generational change by holding his parents' generation responsible for losing its grasp on national destiny, for bequeathing to the next generation no world of its own, he appears to have no clear plans for doing something constructive about it. He is certainly prepared to denounce his own generation for getting too used too readily to a diminished role in the world, and one of his recurring gripes is that "Nobody thinks, nobody cares. No beliefs, no convictions and no enthusiasm" (10). Indeed, Jimmy's attacks on Alison repeatedly focus on what he perceives as her lethargy, her timidity, and her readiness to accept whatever comes her way: "She's a great one for getting used to things. If she were to die, and wake up in paradise—after the first five minutes, she'd have got used to it" (10). This is a tendency widespread enough for Jimmy to recognize it in himself (33), but Jimmy's denunciations are usually strengthened rather than weakened by his recognition of dangers to which he too is subject. In his recurring bouts of condemnation, Jimmy exhibits more of an enthusiasm for thinking and caring about issues and people than for acting upon any beliefs and convictions that might significantly change people's lives or the historical direction of England. Though Jimmy is outraged when his friend Hugh decides to emigrate, he cannot produce for Hugh, any more than for himself, a promising English alternative. Jimmy's sense of national duty seems to require him to bear outraged witness to an unalterable national decline, but not necessarily to intervene. He has made no attempt to establish a career, join a political group, or become socially involved in any systematic way.

Jimmy's inability to do anything about the problems that concern him diminishes but does not destroy the credibility of his judgments and the persuasiveness of his enthusiasms, but more important is the light it sheds on the dramatic function of a character whose idiosyncratic sensibility provides the site of dramatization rather than the source of solution to the issues the play confronts. In effect, Jimmy serves more as a means of identifying and amplifying national problems than as a likely instrument of their solution.

His role in the play is consequently not just that of a character with relationships to other characters on stage but also that of an historical voice seeking to relate events occurring here and now to those that occurred earlier or elsewhere. The large cast of characters who never appear thus serves as one of several means of broadening the implied context of a play whose implications become more extensive as the action progresses.

Across the stage of Jimmy's emotional outrage and rhetorical amplification run the assorted social ills of a difficult moment in English history that Jimmy, in effect, helps both to shape and define. It is a world in which disintegrating empire leaves the country with a sense of decline and guilt; one in which bewildered voters return to power (in 1951) the establishment party in place of the party of social reform; Christians trample upon each other to express their residual spiritual enthusiasms; bishops give speeches to support the manufacture of hydrogen bombs; literary critics squabble over historical trivia rather than cultural substance; and the young subside into resignation, alienation, or emigration. The picture presented is biased, distorted, and exaggerated, but sufficiently true to speak of a generation, though not necessarily for them. But this recognition returns us to one of the vexed problems presented by this putatively historical voice: while generationally engaged, it is not generationally well-situated, for it is neither internally consistent nor externally representative.

To criticize Osborne, however, for appointing the inconsistent Jimmy as the voice of a generation whose views he does not share is not yet to have come to terms with the precarious status of representative voices in a society that is increasingly divided. As a consequence of the discrediting of inherited narratives of national destiny, the world that Jimmy speaks in and for is one whose expectations of consensus foundered early on an increasing recognition of irreconcilable conflicts between people of different ages, classes, genders, education, wealth, religion, and politics. Jimmy himself both exhibits and amplifies some of those conflicts, alternately loving and despising women, attaching himself to Alison while rejecting her social origins, declaring affinity with gay rebels while anticipating that he will be a target of their wrath, trying to overcome the instant dislike Hugh and Alison have for each other, hoping to forge a bond between Alison and Mrs. Tanner, and sympathizing with Alison's father while savagely rejecting her brother:

> Have you ever seen her brother? Brother Nigel? The straight-backed, chinless wonder from Sandhurst? . . . you've never heard so many well-bred commonplaces come from beneath the same bowler hat. The Platitude from Outer Space—that's brother Nigel. He'll end up

in the Cabinet one day, make no mistake. But somewhere at the back of that mind is the vague knowledge that he and his pals have been plundering and fooling everybody for generations. (14)

This is, of course, a very different view of England's military might and political establishment than that exhibited in his response to the career of Colonel Redfern. But Jimmy's inconsistencies are not mere inconsistencies. They are symptomatic of the divided perspectives that characterize both his function as an intergenerational historical voice and his function as a generationally situated character in the play.

The polyvalent Jimmy Porter voice that constantly threatens to drown out those of Alison, Cliff, and Helena is the voice of a larger than life character who functions for his own generation not as someone just like them or as someone completely remote from them, but as someone who seems something of a monster in their midst. They share his Englishness, his youth, and his concerns, but not the fury or the fatalism that give the country's problems for him such power, proportion, and preposterousness. But the odd dynamic of the interaction between Jimmy and the other characters, a dynamic described by Osborne as an *"uneasy polyphony"* (2), is characterized less by disagreements over substance than by disproportion of scale. Though Jimmy rails about politics and religion, he neither addresses nor offers arguments of political or religious scope. And a play that focusses extensively on issues related to empire and equity is also likely at any moment to deal with sweet stalls, tabloid gossip, and jazz bands. These oscillations between events of contrasting scale are partly the consequence of the ironic humor Jimmy adopts throughout the play, but they also prepare the way for a puzzlingly downbeat ending about stuffed squirrels and toy bears. Somewhere in this downbeat ending the concerns of Jimmy as divided historical voice and Jimmy as divided character merge, as personal, national, and cultural reasons for uncertainty and inaction lead inexorably toward issues of diminished scale.

From the outset, issues of historical change, social division, and diminished scale are given visual linkage in a stage setting that situates Jimmy and the other characters in a world of multiple transitions. The scene, we are told, is set in the present with Jimmy and Alison living in *"a fairly large attic room, at the top of a large Victorian house"* (1). The attic room is full of old furniture, some of it from the Victorian era, and its ceiling slopes down sharply to increase the sense of displacement, confinement, and constraint in an otherwise significant space. As Alison later on recalls the evenings she spent with Jimmy in this room, she describes them as "suspended and rather remote" (109). This constrained attic setting with its substantial Victorian foundations gives visual form to one of the unbridgeable and unacceptable historical divisions in Jimmy's life. Alison's and Helena's clothes, when the two are living with Jimmy, register similarly unbridgeable and unacceptable class divisions. Both wear an odd mixture of their own expensive clothes and Jimmy's more utilitarian ones. The Sunday ritual of reading the newspapers provides more examples of the social divisions that drive Jimmy to distraction, and his rhetorical question, "Why do I do this every Sunday?" (3), gives formal shape to a question generated by the whole set, by Jimmy's biting irony, and by much of the early action: why does Jimmy situate his personal life so insistently in the context of England's social history and social divisions?

It is central to the evolving relationship between Jimmy as intergenerational voice and Jimmy as generational character that we recognize that there are personal and not just historical reasons for Jimmy's insistence, in opposing Hugh's decision to emigrate and elsewhere, upon the importance of living nowhere else but England, even at a time when national issues generate more pain than pleasure. Jimmy has an evident personal need to maintain links with earlier generations of English people, whose strengths and weaknesses provide an inheritance with which he feels obliged to come to terms. And coming to terms with that inheritance involves the constant adjustments of scale that complicate Jimmy's life and the lives of everyone else who is haunted by issues of historical consequence and proportion.

The personal basis for Jimmy's intergenerational concerns can be traced back to the early death of his father, and to attend to that story is to encounter some of the reasons why Jimmy's anger is not matched by his actions, and to understand why the intensity of his concerns might captivate other members of his own generation who, though not sharing his anger, feel compelled to respect it. Jimmy had a father who believed there were still, even after the slaughter of the first World War, causes good enough to fight for and collective actions worthy of individual support. In the 1930s he joined in good faith the International Brigade that set out to rescue Spain from fascist domination. He returned, seriously wounded and defeated, to find that his idealistic efforts were greeted not with gratitude, but with doubt and suspicion. Jimmy then felt the full force of his father's disillusionment and defeat at an age when both were likely to make a large and lasting impression:

> For twelve months, I watched my father dying—when I was ten years old. He'd come back from the war in Spain, you see. And certain god-

fearing gentlemen there had made such a mess of him, he didn't have long left to live. Everyone knew it—even I knew it. . . . But . . . I was the only one who cared. (*Turns to the window.*) His family were embarrassed by the whole business. Embarrassed and irritated. . . . All that that feverish failure of a man had to listen to him was a small, frightened boy. I spent hour upon hour in that tiny bedroom. He would talk to me for hours, pouring out all that was left of his life to one, lonely, bewildered little boy, who could barely understand half of what he said. All he could feel was the despair and the bitterness, the sweet, sickly smell of a dying man. (*He moves around the chair.*) You see, I learnt at an early age what it was to be angry—angry and helpless. And I can never forget it. (*Sits.*) I knew more about—love . . . betrayal . . . and death, when I was ten years old than you will probably ever know all your life. (68–70)

Though Jimmy's recurring self-concern and self-pity are as evident here as elsewhere, they do not suffice to eradicate the impact of his experience on the dramatic situation emerging in the play. Jimmy as an individual character, as distinct from Jimmy as an amplifying voice, has personal as well as historical reasons for doubting the value of radical social intervention. His father's death provides the testimony of experience to oppose any testimony youth might offer that strenuous effort will produce its just reward or be its own reward. But worse than that, what the death of his father exemplifies is what the slaughter of world war had exemplified and would exemplify again: that the scale of the effort needed to produce significant change is not proportionate to the probability of success or to whatever might be conceived as constituting success. The death of Jimmy's father provided an early personal encounter with a widely resisted public recognition of the appalling individual costs involved in national responsibilities or national ambitions of imperial scale. And behind the issue of competing public and personal scales lurk questions both about the value of imperial victories so dearly bought and about the value of less visible achievements more locally situated and enjoyed. If no newly defined England could hope to match the scale of achievement that the efforts of earlier generations had, however ill advisedly, produced, what could or should serve, instead, to satisfy the youthful aspirations and ambitions of succeeding generations?

When Colonel Redfern left England in 1914 and returned in 1947, the dates mark key points in the national transition between counting gains and counting costs for large ambitions in the world. Colonel Redfern returns to an England widely regarded as "going to the dogs" (83) but unable to sustain by moral argument or force of arms the scale of its earlier achievements. It is this problem of historical transition and historical scale that makes the English condition in this moment difficult for the generation growing old to accept, but even more difficult, as we have noted, for the young to deal with.

Jimmy as historically situated character is most fully in tune with his own generation when he addresses the issue of being young in England in the period after the second World War. His early comment that their "youth is slipping away" (8) captures a feeling that all the younger characters, in different ways, share. When Alison tries to explain to Helena why she married Jimmy, she describes the youthful fire that seemed to emanate from him and elevate him beyond his much less historically aware peers:

> It had been such a lovely day, and he'd been in the sun. Everything about him seemed to burn, his face, the edges of his hair glistened and seemed to spring off his head, and his eyes were so blue and full of the sun. He looked so young and frail, in spite of the tired line of his mouth. I knew I was taking on more than I was ever likely to be capable of bearing, but there never seemed to be any choice. (50-51)

Later, alone with Cliff, pregnant, and near despair, she responds to Cliff's argument that she is "too young to start giving up" (26) with a despairing acknowledgement that youth has little purchase in a world of inherited decline:

> I keep looking back, as far as I remember, and I can't think what it was to feel young, really young. Jimmy said the same thing to me the other day. I pretended not to be listening—because I knew that would hurt him, I suppose. And—of course—he got savage, like tonight. But I knew just what he meant. (26)

The larger implications of Alison's "I knew just what he meant" help her understand his savagery and help bind all the younger characters to each other whatever their differences. To be young in an aging country is to lose too early the possibilities that youth might otherwise supply and to encounter too early losses that age more regularly supplies. As Jimmy puts it, "I seem to spend my life saying goodbye" (104). But this is a process Jimmy can neither escape nor accept, and his ill-focussed rage is often an expression of the conflict between acceptance of the necessity for change and intolerance of its implications. Alison first regards Jimmy as someone whose youthful vigor can transcend the problem, and then as someone whose mercurial behavior can at least authentically exhibit it, but eventually she comes to see him, as the action of the play suggests we see him, as someone whose idiosyncratic way of dealing with the problem raises further possibilities. And it is in defining the nature of these further possibilities and their relationship to problems of scale that the action of the play clarifies the representative status of Jimmy's otherwise unrepresentative voice.

Alison admires the rigor but is exhausted by the consequences of Jimmy's determination to resist false narratives of national destiny without opposing them with some new one of his own. Jimmy's "blistering honesty" is the honesty, however intemperate, of someone who refuses either to disguise or dismiss temporal and social divisions but seeks to affirm them and try to live through them. Just as he insists upon Alison denouncing him if she feels justified in leaving him, he wants all his relationships to work through their local complexities, rather than work around them in the false name of historically characterized romance or nationally defined destiny. This determination to confront local differences is not for Jimmy a means of destroying larger patterns, but the only means by which he can sustain the possibility that larger patterns might eventually emerge.

Discussing with Helena the rather visible affection she shares with Cliff, Alison tries to describe the relationship in Jimmy's terms:

> It isn't easy to explain. It's what he would call a question of allegiances, and he expects you to be pretty literal about them. Not only about himself and all the things he believes in, his present and his future, but his past as well. All the people he admires and loves, and has loved. The friends he used to know, people I've never even known—and probably wouldn't have liked. His father, who died years ago. Even the other women he's loved. (46–47)

Though Jimmy's self-concern often borders on the insufferable, it is not without its social implications. Relationships survive for Jimmy not on the basis of traditional rights that disguise differences of opinion and value but on the basis of shared achievements that provide bridges across persisting differences. And here Jimmy's attitude strikes Alison as both timely and persuasive:

> Helena—even I gave up believing in the divine rights of marriage long ago. Even before I met Jimmy. They've got something different now—constitutional monarchy. You are where you are by consent. (109)

Such consent does not constitute a permanent commitment, but a repeatedly renewable one, and the implications of that renewal raise in another context the issue of scale that recurs throughout the action. Jimmy wants relationships to be contingent and contractual, but also to exceed their local origins and endure. As Alison points out, Jimmy wants to hold onto everyone he has ever loved, even as he wants love to be based upon freedom, contingency, and ever-revisable consent. He wants relationships to dictate their own terms but also to achieve a depth of intensity and breadth of scale if they are to be significant to him. And startlingly, this peculiar conjunction of convictions results in Jimmy's wife and Jimmy's lover both characterizing the play's most iconoclastic figure as something of an anachronism:

> Helena: He was born out of his time.
> Alison: Yes. I know.
> Helena: There's no place for people like that any longer—in sex, or politics, or anything. That's why he's so futile. Sometimes, when I listen to him, I feel he thinks he's still in the middle of the French Revolution. And that's where he ought to be, of course. He doesn't know where he is, or where he's going. He'll never do anything, and he'll never amount to anything.
> Alison: I suppose he's what you'd call an Eminent Victorian. Slightly comic—in a way. . . . (111)

Slightly comic, of course, not just because of his anachronistic status but also because his concern for historical scale impels him to live his personal life in impossibly public terms, because his uncompromising investment in generational responsibility sustains the very sense of Englishness that he seems otherwise to despise, and because his impossible demands are uttered with the self-deprecating irony of someone who recognizes that his determination to define himself as a lost cause is both a contemporary indulgence and a historical necessity.

Though Jimmy is, indeed, something of an anachronism, he manages not to be a mere anachronism. Somehow, his intergenerational concerns enable him to function simultaneously as a voice of outraged youth, a voice of semi-skeptical modern nostalgia, and a voice of imperious Victorian expectation. The divided voice is divided not just by differing values, but by differing senses of what suffices to constitute value. The differing value judgments of different eras, the differing expectations of what individual action can accomplish, and the differing scales for judging what gives an individual life sufficient shape and sufficient point make Jimmy's attempts to amalgamate them impossible. Such incompatibilities of both substance and scale are amplified by Jimmy's rhetoric and given visual and aural exemplification in the contrast established between the church bells, whose chimes drive Jimmy to distraction every Sunday, and the jazz trumpet that he plays to drown them out. In the differing balance they invoke between convention and innovation and in their significant differences of size and scale, the huge bells and the jazz trumpet offer very different possibilities for individual improvisation and control. And the comic contrast between these competing sounds returns us to the significance of the play's similarly comic ending in which toy squirrels and bears supply a complex context of diminished scale to earlier issues of much larger moment.

Helena is startled when she first encounters the stuffed teddy bear and squirrel in the Porter's flat, and even more startled when she learns that they have an established role in the Alison/Jimmy relationship. Alison explains it at first in terms of sheer escapism:

> Alison: It started during those first months we had alone together—after Hugh went abroad. It was the one way of escaping from everything—a sort of unholy priest-hole of being animals to one another. We could become little furry creatures with little furry brains. Full of dumb, uncomplicated affection for each other. Playful, careless creatures in their own cosy zoo for two. (54)

And it is in just these terms that we see Jimmy and Alison playing this game with each other early in the play. The localizing of context and concern is indeed a temporary means of escape from the brawling over large scale issues of politics and religion. When Jimmy and Alison return to the game at the play's conclusion, however, it is in the generational context of their lost child and recent separation. No longer a means of escaping their problems, the game becomes a means of renewing a relationship whose complexities have become more apparent to them both. The game is no longer a mere escape from the past or an avoidance of the present but a means of engaging the future through a painful but pleasurable "*comic emphasis*" (119) on the value of the divided perspectives that they both now ruefully acknowledge. Their mutual sympathy and individual differences are exhibited in the remarks "Poor squirrels" and "Poor bears" (119). Their reconciliation is one that takes as its point of departure a "*mocking, tender irony*" (119) that is less negative than Jimmy's earlier savage irony and more authentic than the simplistic platitudes of Nigel and his like. In its tender acknowledgement of difference, the reconciliation offers a means of accommodating without equating differing scales of value, expectation, and duration, of coping with local situations saturated with larger generational concerns, of resisting false optimism and premature despair, of deciding to build, with whatever difficulty, from here.

Whether we think that this registers for Jimmy a significant defeat or a significant victory depends on how we evaluate the anger and aggressiveness he was earlier seeking to validate. To be young and English in the 1950s was for him to be trapped, as the Victorian attic setting suggests, in the debris of a dying civilization that not only restricted one's present but nurtured and contaminated one's roots. To live in any way, it was necessary, as Jimmy intermittently recognized, to die in some way. And the transition Jimmy and Alison undergo in the play is one of lowering the scale of imperial expectations in order to sustain any expectations at all. Their adjustment is indeed to one of reconciliation with the smaller world to which Jimmy is initially so opposed, but what is at issue is the nature of the reconciliation that Jimmy had so far steadfastly resisted. For it is the assumption that reduction in scale must imply a reduction in substance that has made Jimmy so frantically determined to affirm both local authenticity and larger significance, with or without an accompanying irony. The most famous lines of the play address directly the shift of national scale and its personal implications, but as we noted earlier, they are spoken in Jimmy's *"familiar, semi-serious mood"*:

> There aren't any good, brave causes left. If the big bang does come, and we all get killed off, it won't be in aid of the old-fashioned, grand design. It'll just be for the Brave New-nothing-very-much-thank-you. About as pointless and inglorious as stepping in front of a bus. (104–05)

The challenge for the Jimmy/Alison generation as it succeeded that of its parents is to find some point to a world no longer glorious, to find a way beyond demanding or denouncing glory on an imperial scale, to find some means of measuring value that does not reduce to triviality, or worse, whatever is available in contexts of diminished scale.

Jimmy's *"semi-serious"* speech on good, brave causes is, in fact, precipitated by his acknowledgement that he would be prepared to sacrifice his friendship with Cliff to any woman whose romantic potential might provide in the personal realm a scale of experience that earlier generations enjoyed in the public realm. Jimmy, in characteristic fashion, both affirms and denies the possibility:

> It's a funny thing. You've been loyal, generous and a good friend. But I'm quite prepared to see you wander off, find a new home, and make out on your own. And all because of something I want from that girl downstairs, something I know in my heart she's incapable of giving. You're worth a half a dozen Helenas to me or to anyone. And, if you were in my place, you'd do the same thing. . . . Why, why, why, why do we let these women bleed us to death? . . . I suppose people of our generation aren't able to die for good causes any longer. We had all that done for us, in the thirties and the forties, when we were still kids. (*In his familiar, semi-serious mood.*) There aren't any good, brave causes left. . . . there's nothing left for it, me boy, but to let yourself be butchered by the women. (104–05)

Jimmy's characteristic irony both elevates and deflates what romance so conceived has to offer, and his actions are likewise inconsistent. Within minutes he is planning to make a new start to his life with Helena (107), later accepting her departure with resignation, then trying to reestablish his relationship with Alison through the squirrel and bear routine. But there is much to suggest that both Jimmy and Alison have learned something in the process. The reconciliation is, in effect, one that takes as given what the squirrel and bear game suggests: the smaller scale, more local context, and less grandiose expectations of a life in which personal relationships are not to be measured primarily on an imperial scale of public achievement. But this adjustment to the smaller scale is no longer treated as a matter of temporary escapism or long-term defeat. This context is treated more as a point of departure than as a necessary destination. The shared irony at the end neither precludes nor predicts significant depth, devotion, or duration, but it clearly suggests that matters of personal scale need be dominated neither by the national narratives of earlier generations nor by the diminished contexts of this. Furthermore, in establishing the issue of diminished scale as central to the play's conclusion, Osborne made the personal concerns of Jimmy and the national concerns of England resonate with larger cultural concerns whose implications have become clearer with the passing of time, but particularly with the performance and publication of his final play, *Déjàvu*.

Dealing with life in intergenerational terms gives the Jimmy of 1956 many problems, not the least of which is an uncertainty over the scale of the picture he needs to draw to make sense of his own life. His efforts to think intergenerationally put him at odds with his own generation and its inclination to narrow its concerns to what it can actually control. Jimmy's idiosyncratic voice achieves a larger resonance by resisting, initially, the retreat to smaller pictures and smaller values and, subsequently, the equation of smaller pictures with smaller values. Look Back in Anger achieved its initial impact in part because the depiction of historically situated and idiosyncratically articulated youthful alienation was able to speak beyond its historical moment by being so thoroughly situated in its historical moment. The role of Jimmy as amplifying voice increased the impact of Jimmy the historically situated character by relating it to and giving it implications for other youthful moments. But Osborne had his finger on the pulse of history in more ways than one. In recognizing that the issue of changing scale was as important to Jimmy as any issue of substance (Jimmy juxtaposes "pointless and inglorious"), he was tracing a larger cultural shift from the large ambitions of both Victorians and modernists toward those lower-scale ambitions of the postmodernists that were to come. Jimmy, a threshold character, was caught in a dilemma that we are only now beginning to be able to articulate, but which we can see much more clearly because of Osborne's 1991 sequel to the play, *Déjàvu*.

Much of the discussion of postmodernism as a cultural category or historical moment has hinged upon a disagreement over the implications of the term itself. As many have pointed out, the sense of a new era is conveyed by the term "post," but to describe the new era as "post" the one before is to anchor it to what it appears to transcend. This ambiguity in the term is further exacerbated by a famous argument from Jean-François Lyotard that postmodernism is not something that succeeds modernism but is, in fact, a recurring aspect of it.[5] Whether postmodernism precedes, accompanies, or succeeds a modernism itself very difficult to define has thus become a major bone of contention, one that puts at particular risk those who seek to discuss postmodernism primarily in terms of documents with some new kind of style that have appeared only in recent years.

To avoid that limiting presupposition and to consider postmodernism continually in its relationship to modernism is to adopt precisely the kind of inter-era/intergenerational perspective that makes Jimmy Porter's voice so powerful, so inconsistent, and so surprisingly authentic in *Look Back in Anger*. Indeed, one of the early theorists of postmodernism, Ihab Hassan, argued, in a famous essay, both that postmodernism marks a decisive break with modernism and that, in spite of the radical nature of period transitions, we are all something of Victorians, modernists, and postmodernists at once.[6]

To take such a view is to recognize that the divided perspective and intergenerational concerns of Jimmy Porter capture not just something of the youth of a particular character or of a moment in the decline of a particular nation but also something of a moment of cultural transition, one that has resonance for everyone concerned with what comes after modernism as a cultural movement and with what should happen to the modernist social values that accompanied it. Osborne's peculiarly structured play, with its insistent focus upon the divided sensibility of a central character, achieved and retains its historical importance because of the resonance it establishes between personal, political, and cultural issues at a moment of triple transition. In each of the three spheres, relationships between successive generations, competing values, and shifting scales are of central importance. Indeed, the issue of contrasting scales, so evident in the play's concluding images of squirrels and bears, marks a key difference between the Victorian/ modernism transition, where it was a less important issue, and the modernism/postmodernism transition where it becomes an obsessive concern. Much of Lyotard's famous argument hinges upon the lost credibility of large unifying community narratives and upon their replacement by local group commitments of limited scope and durability. Cultural change, so conceived, intersects with the trajectory of post-imperial England's social change to generate Jimmy's persistent anger about the (often unwitting) betrayal by the previous generation and about his own generation's acquiescence, timidity, and general lack of aggression and enthusiasm. In *Déjàvu*, written thirty-five years later, Osborne voices his worst fears of where things might be headed, rather than the qualified hopes exemplified in the final pages of *Look Back in Anger*.

In *Déjàvu* (1991) Jimmy Porter is thirty years older and has found a way of surviving, even of thriving, but in a characteristically idiosyncratic fashion, rather than one he might recommend to anyone else. Still a determinedly unrepresentative figure, he is, he argues, "a spokesman for no one but myself."[7] Jimmy's marriage to Alison has ended in divorce, and much of the action of the play is devoted to Jimmy directing at the children of his second marriage the same scathing, but not always unsympathetic, irony that he once inflicted upon his parent's generation. The toy bear, which had once suggested the positive possibilities of life at a reduced scale, now exhibits only the negative possibilities of narrowness, conformity, political correctness, and stunted growth. Though seriously interested in such things as "meaningful relationships" (11), Teddy has been encouraged to avoid unusual "forms of self-expression" (86), to indulge only in "safe sex" (12), to consider himself a likely victim of oppression (74), to seek redress in a "European Court of Teddy Rights" (85), to degenerate into a "cuddly conformist" (63), to aspire no higher than "mediocrity" (101), and, in effect, to exemplify what J.P. regards as the worst of the post-Jimmy generation:

Cliff: Damn it, J.P., he's only human—
J.P.: Damn *you*, that's just what he's not. It's what he's been told.
(85)

The usual layers of irony confirm that, from Jimmy's point of view, the possibility of building from the local something larger has collapsed into a collective myopia that diminishes both the scale and substance of the next generation's concerns. Oblivious to the potential virtues of the intergenerational perspective that has characterized, divided, and tormented his own life, the next generation deals with generational change, social diversity, and cultural transition by developing fashionable and fleeting means of unifying the otherwise un-unifiable. To Jimmy, the new generation seems determined to compromise its way into consensus, to become "unconnected to the past" (64) in general, and even to "erase the past" (83) whenever it suggests reasons for dissatisfaction with the current state of affairs.

The self-congratulatory disruption that Jimmy sought to impose upon his own quietly divided generation has little purchase on the next generation, which, to Jimmy's mind, has abandoned self-determination and individual responsibility for collective counselling, "sloppy fads" (57), mass opinion, "mob philanthropy" (75), and unearned European solidarity. The unifying imperial narrative of English destiny that pressured individuals to elevate their concerns to the rhetorical levels of the few born to lead have given way to random narratives that briefly unify otherwise disparate groups by appealing to the lowest common denominator, to the life of least disruption, to the path of least resistance. Jimmy's summarizing image is of mass attendance at a pop concert at which the audience members engage in a collective wave motion to exhibit the coherence and comfort of a "wave new world" (34). As church bells once more ring out in the background, Jimmy's critique of the succeeding generation echoes the one he had earlier made of the preceding generation: "against the noise and clamour of those who would impose their certainties upon us. God *rot* their certainties" (101).

Jimmy's daughter, Alison, spends much of the play at the ironing board once occupied by his first wife; she wears the ubiquitous earphones of a generation turned largely within rather than without, but attending within only to what has been collectively affirmed without. Jimmy's savage images of this generation, like his savage images of the preceding generation, are not without their justification, but, as the earphones suggest, his ability to attract attention has, like much else in the world, diminished sharply. To Alison, Jimmy is someone who has devoted himself to "a lifetime of useless snarling" (39), and it is evident in this play, as in *Look Back in Anger*, that Jimmy's function is to focus and amplify generational issues rather than to resolve them. And as in *Look Back in Anger*, Jimmy's idiosyncracy, inconsistency, and excess serve more to extend the play's range of awareness than to provide a model for others to follow.

Jimmy's mode of self-justification has, however, progressed one step further. The difficulty he encountered in the earlier play of affirming both the integrity of local events and the importance of imperial scale has been transformed from a baffling inconsistency into a paradoxical affirmation. In the face of a new generation's debilitating readiness to conform to fashionable narratives of many kinds, whether based upon nationality, class, gender, race, religion, or anything else, Jimmy preaches the virtues of the very inconsistency his intergenerational perspectives have repeatedly exhibited. Refusing to become anything so assimilable as "a member of the public" (9), the erstwhile jazz player argues in exasperation that "coherence isn't all," that "coherence . . . conceals as much as is revealed to the lost like me who contemplate the wreckage" (51). Jimmy revels in the "mess" of "muddled enthusiasm" (94), in the "rowdy passion" that once typified English life, and in that splendidly "English virtue" of "irony" (81), an irony that multiplies perspectives so rapidly and unceasingly that any affirmation of it is itself rendered irreducibly and comically ironic:

> (*Very crisply, like battle commands.*) Endow us with the courage of uncertainty. Accept an unruly but contrite heart. And in that frailty of disbelief we cannot overcome let us seek remedy from within ourselves and offer mercy that the world cannot give among the perils etcetera, etcetera. (101)

Jimmy's contingent affirmation of contingency parodies the style and conviction of the fashionable preacher, "the Rev. Ron" who has joined the successor to the former play's Bishop of Bromley in establishing a "liturgical leisure centre" and "liturgical café" at which various kinds of "pop chat" reassure the masses that the responsibility for aberrant behavior lies not with the individual but the state (98, 45, 76). Jimmy supplements his own characteristically modernist irony with a characteristically postmodern investment in parody to challenge both the "dumb pieties" (63) of the next generation (34–36) and whatever platitudes he feels himself inclined to offer as a substitute (49–51). To Cliff's plea for "No more questions," Jimmy retorts, "No more *answers*" (83), seeking always to situate himself intergenerationally between competing worlds. And to see Jimmy's divided sensibility as an exemplification of generational supplementation as opposed to generational supplantation is to recognize what Osborne was seeking to achieve by exploring cultural and national issues through the shifting sensibilities of an idiosyncratic and unrepresentative character. Strangely enough, it is Jimmy's very refusal to restrict his views to that of a single era, to unify his convictions into a single world view, or to align his actions with his assertions, that makes him serve as an unexpectedly successful site of dramatic engagement with the idiosyncratic shape of individual lives, the multilinear history of an evolving nation, and the contested development of a cultural process in a period of major transition.

Jimmy's inconsistency and excess mark him not as someone whose views we are expected to share, any more than the other characters share them, but as someone who provides, in spite of his many faults, a powerful and varied means of measuring those worlds that seek to exclude him. His excess, like Falstaff's in another era, prevents him from representing a world that any collectivity could occupy, but the vitality that accompanies it both measures and is measured by whatever seeks to oppose or ignore it. The "rowdy passion" that Jimmy both exemplifies and extols invokes a tradition of English irreverence that was already well established in the drama and poetry of medieval England and has persisted ever since.

Jimmy's divided sensibility provides a canvas wide enough to accommodate conflicting personal, national, and cultural issues. It shows how these issues can be mapped without being unified, can be related without being equated, can be measured without being standardized. Jimmy's determinedly intergenerational perspective exhibits inconsistencies whose virtues are clarified by an implied contrast with the costs—personal, social, and cultural—of any unified perspective, whether it be that of a generation, an era, a nation, a religion, a political philosophy, a cultural moment, or an aesthetic theory. What happens when a generation rejects too readily the voices of generations that have preceded or are succeeding it and settles for something currently fashionable is that the social divisions that generate future change are disguised rather than demolished, and a personal, national, and cultural resource is squandered. Jimmy, inconsistent and excessive, self-absorbed and generationally obsessed, seeks to be true to his own time by relating it continually and contentiously to the voices of other times. As inconsiderate of the pieties of one generation as of another, and of his own, Jimmy does, indeed, indulge in relentless "snarling," but its value depends upon its capacity to persuade us of the falseness of the hope that peace can be born of coherence, consistency, or consensus.

Osborne, by ruthlessly cataloging Jimmy Porter's faults before the action of *Look Back in Anger* begins, challenges himself to find the means of making a disagreeable voice theatrically viable and an idiosyncratic personal voice nationally and culturally functional. The revolutionary play he was soon to describe as "rather old fashioned" mixed old and new in ways that captured a pivotal moment in the history of England and a pivotal moment in the development of modernism. The theatrical function of the main character is not to provide the audience with an example for admiration or emulation but to supply an idiosyncratic site of exploration for the issues that bind and divide citizens of a nation in flux. Like the jazz trumpet that selects from and recombines a history of possibility, Jimmy Porter finds his way beyond the homogenizing imperatives and linear expectations of imperial or post-imperial scale. His extravagant irony might indeed reduce his life to one of "useless snarling," but his persistent search is for a "snatch of harmony" (51) that might, like the rhythms of the jazz trumpet and the games with squirrels and bears, resonate both at some smaller scale and at some larger level of social and cultural development, thereby suggesting larger human bonds and more complex historical patterns than any he can ever hope to summarize, circumscribe, or define:

> J.P.: (*Softly.*) . . . Anger is not hatred, which is what I see in all your faces. Anger is slow, gentle, not vindictive or full of spite. Also, it comes into the world in grief not grievance. . . . (*Still softly.*) "What's he angry *about*?" they used to ask. Anger is not *about* . . . It is mourning the unknown, the loss of what went before without you, it's the love another time but not this might have sprung on you, and greatest loss of all, the deprivation of what, even as a child, seemed to be irrevocably your own, your country, your birthplace, that, at least, is as tangible as death.
> *(Alison "waves" defiantly. Deliberately, J.P. removes her headphones, picks up the attached instrument, drops it to the floor and steps on it. It crackles and breaks.)*
> Alison: (*Presently.*) Oh—well done, J.P.
> J.P.: I do try not to behave like the people I most despise. (36–37)

NOTES

1. John Osborne, "That Awful Museum," *Twentieth Century* 169 (1961): 216.
2. David Hare, cited in "Introduction," Hersh Zeifman and Cynthia

Zimmerman, eds., *Contemporary British Drama 1970–1990*, (London: Macmillan, 1993) 2–3. See also Zeifman's accompanying discussion.

3. John Osborne, *Look Back in Anger*, (New York: Bantam, 1971) 2. Subsequent page references are to this edition.

4. See, in particular, Jimmy's remark, "Our youth is slipping away" (8), and Alison's, "I can't think what it was to feel young, really young" (26).

5. Jean-François Lyotard, *The Postmodern Condition: A Report on Knowledge*, trans. Geoff Bennington and Brian Massumi, (Minneapolis, MN: U of Minnesota P, 1984) 79–82.

6. Ihab Hassan, "Toward a Concept of Postmodernism" in *The Dismemberment of Orpheus: Toward a Postmodern Literature*, (Madison, WI: U of Wisconsin P, 1982) 259–71.

7. John Osborne, *Déjàvu*, (London: Faber and Faber, 1991) 97. Subsequent page references are to this edition.

Osborne on the Fault Line

Jimmy Porter on the Postmodern Verge

William W. Demastes

The unsavory impression that Jimmy Porter creates for audiences (and most readers) of *Look Back in Anger* is possibly the single most troubling aspect of this powerful but problematic play. At one very simple level, one must be reminded that, as Arnold Hinchliffe observes, "the original interpreters of Jimmy Porter—Kenneth Haigh and Richard Burton—were not weedy neurotics the text rather invites but substantial, even heroic, figures" (22–23). These actors' charismatic qualities probably did much to make this character more appealing than he appears to be today in text. In fact, these actors' interpretations of Porter in 1956 were essentially the English equivalents of the American Marlon Brando's Stanley in Williams's 1949 *A Streetcar Named Desire*.

Working beyond fundamentally different cultural preferences (a more cerebral element among the British and a more earthy, animalistic strain among the Americans, for example), the similarities in roles are striking. Both characters bully the women they encounter, though the women seem nonetheless strangely/perversely attracted to the two men. Indeed, it is even perhaps because they bully the women that the women are attracted. And both characters are insensitive to the needs of everyone around them, trampling on whatever they personally believe has no value. From these similarities in roles, the actors mentioned above added a complexity not always evident by merely reading the texts, for though we may be intellectually repelled by these characters in the text, our emotions are quickly engaged by the power exuded by these characters when transformed by charismatic actors to flesh and blood on stage. A lesson can be learned here about the fundamental differences between seeing a play as "drama" (as simply a text) and a play as theatre (with the full complement of performance machinery).

But this approach to the character of Jimmy Porter, this effort to salvage Porter as a "likeable" person by casting an appropriate actor, is a fairly traditional one that presumes the central character requires empathic qualities. Even though Haigh and Burton did—and others doubtless still do—bring a degree of empathy to the character Jimmy Porter, it is not entirely clear that a production needs to create a sympathetic Porter for this play to be successful. Apparently Osborne himself felt otherwise when he reported in 1974, "I thought *Look Back in Anger* was quite a comedy" (qtd. in Amory 34), and when he defended Porter earlier in 1957: "Jimmy Porter isn't unpleasant, really; he is careful, good-humoured and honest, although he may be wrongheaded sometimes" (qtd. in Dempsey 27). Obviously, however, audiences see something different than Osborne may have intended, at least something different when not afforded powerful dramatic interpretation/ transformation by the actor portraying him.

Osborne's traditionalist view of his play is more appropriately a view necessary for *Streetcar Named Desire* to succeed than for *Look Back in Anger*. Williams structurally and thematically needs his audience to experience an ambivalent feeling that simultaneously includes revulsion from and empathy toward Stanley in order for *Streetcar* to succeed. The very issue of ambivalence is at the center of *Streetcar*, after all. But *Anger* functions differently. Though ambivalent feelings toward Porter may exist among audiences, it is not essential for Porter to have been created in the image of empathic, positive heroes of pre-twentieth-century drama, nor to have created him even in the image of ambivalent heroes of early- to mid-twentieth-century drama.

Furthermore, seeing Porter as dominatingly central to this play, as traditionalist interpretations have, leaves the audience inclined to see Porter as not just the messenger but rather as the message of the play. Hayman echoes the sentiments of many when he says, "*Look Back in Anger* is the one-man play *par excellence*" (17). If Porter is indeed everything to the play, then our response to Porter in turn becomes a response to the message of the play as a whole, whatever that may be. While this star-quality approach to drama and theatre is perhaps integral to a Williams play—indeed, while it is often integral to most modernist and classical drama—it is counterproductive to pursue this approach with either Porter or with a good deal of postwar/postmodern drama. While Osborne himself follows a long line of critics in reading Porter from this traditional perspective, a more fruitful option exists, one that looks forward (rather than "back," as the author desires and critics oblige) to an egalitarian strain in postmodern drama that strives to empower the audience over any authority either on or off stage. That includes Porter and even his creator/author/alter ego, Osborne. This play works much more effectively not as a piece that leads its audience to answers but rather as a work that pushes its audience to derive its own answers and conclusions.

Often, when an audience fails to accept its own empowerment, then the actor must essentially "recreate" Porter into an empathic character who will lead a resisting audience. From a traditionalist's perspective, if this empathic transformation does not occur, then the play fails, or at very least its effects become negative and depressing. When Porter is not heroically cast, the play becomes listless. The confused and mixed reviews of the premiere and the heated debates that followed are the best evidence that audiences refused to relinquish their old, established preferences in 1956 to be led by empathic characters. And many audiences and readers today still hold to those preferences. We want to be attracted to, not repulsed by, central characters. But although such repulsion is theatrically disturbing from a traditionalist's perspective, this overturning of traditionalist audience desires can in fact be seen from another perspective as integral to the success of the play. When audiences are more willing to abandon their desire to be led empathically to a message/theme by a leading character, then this play truly assumes great power and succeeds at a level unseen by the traditionalists. Ultimately, it is more a matter of audience perception/reception than it is merely a matter of production (though production may help redirect us). We can be traditionally tantalized by a Kenneth Haigh or Richard Burton, but finally such engaging performances are not essential to the success of a production, unless financial success based on drawing in traditionalist-trained audiences is perhaps the goal.

What I am suggesting is that *Look Back in Anger* is a play settled on a theatrical fault line, riding upon ground moving in two opposite directions, and being fully part of neither. One perspective reveals it is moving in a traditional, naturalist direction, while another perspective suggests it has been caught in the flow of a burgeoning, new, postmodern movement. As a hybrid, anchored exclusively in neither, it cannot fully find its "place" in the descriptions of either.

Clearly, most scholars, critics, general audiences, and readers have worked to force the play into the traditionalist/naturalist category. Osborne himself has confirmed and encouraged such thought by observing in 1961, "I thought *Look Back in Anger* was a formal rather old-fashioned play" ("That Awful Museum" 214). But perhaps even he did not see what he had created until much later, when he confessed in 1974, "I took a lot of daring risks" (qtd. in Amory 34), including, significantly, multiple references to nonpresent characters, a practice not condoned by the naturalist/modernist theatre of 1956. For us, too, perhaps a reevaluation of where the play "fits" in dramatic terms is necessary.

Our traditionalist desire for consistent characterization, logical unity, direction, and closure lead us, naturally enough, to long for "realist" texts. *Look Back in Anger* obviously grants us that option. But we can also study the question of Porter's presence in ways that speak beyond the issue of consistent characterization or rounded personality, and move toward seeing Porter more indeterminately as a presence beyond a flesh-and-blood, naturalistically created character.

When an audience moves away from having its response to Porter's personality be also the response it has to the play, it moves closer to embracing the overall effect of *Look Back in Anger*, and a different, nontraditional effect surfaces. Despite all appearances, this play is more than a psychological study about a disenfranchised everyman. For although Porter's actions on stage give the play dramatic force, those actions effectively background Porter (and even Osborne) as an authority to be listened to. Just as Cliff and Alison often background Porter on stage, not seriously drawn in by his verbal assaults, so the audience invariably backgrounds Porter as an authority, accepting him as less worthy of hero worship with every passing speech. Theatre presence/foregrounding does not necessarily lead to authority foregrounding.

So the process is such that we first must separate our impressions about Porter the stage presence from Porter the authority, and then we must further separate our various impressions about Porter from our overall impression about the play. If we distinguish these responses, then we should likely come to a realization that Porter's dominant stage actions repel and undermine his effective presence as some traditionally based leading spokesperson of a cause. The play has a "hero" in that it has a main character, but it has no "hero" in the sense of having someone to follow.

This conclusion is perhaps a damning one from a traditional perspective that insists on guidance and resolution. But from a more postmodern perspective, this conclusion opens the play to a diversity of directions, a defeat of linearity and encouragement of spatial direction. In essence, this perspective empowers the audience over both Porter and Osborne, leaving the audience open to determine its own destiny, without the clear guidance of either Porter or Osborne. The character of Porter—and of Osborne, the man behind Porter—essentially deconstructs before our eyes, leaving a void that the audience must fill.

The most critical passage in the play to support this perspective is the one when Porter summarizes his father's life, a man who died as a result of fighting against tyranny in the Spanish Civil War:

His family were embarrassed by the whole business. Embarrassed and irritated. . . . As for my mother, all she could think about was the fact that she had allied herself to a man who seemed to be on the wrong side in all things. My mother was for being associated with minorities, provided they were the smart, fashionable ones. (57)

Porter—and Osborne—are here attacking a phenomenon visible in the 1930s, '40s, and '50s, and that is perhaps even more evident (and the attack still relevant) today: the bandwagon desire to be politically fashionable by supporting causes that require little real commitment and demand little if any real risk. Consider the world-wide "Band-Aid" and American "Farm-Aid" campaigns of the '80s, as well as such causes that pay lip service to eradicating drug abuse or homelessness. As long as the causes do not require real commitment and risk, as long as they are "smart" and "fashionable," many self-proclaimed liberals will emerge with vocal (and sometimes even nominally material) support. Rarely, however, does such commitment result in any real risk or commitment—few ever give or sacrifice more than what is superfluous to their lives. Ultimately, the degree of commitment is indeterminable because the causes—though perhaps in real need of backing—are safe and the sacrifices have not entailed demanding personal risk.

Jimmy Porter's own all-embracing "cause" is vaguely described as a struggle to rekindle human "enthusiasm." By being as vague as he is, Porter fails to validate any cause, which is yet another characteristic that invalidates much of his energy on stage as a traditional authority. But though critics often condemn this vagueness as they do Porter's negative personality, I see several strengths in this characterization. Even if we look to see Porter's energy on stage as potentially positive, this desire to see potential is thwarted by a lack of specific, traditionally sited direction. With so much informing against this stage presence, with so much negating this stage presence, we as audience must in turn fill the void that Porter points to but himself leaves vacant. Ultimately, we must find our own concrete direction for the play, or, more generally, we must extend the activity begun by Porter and the play, and find a direction for our own visions of "causes" outside the play. Porter is a catalyst awakening us to the issue of commitment, Porter's cause is a vacuum into which we as audience are activated into envisioning any number of specific possibilities.

And because Porter drifts without direction, we as audience must determine to forge paths on our own. Left "leaderless" in this play, audiences are forced into an active rather than traditionally passive role in order to derive real value and meaning from the play, something positive with which they can leave the theatre. This process, of course, runs contrary to traditional audience/reader expectations of being directly told by a playwright—as, say, Shaw does—what "right action" is. What *Look Back in Anger* has become is a catalyst to stimulate audience (re)action rather than a reflection of the playwright's personal vision of right action. Following Porter's lead just will not do. Determining what is right behavior is left to the audience, as is determining what are real causes since, at very least, the play does not offer any "smart, fashionable" ones to bandwagon onto.

If Porter had been created to speak eloquently for a cause in a more traditional vein, and if he himself were an unambiguously empathic character, then it is very likely that audiences would actually leave the theatre supporting, in a "smart, fashionable" way, the cause Porter (and Osborne) hypothetically endorsed. Of course, no endorsement exists in the play. But if given traditionalist circumstances where an endorsement were made, how can we truly measure the degree to which we are supporting the cause if the cause is so easy to support, by way of merely bandwagoning onto the message of the theatre event? How much investment, even in original thought, have we made? Both previous questions in fact are questions postmodern artists generally ask about the value of the traditional approach to message in art. And an additional question would also linger when it came to creating a charismatic central figure: are we even at very least fashionably supporting the cause, or is the commitment even less, merely a sign of commitment to a messenger of the cause?

As the play stands, Porter has proven himself incapable of speaking for the cause (for any cause), and even if he did speak for a specific, directed cause, would not the cause be crippled by the negative feelings felt for the spokesman? Leaving his specific cause as vague as Osborne does effectively works to avoid placing a "Porter" stigma on any cause that may gather audience support.

In fact, to a certain degree, seeing Porter as a negative presence even succeeds on a traditionalist level as well, though less effectively. It succeeds at a level that focusses on characters on stage rather than audience engagement and activation as described above. These characters do become something of models for audience behavior and reaction. Looking back to 1956 and assuming a traditionalist's posture, we can see that what Porter did demand of his onstage audience was genuine commitment, genuine "enthusiasm," something that must be generated before any movement toward specific causes can occur. But even in this case, once again, Porter is merely a catalyst and not a prime example, for he offers his roommates (or cellmates) nothing tangible to stand up for or against (except, generically, the "status quo"). Porter really teaches nothing, even in this traditional sense, because though he sensitizes other characters into a need for greater awareness, he remains hopelessly unfocussed.

But in offering Alison as its particular case study (in moving beyond the centrality of Porter), the play moves beyond a limited one-man show and offers something of a model to follow, one that nominally conforms to traditionalist expectations. Attached before the play begins to Porter as the result of a sort of fashionably rebellious move against her parents, Alison eventually enters Porter's house of pain as a result of her losses away from Porter, mainly as a result of her miscarriage and resulting sterility. When she finally returns to Jimmy, Alison proclaims, "I was wrong, I was wrong! I don't want to be neutral. I don't want to be a saint. I want to be a lost cause. I want to be corrupt and futile!" (95). Settling into "the mud at last" (95), Alison has experienced the pain of existence that Jimmy raves against, and she is now on her way to truly being Porter's kindred spirit. But the transformation has little really to do with Porter; he doubtless paved the way, but events beyond his ken transform Alison.

Alison's transformation occurs very much in the traditional vein of standard naturalist theatrical events: an impervious spirit is assaulted but resists, only to succumb to unexpected events which lead to an epiphany and promise of transformation. Osborne's goal of awakening a generation finds its reflection more in Alison than in Jimmy Porter. Though clearly a lightning rod, Porter's white-light intensity actually only brings an audience to a focal point; it does little to direct us toward an awakening. Alison specifically shows us the way.

But Osborne keeps her as vague as Jimmy when it comes to what to do and against what injustices; after all, it is difficult to envision a cause that could succeed at eliminating miscarriages (the source of her epiphany). And here is where we return to the above position. First, *Look Back in Anger* is more than a one-man show. Second, this one man's incredible stage presence turns into a black-hole performance, falling back into itself so powerfully that anything positive it tries to emit simply cannot escape the imploding force of his anger. If that anger is to ever move outward in a positive way, it will require a different mechanism than what Porter and Alison (and perhaps Osborne as well) are equipped with. Alison offers us a sign that general awakening is possible, that the fact of personal disaster can be the signal for change rather than a prelude to surrender. Porter presents the impotent rage of looking back. The play itself offers signs—indeterminate, but signs nonetheless—that looking forward is the only hope.

The direction Jimmy and Alison may look following the play's conclusion is, of course, not clear. If Alison completes—or at least begins—a naturalist/traditionalist transformation, that transformation is nonetheless undeveloped and ultimately unfulfilling from a traditionalist audience's point of view in that it does not offer a full-fledged pattern, complete with specific target, to follow. And Jimmy is, of course, not a guiding star by any means. In fact, given the apparent actual design of the play—to insist that we all begin to evolve and aspire to our own goals—traditional guidance would defeat itself in that it would present a model to *follow* rather than insist on individual initiative.

The effect of the play overall moves beyond the characters, a perspective that turns the characters' undeveloped states into dramatic and rhetorical strengths from a postmodern perspective rather than weaknesses or flaws of craft from a traditional perspective. Jimmy looks back with rage at his father's life and death, but perhaps the audience—alienated from this father's son—can see what Porter does not because Porter is not in the audience watching himself. In almost Brechtian fashion, the distance we are forced to keep from Porter allows the audience to draw conclusions that neither Porter nor possibly even Osborne saw: there is a need to discover and commit to much more than popular causes, that looking back may be a first step, but it is only a transitional step to moving forward, and moving forward under one's own power.

The play has rightly been identified as revolutionary in introducing a new class of characters on the British stage. But that sort of recognition of revolutionary redirection identifies, ultimately, only a refinement of naturalist processes. This sort of revolution affects the traditional ground of British theatre. Footed on the other side of the fault line, the play perhaps more profoundly, and more revolutionarily, steps onto new ground by neutralizing the authority of the central character and its creator and by empowering the audience in their stead. Though such efforts at audience empowerment had been made by the experimental advances of Pirandello, Brecht, and other predecessors, Osborne's singular achievement is that by positioning himself between two movements—the traditional and the experimental or avant garde—he brought such techniques to mainstage, popular theatre.

In fact it is very likely that the critics in 1956, and even today, responded so violently to *Look Back in Anger* less because of the new language and class of characters on stage—the ostensible and articulated reasons—than because of the introduction of a new dramatic methodology so subtle that it escaped the conscious attention of virtually everyone. Consider the following:

> John Osborne didn't contribute to the British theatre: he set off a landmine called *Look Back in Anger* and blew most of it up. The bits have settled back into place, of course, but it can never be the same again. (Sillitoe qtd. in Taylor, ed., 185)

If Osborne blew up the British theatre, more than dialogue and character types were involved. The form itself altered, and on closer scrutiny I do not think one can say things actually settled back into place, for what Osborne may have unwittingly introduced to the British stage has become more and more the new tradition. And Osborne is no longer the lone proponent. Edward Bond's dramas of antiheroes and spiritual voids, as well as Joe Orton's, John Arden's, and Harold Pinter's, are less revolutionary because of their subject matter than because of the patently inconclusive nature of their works. If Osborne's *Look Back in Anger* provides a formal theatrical closure not often found in his successors, that is because Osborne had his foot in the past as well as in the future. But bridging the gap, Osborne opened the way for these others. And by opening this path for others, he more importantly helped to establish a new kind of serious theatre that insisted on audiences participating—cerebrally at least—in the dramatic idea, or theme, rather than entering the theatre with the intention of being fed a message or to find out what the author wants us to do.

The world's ills will find curatives through myriad separate conclusions. And if we choose to accept what Sillitoe concludes, then as the exploded pieces of traditional British theatre have fallen back into place, the resulting mosaic produced only a superficial reflection of the old form.

WORKS CITED

    Amory, Mark. "Jester Flees the Court." *Sunday Times Magazine* 24 November 1974: 34.
    Dempsey, David. "Most Angry Fella." *New York Times Magazine* 20 October 1957: 22, 27.
    Hayman, Ronald. *John Osborne*. London: Heinemann, 1968.
    Hinchliffe, Arnold. *John Osborne*. Boston: Twayne, 1984.
    Osborne, John. *Look Back in Anger*. New York: Criterion, 1957.
    ———. "That Awful Museum." *Twentieth Century Literature* 169 (February 1961): 212-16.
    Taylor, John Russell, ed. *John Osborne: "Look Back in Anger," A Casebook*. London: Macmillan, 1968. 2.

The Logic of Anger and Despair

A Pragmatic Approach to John Osborne's *Look Back in Anger*

Luc M. Gilleman

John Osborne once said "I want to make people feel, to give them lessons in feeling. They can think afterwards."[1] It is long "afterwards" now, more than thirty-seven years since Osborne's first successful play, *Look Back in Anger*, was staged at the Royal Court Theatre in London. Yet today a sound articulation of the structure responsible for that play's oft-celebrated emotional impact is still lacking. In fact, although never passed over in accounts of literary history, *Look Back in Anger* is mainly remembered as a play "in which rebelliousness and disillusionment shout themselves hoarse *for no reason at all* in the person of Jimmy Porter."[2] Because of this lack of critical understanding, the play's historical importance is not so much recognized as grudgingly granted. Since we are obviously stuck with the play, as literary historians seem to imply, let us try once more to find out why Jimmy is angry and desperate.

Looking for an answer to the problem of Jimmy's moods may seem trivial yet is only apparently so. We are, in fact, interested in the line of plausibility that made this play a credible or truthful emotional experience for so many spectators. By solving the problem of motivation we, in other words, discover the play's implied logic of realistic representation or its *vraisemblance* that, in turn, reflects historically changing perceptions of the real. I will argue that the play's logic of anger and despair, which appears after a pragmatic analysis, reflects a systemic functionalist convention of reality. At the end of this article, we will have occasion to deal very briefly with some of the aesthetical and ideological consequences of this particular *vraisemblance*. After the war, such a systemic structuring of reality was perceived as breathtakingly "real" in comparison to a more mechanical way of organizing the representation of reality that had by then become a stale convention. The inability of many critics to account rationally for the audience's strong emotional experience signifies that this change in the convention of the real had not yet found adequate conceptualization.

Osborne obviously rejects the more conventional mechanistic paradigm of playwriting with which critics of realistic plays are more familiar. Like Harold Pinter in "Writing for the Theatre" (1962), Osborne in "They Call It Cricket" complains that the critic expects to be confronted with reliable characters whose words reflect their intentions, whose language, in other words, is transparent. The type of critic Osborne has in mind is obviously spoiled by a tradition of didactic realism and assumes with Aristotle that "even if inconsistency be part of the man before one for imitation as presenting that form of character, he should still be consistently inconsistent."[3] Osborne, on the contrary, wants to put people of flesh and blood on the stage who exhibit a "natural" fitfulness. "It seemed that Osborne had ripped out an inner part of himself and tossed it, bleeding, onto the stage," says Alan Carter.[4] This flattering appraisal of Osborne's artistic skill should not prevent one from realizing that the language of the gut is not less convention-bound than that of the brain. In fact, in a less violently creative moment, Osborne has formulated his own view of what constitutes "reality" on the stage quite rationally:

> Drama rests on the *dynamic* that is created *between* characters on the stage. It must be concrete and it must be expressed, even if it is only in silence or a gesture of despair. The theatre is not a school room, nor is it, as many people seem to think, a place where "discussion" takes place, where ideas are apparently formally examined in the manner of a solitary show-off in an intellectual magazine.[5]

With these words, Osborne distances himself from a realism inspired by the Aristotelian tradition. He also tells us effectively that it is as pointless to interpret isolated utterances in his plays as it is to catch the whole nature of a dance from a snapshot. And, most important, these words draw attention to a method of recreating reality, a new *vraisemblance* that, as I will conclude at the end of this study, turns *Look Back in Anger* into one of the first examples of postwar language-oriented realism.

And yet, we may well question the justness of John Osborne's attack on those critics who, because of their insistence on a conventional content-analysis of *Look Back in Anger*, were "incapable of recognizing the texture of ordinary despair, the way it expresses itself in rhetoric and gestures that may perhaps look shabby, but are seldom simple."[6] The play, after all, shares many characteristics both in terms of content and form with a conventional "well-made play," such as *Table by the Window*, the first of the two plays of Terence Rattigan's *Separate Tables* (1954). The action both in *Look Back in Anger* and *Table by the Window* requires characters to be isolated from the outside world in an entrapping room. Both plays deal with a troublesome marriage across class barriers and with two kinds of love—the one comfortable but emotionally dissatisfying, the other intense yet requiring perhaps more "muscle and guts" than the characters can endure. The passionate dialogues in both plays are "full of tenderness and pain," i.e., in accordance with the literary convention of a love-hate relationship. And the final reconciliation scene between the warring couples is underscored by symbolism indicating hope while leaving a certain degree of ambiguity so that discussion after the play is guaranteed. All these similarities with conventional realism would justify a content-oriented approach.

A closer look, however, reveals that both plays are based on a distinctly different *vraisemblance*, or logic of realistic representation. As far as *Table by the Window* is concerned, the pattern is distinct: characters are introduced with their past and present idiosyncracies, a secret is hinted at, a conflict emerges. From that moment on, the scene is set like an alarm clock and the action ticks off toward its resolution with for some depressing, for others comforting, logicality. Most important, this process of reordering an initial configuration of characters and tensions is established and clarified through dialogue, even to the extent that we are literally given the rationale behind the couple's constant bickering and fighting by having one of them solemnly proclaim that "marriage is a kind of war" (*Separate Tables* 46). Analysis of that kind of play asks for a sorting out of the information and a fitting together of character, action, and language, so that, as in a puzzle, a complex, unified image appears.

Critics of *Look Back in Anger*, we may remember, had a harder time putting together character, action, and language. The bravura of Jimmy's anger cannot disguise the unreasonableness of his attacks. Jimmy obviously does not know what he wants; some peevish early reviewers even recommended a forced dip into "a horse pond" or a life sentence of "cleaning latrines" as the only cure for such puerility.[7] If an analysis of character did not provide the key to the play's overall meaning, perhaps action would. This rather claustrophobic room-play certainly compensates for its lack of physical action by Jimmy's acts of verbal virtuosity which, Kenneth Tynan told us, exemplify the effervescence of rebellious youth that lashes out at all and sundry.[8] For Tynan this was sufficient to make watching the play an experience short of revolutionary. However, judged from a more sober social or political perspective, the play offers neither insight nor alternatives. On the contrary, it bears traces of a dubious nostalgia for former imperialistic grandeur. Because of its large range of unfocussed criticism, the play in fact reinforces our fatalistic belief that no adequate solution to existing sociopolitical problems can be found. Perhaps then the play was all about lack of action, but if so, it was hardly relevant to the historical reality it was supposed to portray. Benedict Nightingale was quick to point out that Jimmy Porter's most celebrated line, "there aren't any good, brave causes left," was evidently untrue (84).[9] In the year of the play's performance, the Suez crisis, the Soviet intervention in Hungary, the Campaign for Nuclear Disarmament, and the "threat" of egalitarianism, to name just a few, offered just causes for Right and Left, and effectively divided public opinion. As a result, some critics decided to forget about the topical references. If what Jimmy Porter said made little sense, it was because we were dealing not with social drama but with a case study of a neurotic personality.[10] This did not prove a very fruitful line to follow, however. It may be true that Jimmy's obsession with drinking and eating, his puffing at his pipe, and his logorrhea fit the pattern of anal fixation; elaborating on such a concurrence only makes us wonder even more at the play's general attraction. So critics turned away from character and focussed on language, praising its "Dionysian quality" or its "emotional substructure"—terms that are more evocative than explanatory.[11] John Russell Brown and Andrew K. Kennedy minutely investigated Jimmy Porter's "rhetoric," probably influenced by John Osborne's statement that "although *Look Back in Anger* was a formal, rather old-fashioned play, I think that it broke out by its use of language."[12] They investigated this language mainly stylistically and rhetorically but failed to establish the link between communication and behavior—a remarkable oversight considering that the correlation, or even the coalescence of words and action, is what most clearly distinguishes theatre from literature ("*car là Parler, c'est Agir*," says Abbé d'Aubignac about the theatre as early as the seventeenth century).[13]

    The critics, in other words, were faced with the following problem: *Look Back in Anger* looked like a conventional realistic play but failed to behave as one. The strongly cut characters of Terence Rattigan's *Table by the Window* move like chess pieces on a board in a clearly defined conflict toward the resolution; although apparently moving through a conflict toward a resolution, characters in *Look Back in Anger* display an excess of anger and despair, insufficiently justified by this action. Characters in *Table by the Window* are as clearly defined by their language as chess pieces by their way of moving; language in *Look Back in Anger* suffers too much from inconsistency and ambiguity to be a proper gauge of the characters' "true nature." For these reasons, a content-directed analysis, although sufficiently adequate to articulate our understanding of a conventional realistic play, leads to unsatisfactory results when applied to *Look Back in Anger*. This is either because *Look Back in Anger* is a bad play or because it is founded on a different *vraisemblance*. Much critical acumen and malicious gusto have gone into proving the first explanation to the problem: John Osborne was a young "angry" playwright with more promise than skill. A more satisfying answer can be found if we compare *Look Back in Anger* to an apparently very different kind of realistic play.

Although Harold Pinter's plays differ in style and subject matter, they share with John Osborne's *Look Back in Anger* a foregrounding of language that is ultimately uncongenial with a conventionally realistic development of character, plot, or sociopolitical issues. In predominantly character-, plot-, or issue-oriented realism, language plays a serving role. Revealing crucial aspects of personality, clarifying motivations on which the action is based, conveying ideas that the playwright wants his or her audience to consider are some of the "transitive" functions of language in these forms of realism.[14] On the other hand, language-oriented realistic plays, including those of Harold Pinter and, as I will argue, John Osborne's *Look Back in Anger*, have a tendency to use language "intransitively," i.e., often apparently for its own sake. These plays seek a "truthful" rendition of the rhythm, sound, and structure of communication and are less concerned with the literary conventions of coherence and consequentiality that a more didactic realism prescribes for the presentation of character, action, or ideas. These realistic plays possess a *vraisemblance* that demands from the critic a different analytical approach to articulate the theatrical experience.

As far as Pinter's plays are concerned, the logic of representation on which some of his more realistic plays are based has already been articulated. "The problem [in dealing with Pinter's plays] is as much one of description as one of understanding," says Austin Quigley, who found the methodological solution in Wittgenstein's theory of language games.[15] Quigley thus avoided the "lingering impact of the reference theory" that "encourage[s] us to try to separate the meaning of a sentence from its use."[16] For *Look Back in Anger*, I also propose to follow a pragmatic, i.e., effect- rather than content-oriented approach, but based, in my case, on ideas derived from a "family interactionism" grounded in Gregory Bateson's early work on schizophrenia.[17] From non-mechanistic cybernetics and systems theory, Bateson's pragmatic approach derives its belief that human relationships are circularly patterned, a view which, as we will see, makes the durability of apparently unendurable relationships more intelligible, yet, as I will point out, in a way that some find ideologically objectionable. Systems theory holds that various "negative feedback" or regulating mechanisms counteract behavior that threatens the status quo. Family interactionism, for instance, sees mythmaking as a powerful regulating mechanism: people often put up with a troublesome relationship because its continuation is necessary for the preservation of their self-image.[18] Paradox is another "negative feedback" mechanism: when it forms the dominant characteristic of an interaction, partners can be entrapped in a stalemate relationship, a "double bind," that prevents them from making any move that could bring about change. This impossibility to change often is also the result of an inability or impossibility to "metacommunicate," that is, to comment on the ongoing communication, because in the absence of mutual trust, remarks on the formal aspects of a problematic communication pattern ventured by one of the participants in that interaction are easily drawn into the dispute they try to solve. Finally, and most importantly for this particular play, since systems theory conceives of communication in its broadest sense as responding and responsive behavior, it asserts that "one cannot not communicate."[19] Silence, thus, is no withdrawal from communication; on the contrary, it is a powerful response that serves a purpose.

The pragmatic approach will allow us to formulate a rationale for the characters' excessive anger or despair, different from but not incompatible with their own unsatisfactory interpretations of their behavior. It should also help us to avoid some of the common mistakes that John Osborne has accused critics of committing. Osborne has called drama "dynamic," yet critics have quoted statements pronounced by individual characters as if these words were not born in the heat of a battle between warring factions; Osborne has drawn attention to what happens "between" characters on stage, yet critics have concentrated on what happens "in" Jimmy Porter. The play does not make sense if we listen to *what* the characters say and fail to take into account *why* they say it. This is the domain of "pragmatics." I will adopt this point of view in an attempt to come to a coherent vision of the play.

* * *

Whereas in a conventional critical response to realistic drama, interaction is merely talked of as a function of character, a pragmatic approach foregrounds the interactional dynamics and discusses everything else (character, plot, ideas) as a function of it. The difference in approach becomes crucial in an interaction such as that of *Look Back in Anger*, which consists of a series of withdrawals (on the part of Alison) and provocations (on the part of Jimmy). An interpretation that centers on character rather than on interaction will have to decide which comes first, withdrawal or provocation. However, the 1968 revival production of *Look Back in Anger*, as John Russell Taylor points out, emphasized a new aspect of the play in drawing attention to the way the principal characters are caught in the vicious circle of their interactional responses.[20] In that production, Cliff's comment, "I'm wondering how much longer I can go on watching *you two* tearing the insides out of *each other*" became programmatic [my emphasis] (28). Only some critics, however, have noticed the interactional circularity of Jimmy and Alison's communication, yet they have not given it more than a passing mention.[21] In a conventional, non-pragmatic assessment of such an interaction, one chooses the beginning term of this series of withdrawals and provocations most often in accordance with one's sympathies and allegiances. So, according to the critic's own views of gender relations, Jimmy is either a frustrated husband who is brought to despair by his wife's passivity or a cad who bullies his wife into dejected silence. "It is her quiescence that drives him to an almost insane pitch of frustrated loathing," writes Kenneth Allsop.[22] Carter thinks that "we can appreciate how Jimmy has been pressured by the forces of society to take it out on Alison," and that "it is her lack of response and affection towards Jimmy which causes him to treat her so badly."[23] After all, does Jimmy not complain that "that girl there can twist your arm off with her silence" (59)? Other male critics in a gentlemanly fashion side up with Alison, describing Jimmy as an objectionable young man who constantly tyrannizes his wife.[24] These critics feel themselves strengthened in their opinion by Helena's advice to Alison: "Listen to me. You've got to fight him. Fight, or get out. Otherwise, he *will* kill you" (47).

A conventional character-oriented analysis, in other words, yields a lopsided view of the interaction that is presented as if crystallized in one particular moment of its dynamics. In siding up with one or the other character, the critic only adopts that character's limited view of the cause-effect chain in what could, after all, be an interlocking, reciprocal interaction. A systemic pragmatic analyst would say that such a critic sides up with one character's "punctuation of events."[25] The pragmatic analyst would conceive of Jimmy and Alison as chained prisoners forced to coordinate their moves to avoid tumbling. Whether the net result of an interaction pattern will be disruptive or stabilizing for the relationship as a whole depends on the kind of feedback mechanism that dominates. In a symmetrical interaction pattern, both partners exhibit the same kind of behavior, thus intensifying it by positive feedback. In a complementary pattern, one of the partners exhibits a behavior opposite to the one he/she is faced with, thus counterbalancing the effect by negative feedback.

The provocation-withdrawal interaction pattern in *Look Back in Anger* appears to be "complementary" in that one of the partners reacts with the complementary behavior of submission to the verbal attacks of the other. However, if this submissive behavior functions as a disguised form of aggression, then the relationship, although formally "complementary," has the same effect as a "symmetrical" interaction in which aggression is matched by aggression, and escalation follows. In *Almost a Gentleman*, John Osborne mentions that he created the role of Alison as "a study of the tyranny of negation": "Alison's brutal power lay in the puny crackle of her iron."[26] Alison's words to Cliff corroborate this last view but add an important qualification:

> I keep looking back, as far as I remember, and I can't think what it was to feel young, really young. Jimmy said the same thing to me the other day. *I pretended not to be listening—because I knew that would hurt him, I suppose.* And—of course—he got savage, like tonight. But I knew just what he meant. I suppose it would have been so easy to say "Yes, darling, I know just what you mean. I know what you're feeling." (*Shrugs*). *It's those easy things that seem to be so impossible with us.* [my emphases] (28)

Alison reveals here that her imperviousness is an *unavoidable* strategy of provocation. She also draws attention to what keeps this cruel game going: it is impossible to say the saving words that could prevent a fight.

In the language of pragmatics, the self-perpetuating pattern of Alison's withdrawal and Jimmy's provocative behavior would be explained as resulting from a "failure of metacommunication"; "those easy things" refer, then, to those words that should reach out across and beyond the cross fire of habitual taunt and retort in a gesture that comforts and leads toward a discussion of the relationship. But this is exactly what is "so impossible" in Alison's and Jimmy's relationship. Every attempt at metacommunication fails. On several occasions Alison tries to prevent the interaction from deteriorating. Each time, these attempts are caught up in the quarrel as further evidence of Alison's despicable habit of withdrawing from involvement. Therefore, instead of alleviating the tension, metacommunication in this relationship further increases the conflagration:

> Alison: God help me, if he doesn't stop, I'll go out of my mind in a minute.
> Jimmy: Why don't you? That would be something, anyway. (22)

> Alison: Really, Jimmy, you're like a child.
> Jimmy: Don't try and patronise me. (24)

> Alison: *(Starting to break).* Why, why, why, why!
> *(Putting her hands over her ears).*
> That word's pulling my head off!
> Jimmy: And as long as you're around, I'll go on using it. (54)

> Jimmy: You Judas! You phlegm! She's taking you with her, and you're so bloody feeble, you'll let her do it!
> *Alison suddenly takes hold of her cup, and hurls it on the floor. He's drawn blood at last. She looks down at the pieces on the floor, and then at him. . . .*
> Alison: *(Softly).* All I want is a little peace.
> Jimmy: Peace! God! She wants peace! *(Hardly able to get his words out.)* My heart is so full, I feel ill—and she wants peace! (59)

We see Jimmy's "blocking of metacommunication" also at work in response to Cliff's "You've gone too far Jimmy. Now dry up!" (55).[27] Jimmy disqualifies this restraining move as evidence of Cliff's allegiance to the other side. Moreover, he manages to work Cliff's pacifying move into his ongoing argument with Helena: "I suppose you're going over to that side as well. Well, why don't you? Helena will help to make it pay off for you. She's an expert in the New Economics—the Economics of the Supernatural . . ." (55). Cliff is, of course, far from a neutral ground in this battle between Jimmy and Alison. By either softening Jimmy's cruelty through humor or by repairing excessive emotional damage, Cliff contributes to the negative feedback. Helena's attempt to break through the argument by commenting directly on Jimmy's behavior ("I think you're a very tiresome young man" [50]) is used by Jimmy as evidence of her upper-class background, which becomes now an object of mockery:

> *A slight pause as his delight catches up with him. He roars with laughter.*
> Jimmy: Oh dear, oh dear! My wife's friends! Pass Lady Bracknell the cucumber sandwiches, will you? (51)

Alison's complementary behavior has the effect of a symmetrical response, and she is unable to comment on her plight because, as is born out by the examples cited above, in such relationships "metacommunication, a possible stabilizer, proves to be subject to the same rule of symmetry, and, instead of stopping the conflagration, further ignites it."[28]

Blocking metacommunication is not an uncommon practice, but in *Look Back in Anger* the confusion between the two separate levels of communication, ordinary communication and metacommunication, and between symmetrical and complementary interaction leads to an impasse of a paradoxical nature: Jimmy and Alison are trapped in a "game without end."[29] Their relationship is both complementary (in form) and symmetrical (in effect). Alison's complementary stance toward Jimmy is described by herself, by Jimmy, and by Cliff as a means of attack on Jimmy. Jimmy, on the other hand, torments his wife, allegedly out of despair provoked by Alison's withdrawal tactic. To Jimmy, Alison's withdrawal in daily life means secret provocation; similarly, in their sexual relationship, submission comes to mean secret dominance. "Oh, it's not that she hasn't her own kind of passion," says Jimmy. "She just devours me whole every time, as if I were some over-large rabbit" (37). Again, Alison is put in an untenable position that leaves her no possibility to react properly. Obviously, open signs of sexual desire on her part would likely be interpreted by Jimmy as the proof of the dominance he always suspected. And since he perceives Alison's apparent sexual submission as a hidden dominance, he, in turn, subverts the signs of his desire for women and his victimization by women by constant intimations of homosexuality ("I'm tired of being hetero" [50]).

Caught in this double bind, Jimmy develops an all-encompassing distrust, searching for clues that would corroborate his suspicion. In what Dyson refers to as a "persecution-complex," Jimmy mistrusts Alison's virginity ("as if I had deceived him in some strange way" [30]); he would have distrusted her pregnancy ("He'll suspect my motives at once" and "he'd feel hoaxed" as Alison says to Helena [29]); he distrusts her silence ("that girl there can twist your arm off with her silence" [59]), her loyalty (he searches her correspondence), her passion ("She just devours me whole every time, as if I were some over-large rabbit"[37]) or frigidity ("Do you know I have never known the great pleasure of lovemaking when I didn't desire it myself" [37]).[30] Jimmy's suspicions leave Alison no alternative, no behavior likely to break the circle that imprisons them. Both seem to want something from each other that neither of them can give. Maria Palazzoli has formulated the unspoken wish that fuels this kind of interaction pattern in real life: "It's not that you should *do* something different; you should *be* different. Only in this way can you help me to be what I'm not, but what I could be if you were not what you are."[31] Paul Watzlawick considers this as "probably the most frequent and important way in which paradox can enter into human communication."[32]

In analyzing Harold Pinter's plays, Austin Quigley made the comment that "relationships . . . become major battlegrounds as characters attempt to negotiate a mutual reality."[33] Jimmy and Alison are likewise engaged in a struggle to convince each other of their "punctuation of events," their definition of the relational reality, and it is a battle that is fought rather than discussed because every attempt to discuss it immediately becomes part of the battle. As Alison is unable to react, Jimmy increases his attempts to evoke in her some reaction that would amount either to confirmation or rejection. But the more he rages and shouts, the more she is aware of her untenable position, and the less she can do to get out of it. As long as none of the partners can define the relationship in unequivocal terms, there is neither winner nor loser, and each of the partners can still cherish the hope that one day he or she will be able to convince the other of the "true" punctuation of events. In order to perpetuate this game, each move must be parried with a countermove that disqualifies it. For instance, when Alison finally leaves Jimmy, this is an explicit manifestation of her desire to put an end to an impossible situation. But in *Look Back in Anger* no move is made unambiguously, as Alison's farewell letter shows:

> Jimmy: (to Helena) Did you write this for her! Well, listen to this then! (*Reading*.) "My dear—I must get away. I don't suppose you will understand, but please try. I need peace so desperately, and, at the moment, I am willing to sacrifice everything just for that. I don't know what's going to happen to us. I know you will be feeling wretched and bitter, but try to be a little patient with me. I shall always have a deep loving need of you—Alison.' Oh, how could she be so bloody wet! Deep loving need! That makes me puke! . . . She couldn't say "You rotten bastard! I hate your guts, I'm clearing out, and I hope you rot!" No, she has to make a polite, emotional mess out of it! (72)

Jimmy rages because the couple is more than ever in an "emotional mess." The letter defines her moving out paradoxically: she is leaving him because she needs him—and this is parallelled on a symbolic level by Alison's decision not to take the squirrel, her alter ego, with her but to leave it along with the bear that we by then have come to see as Jimmy's image. Even without Alison's physical presence, the unresolved conflict between Jimmy and Alison prevents the two participants from tearing the bonds that keep them imprisoned.[34]

The final solution to the play comes in the form of Alison's total physical and emotional breakdown. She not only has lost her child but is unable to be pregnant ever again. Sobbing, she falls in Jimmy's arms, and the pair is reconciled in what is a most peculiar happy end. Alan Carter puts it succinctly, although with an alarming lack of irony: "Alison had suffered sufficiently for Jimmy to warm to her, and so a reconciliation could be hopefully effected."[35] This statement is reasonable for someone who throughout his analysis of the play has followed Jimmy's "punctuation of events," and who uncritically accepts Jimmy's professed self-image, namely, that of the "knight in shining armour" who knows all about "love . . . betrayal . . . and death" (45, 57). Through her suffering, Alison, according to that view, has reached some of her husband's heroic and romantic stature. An analysis based on identification with a character that one chooses as the central focus of all action runs the risk of either taking Jimmy's self-image for granted, and then from that point of view declaring rather callously that Alison's tragic return is the price she has to pay in order to be allowed to live in the shadow of his romantic grandeur, or silently disregarding that self-image, and in that case suffering the embarrassment of witnessing what is then described as the "painful whimsey" of this last reconciliation scene.[36]

But Alison's return can also be analyzed for its effect on the two most powerful negative feedback mechanisms that keep this relationship from changing, namely, the family myth and paradox. The shared "family myth" consists of a silent agreement among members concerning their mutual position and their respective roles in the interaction. This myth is the "official party line" of the family, even if it constitutes a "group departure from reality." It may be imaginary in content, says Paul Watzlawick; the interaction, however, is real, and "the nature of this interaction" is important.[37] As it requires all members to collaborate in a stable coalition, family myth helps to preserve homeostasis. In fact, we find Alison, of all people, instructing Helena in the official Byronic image of her Jimmy, the wild and sad outsider, burningly vitalistic and deeply despairing, whose "hair glistened and seemed to spring off his head" but whose face is marked by "the tired line of his mouth" (45). At the same time, the heroic image of Jimmy as a Don Quixote fighting windmills, a revolutionary in a stagnating world, provides the much needed rationale without which some of his excessively cruel attacks would be unbearable to his victims. However, if we believe John Osborne's comment that it is not good enough to take Jimmy on his word when he says that "there aren't any good, brave causes left," neither is it necessary nor wise to take this self-image for granted of a man who, as we know, spends his time working at a sweet-stall during the week, reading the "posh papers" on Sundays, and having the occasional beer in the local pub. Osborne's advice supports our view that there are no statements in *Look Back in Anger* that do not function primarily as strategic moves in a relational game—and that applies equally well to Jimmy's self-image.

If the dominant characteristic of Jimmy and Alison's relationship was its ambiguity, Alison's return forces them to place the cards on the table once and for all. Jimmy is now forced to take the consequences of his wish: "If you could have a child, and it would die. Let it grow, let a recognisable human face emerge from that little mess of indiarubber and wrinkles. . . . Please—if only I could watch that" (37). He has further mortgaged his future actions by describing how he would behave in that case:

> Perhaps, one day, you may want to come back. I shall wait for that day. I want to stand up in your tears, and splash about in them, and sing. I want to be there when you grovel. I want to see your face rubbed in the mud—that's all I can hope for. There's nothing else I want any longer. (59–60)

Nothing in this wish is incompatible with the family myth. It shows Jimmy as a hard, cruel, and desperate man who knows that "there are no dry cleaners in Cambodia" and that love "takes muscle and guts" (50, 93). Because of Alison's return, Jimmy has now to live up to his words or the couple has to reconsider the family myth and rebuild their relationship on a different basis.

From the point of view of pragmatics, Alison's return has created the counterparadox that resolves the paradox of their peculiar interaction. If change is to be brought about in a relationship that through strong negative feedback is frozen into a double bind, it will have to be induced without resorting to comments or criticism or any other form of metacommunication. As all comments on the illogicality or the impossibility of the situation are immediately subjected to the same rules that lead to a symmetrical escalation, the intervention must take a form that can neither be refused nor disqualified while remaining in accordance with the family myth. Alison's utter submission takes the form not of subjection but of a demand to undergo the treatment Jimmy claimed he would have in store for her: "This is what he's been longing for me to feel. This is what he wants to splash about in! . . . Don't you see! I'm in the mud at last! I'm grovelling! I'm crawling!" (95). But not surprisingly this apparent rigid complementarity is also very ambiguous. The victim who asks for torture puts the torturer in a quaint position: whether he complies or not with this wish, the torturer loses his superior position. Jimmy cannot disqualify Alison's move, nor can he escape the paradox he is confronted with. In this crucial moment, the old family myth collapses. His doubts are voiced in a magnificent metaphor: the image of the bear can stand for the power and strength of the outcast, but may as well allude to the toy bear, the consoler of a frightened child:

> Was I really wrong to believe that there's a—a kind of—burning virility of mind and spirit that looks for something as powerful as itself? The heaviest, strongest creatures in this world seem to be the loneliest. Like the old bear, following his own breath in the dark forest. There's no warm pack, no herd to comfort him. That voice that cries out doesn't *have* to be a weakling's, does it? (94)

The bear-squirrel ritual that now follows resembles the previously enacted one in that it is an interaction of mutual confirmation, yet it is also significantly different in that it prefigures the abandonment of the family myth and the institution of a new interactional pattern. Ritual not only acts as safety zone, as was the case in the bear-squirrel game of Act I, but can also be an intermediary step in the process of rule change, as is the case here.[38] The "super," "marvelous" bear, which was just another representation of the "knight in shining armour," has made place for a "soppy, scruffy sort of a bear." Both bear and squirrel face now the fact that maybe they are "rather mad, slightly satanic, and very timid little animals" (96). Far from dismissing this ending as romantic escapism or childish fantasy[39] (or in the more visceral language of Faber's psychoanalytic verdict as a "return to the womb"[40]), a pragmatic view draws attention to the functional role of this bear-squirrel communion as a tentative working toward a new self-image with both positive and negative characteristics: the bear has "claws" but is also "sloppy"; the squirrel is "beautiful" but "none too bright either." Horst Oppel's pessimism in considering the play's ending as only a temporary truce between Alison and Jimmy ("*Nichts deutet darauf hin, daß diesem Gefühl der Harmonie Dauer beschieden werden kann*")[41] is matched by that of Dieter Schulz, who stresses the fact that the ending is positive in presupposing a desire to overcome the difficulties of life, but negative in expressing this desire in a regressive, animalistic way.[42] A pragmatic analysis, on the contrary, considers the bear-squirrel ritual as an intermediary step toward establishing a new code of living together, a tentative enacting of new relationship rules. Although it remains an open question whether Jimmy and Alison will be able to translate this symbolic enactment of their new relationship into a contract for daily living, everything in this last ritual points toward a new on mutual confirmation and care: "you'll keep those big eyes on my fur. . . . And I'll see that you keep that sleek, bushy tail glistening as it should . . ." (96).

* * *

A systemic pragmatic analysis, as is demonstrated in the preceding pages, results in an understanding of the characters in the play that goes beyond the way in which they define themselves or are defined by others. Alison's role has been qualified: she not only silently endures; she also plays an important role in sustaining the interaction by withdrawal and imperviousness, which are now seen not as absence of communication but as active responses. Emphasizing the effect rather than the content of language has prevented us from being led astray by appearances (a man is tyrannizing his wife) and has produced insight into what critics have called "the emotional substructure" of the play: the couple's despair, their paranoid feelings of entrapment, result from a double bind relationship that is resolved by a counter double bind at the end of the play. Look Back in Anger, we can now conclude, is a play whose dynamic depends on a central paradox and whose resolution is equally paradoxical. It is not a play *about* paradox, however, but about passion. As driving principle, the central paradox remains hidden, and it is this concealment of what triggers the violent emotions that makes the play so effectively realistic. Through its empathy with the characters' suffering, the audience experiences the paradox without being offered insight into it. Indeed, the theatre, according to Osborne, is not a schoolroom, and insight has to be acquired on one's own and at one's own risk. In conceptualizing this experience, attention for interaction patterns rather than for single statements is warranted by John Osborne's reference to the play's "texture of ordinary despair," which indeed calls up the image of an intricate woof in which utterances cannot be isolated but are part of a "dynamic that is created between characters on the stage." A pragmatic analysis thus provides the logic behind Jimmy's impotent anger and prevents the customary dismissal of the play on grounds of alleged unreasonableness.

Look Back in Anger then acquires a new importance as the play that functioned as bridgehead into the new territory of language-oriented realism. Harold Pinter would further file away at some of the conventions from character-, issue-, and plot-oriented realism that still survive in Look Back in Anger. Indeed, the latter's formal three-act structure, the apparent centrality of one of its characters, and other overall resemblances with conventional well-made plays invited criticism that concentrated on character or on social and political issues instead of on interactional dynamics. However, the fact that a systemic pragmatic rather than a content-oriented analysis reveals the logic of its realistic representation aligns *Look Back in Anger* not with a conventional realistic play such as Terence Rattigan's *Table by the Window*, but with the language-oriented realistic plays of the postwar era.

One can still object that although a systemic pragmatic analysis is more suited to analyze the logic of representation of a language-oriented realistic play such as *Look Back in Anger*, it leads to a politically neutral (and, therefore, reactionary) reading. In such an interpretation, even explicit references to class or gender are only considered for their contribution to the overall interactional dynamic. As a result, *Look Back in Anger* is given an easy escape from the many serious accusations that, notably, feminist critics have directed against the play. Some have indeed taken offense with Jimmy's misogynist language and even with the fact that a female character does the ironing on Sundays while her husband and his pal are reading the papers.[43] Such criticism, however, questions the play in a language that it cannot understand as it is animated by a different logic—that of the medium of communication rather than that of its participants. Thematic, content-oriented feminist criticism offers interesting sociological observations that, however, are better pursued in a larger historical context in which drama only plays a minor role; as far as *Look Back in Anger* is concerned, such criticism only touches the surface of the play and does not contribute to a better understanding of what the play is most concerned with. In fact, the relationship portrayed in *Look Back in Anger* only becomes interesting when such self-evident observations do not dominate the analysis.

Feminist critique should be directed not against the play as such but rather against the kind of convention of the real that the play takes for granted and against the implicit logic that constitutes its *vraisemblance*. The axiom of the circularity of all human interaction—central in a systemic, functionalist convention of the real—ties the apparent victim to the apparent victimizer in complicity, prevents the "us against them" dichotomy on which effective political or feminist criticism and action are based.[44] The logic of the play implies that while ostensibly battling each other and their environment, Jimmy and Alison are in reality grappling with the inexorable laws that determine their communication. Such a functionalist paradigm, it can rightly be argued, rationalizes the male chauvinist myth that posits a fundamental human solidarity between sexes despite evidence of a concretely lived inequality between men and women in the larger socioeconomic context. Inexorable laws of communication are neither natural nor objectively given but phallocentric.

However, a wholesale rejection of a fine and sensitive play on the basis of arguments that are rooted in a more ideologically aware present prevents us from seeing what the play has to offer. It is true that *Look Back in Anger* asks us to believe that men and women are living in inextricably bonded relationships, that Alison can be humiliated all along yet that the humiliating man can also truly suffer, that Alison can wish to come back and that a reconciliation can follow. We are also asked to understand that Alison has managed to take up the challenge and has emerged at the end of the play as a paradoxical winner— paradoxical because she can only win by losing, in the same way as Jimmy's triumph takes the form of an admission of defeat. However, despite its ideological limitations, the systemic functionalist convention of the real (on which not only *Look Back in Anger* is based but also other plays of the same period such as Edward Albee's *Who's Afraid of Virginia Woolf* [1962], James Goldman's *The Lion in Winter* [1964], and Edward Bond's *Saved* [1965]) can yield important insights that any political critique should dare to face. Looking beyond the direct appearances of things, it draws a more intricate picture of lived and living reality that defies the arbitrarily drawn lines of political partisanship and that force the latter constantly to reexamine its too facile dichotomies. Plays whose *vraisemblance* is based on such a convention of the real heighten our awareness of the reciprocal dependence, the hubris, and the self-enslavement that makes the dominant-submissive, sadomasochistic relationship of the *folie à deux* so durable despite the pain and despair it generates. Such plays require that we move from empathy with a single character's "punctuation of events" to a study of the ways in which both men and women are responsible for creating the interactional micro- and macroenvironment of family and society that double-bind them in such a way that either protest or acquiescence only serve to strengthen their chains. It is true that class and gender conflicts are in this way made secondary to the portrayal of the centripetal mechanisms of the interactional machine. It is with the latter, however, that *Look Back in Anger* is mainly preoccupied, and it displays these complex processes with a profound experiential knowledge.

NOTES

1. John Osborne, "They Call It Cricket," *Declaration*, ed. Tom Maschler (London: MacGibbon & Kee, 1957) 65. Page references in the text refer to John Osborne's *Look Back in Anger* (New York: Penguin Books, 1982). Page references to Terence Rattigan's *Table by the Window* come from *Separate Tables* (New York: Samuel French, 1984).

2. Harry Blamires, *A Short History of English Literature*, 2nd ed. (London: Methuen, 1979) 408. All emphasis in quotations of secondary sources throughout this paper is mine. Emphasis in quoted primary material is mine only where indicated.

3. Aristotle, *Poetics*, trans. Ingram Bywater, *Introduction to Aristotle*, ed. Richard McKeon, 2nd rev. and enlarged ed. (Chicago: U of Chicago P, 1973) 689 [15. 1454a 16–40].

4. Alan Carter, *John Osborne*, 2nd ed., Biography and Criticism 14 (Edinburgh: Oliver and Boyd, 1973) 22.

5. John Osborne, preface to an excerpt of *The Entertainer* in *Writers' Theatre*, ed. Keith Waterhouse and Willis Hall (London: Heinemann, 1967), and qtd. in Alan Carter as motto to his monograph, *John Osborne*.

6. John Osborne, "They Call It Cricket" 69.

7. Stephen Williams in the *Evening News*, rpt. in *John Osborne: "Look Back in Anger," A Casebook*, ed. John Russell Taylor (London: Macmillan, 1968) 43.

8. Kenneth Tynan in *The Observer*, rpt. in *John Osborne*, ed. John Russell Taylor, 49–51.

9. Benedict Nightingale, "The Fatality of Hatred: On John Osborne," *Encounter* 58 (1982): 64.

10. See, for instance, Jean Selz, "John Osborne et Jimmy Porter," *Les Lettres Nouvelles* 61 (1958): 908–911; Graham Martin, "A Look Back at Osborne," *Universities and Left Review* 7 (1959): 39; Roy Huss, "John Osborne's Backward Half-Way Look," *Modern Drama* 6 (1963): 20–21; M.D. Faber, "The Character of Jimmy Porter: An Approach to *Look Back in Anger*," *Modern Drama* 13 (1970): 77.

11. G. Wilson Knight, "The Kitchen Sink: On Recent Developments in Drama," *Encounter* 11 (1963): 48; Steven H. Gale, "John Osborne: Look Forward in Fear," *Essays on Contemporary British Drama*, ed. Hedwig Bock and Albert Wertheim (Munich: Hueber, 1981) 5.

12. John Russell Brown, *Theatre Language: A Study of Arden, Osborne, Pinter and Wesker* (London: Allen Lane, 1972): 118–157; Andrew K. Kennedy, *Six Dramatists in Search of Language: Studies in Dramatic Language*, 2nd ed. (Cambridge: Cambridge UP, 1976). John Osborne, "That Awful Museum," *John Osborne*, ed. John Russell Taylor, 66.

13. François Hédelin (Abbé d'Aubignac), *La pratique du théâtre, La pratique du théâtre und andere Schriften zur Doctrine classique. Nachdruck der dreibändigen Ausgabe Amsterdam 1715 mit einer einleitenden Abhandlung von Hans-Jörg Neuschäfer*, ed. In Hans-Jörg Neuschäfer (München: Wilhelm Fink Verlag, 1971) 260.

14. Language "transitively" used functions as "a means of communication and description." "Intransitively" used, language "emphasizes itself as primary to the phenomena it describes" and functions mainly as a means of "organiz[ing] reality." Betty Jean Craige, *Literary Relativity: An Essay on Twentieth-Century Narrative* (Lewisburg: Bucknell UP; London: Associated UP, 1982) 105.

15. Austin E. Quigley, *The Pinter Problem* (Princeton: Princeton UP, 1975) 18.

16. Quigley 46.

17. Gregory Bateson, *Steps to an Ecology of Mind: Collected Essays in Anthropology, Psychiatry, Evolution and Epistemology*, 2nd ed. (London: Paladin Granada, 1978). The coinage "family interactionism" is Peter Sedgwick's, used in his review "Laing's Clangs," *New Society* 15 January 1970.

18. Antonio J. Ferreira, "Family Myth" (1966), *The Interactional View: Studies at the Mental Research Institute, Palo Alto, 1965–1974*, eds. Paul Watzlawick and John H. Weakland (New York: Norton, 1977) 49–55.

19. Paul Watzlawick, Janet Helmick Beavin, and Don D. Jackson, *Pragmatics of Human Communication: A Study of Interactional Patterns, Pathologies, and Paradoxes*, Mental Research Institute, Palo Alto, California (London: Faber and Faber, 1968) 51.

20. John Russell Taylor in *Plays and Players* January 1969, qtd. by Arnold P. Hinchliffe, *John Osborne* (Boston: Twayne, 1984) 23–24.

21. Ronald Bryden, in *The Observer* 3 November 1968, mentioned that "the conflict of husband and wife is fierce and equal, as roundly theatrical as *Virginia*

Woolf." Kenneth Tynan observed the circularity of the interaction as early as 1957: "[Osborne] shows us two attractive young animals engaged in competitive martyrdom, each with its teeth sunk deep in the other's neck, and each reluctant to break the clinch for fear of bleeding to death" (*The Observer* 30 December 1956). A.E. Dyson makes a similar observation in an article first published in 1959 and later reprinted as "Look Back in Anger," *Modern British Dramatists: A Collection of Critical Essays*, ed. John Russell Brown (Englewood Cliffs, NJ: Prentice-Hall, 1968) 47-57.

22. Kenneth Allsop, *The Angry Decade: A Survey of the Cultural Revolt of the Nineteen-Fifties*, 4th ed. (London: Lowe & Brydone, 1969) 114.

23. Carter 56.

24. Wayland Young, "London Letter," *Kenyon Review* 17 (1956): 647.

25. Paul Watzlawick et al., *Pragmatics of Human Communication: A Study of Interactional Patterns, Pathologies, and Paradoxes* 95. Definitions of other terminology such as "complementary" and "symmetrical" interaction patterns, "failure of metacommunication" used further on in this article, can also be found in this work that is heavily indebted to Gregory Bateson's theory of schizophrenia.

26. John Osborne, *Almost a Gentleman: An Autobiography*, Volume II, 1955-1966 (London: Faber and Faber, 1991) 17.

27. Watzlawick et al. 197.

28. Watzlawick et al. 158.

29. Watzlawick et al. 233.

30. A.E. Dyson, "Look Back in Anger" 52.

31. Maria Selvini Palazzoli, Luigi Boscolo, Gianfranco Cecchin, and Giuliana Prata, *Paradox and Counterparadox: A New Model in the Therapy of the Family in Schizophrenic Transaction*, trans. Elisabeth V. Burl, 5th ed. (New York: Jason Aronson, 1983) 36.

32. Watzlawick et al. 115.

33. Quigley 54.

34. Among the titles that John Osborne considered for his play was the awkward but nevertheless revealing "Close the Cage Behind You." See John Osborne, *Almost a Gentleman* 63.

35. Carter 57.

36. Kenneth Tynan in *John Osborne*, ed. John Russell Taylor 50.

37. Watzlawick et al. 172-74. Antonio J. Ferreira in "Family Myth" 51 claims that "[a]lthough to an outsider they may appear as blatant misstatements of the facts in the family, these organized beliefs—in the name of which the family initiates, maintains, and justifies many interactional patterns—are beliefs shared and supported by all family members as if they were some sort of ultimate truths beyond challenge or inquiry."

38. See Watzlawick et al. 104, Palazzoli et al. 96, and Harley C. Shands, *The War With Words: Structure and Transcendence* (The Hague & Paris: Mouton, 1971) 80.

39. Ian Scott-Kilvert, "The Hero in Search of a Dramatist: The Plays of John Osborne," *Encounter* 9 (1957): 29; Emmy Van Lockhorst, "Toneelkritiek: Wrok tegen het verleden," *De Gids* 12 (1957): 406; Nona Balakian, "The Flight from Innocence," *Books Abroad* 33 (1959): 264; Bamber Gascoigne, *Twentieth-Century Drama* (New York: Hutchinson, 1962) 196; Patricia M. Spacks, "Confrontation and Escape in Two Social Dramas," *Modern Drama* 11 (1968): 70; Dieter Schulz, "Ritual und Spiel in John Osbornes *Look Back in Anger*," *Sprachkunst: Beiträge zur Literaturwissenschaft* 9 (1978): 178.

40. Faber 75.

41. Horst Oppel, "John Osborne: *Look Back in Anger*," *Das moderne englische Drama: Interpretationen* (Berlin: Erich Schmidt, 1963) 322.

42. Schulz 178.

43. See, for instance, Michelene Wandor's remark, in *Look Back in Gender: Sexuality and the Family in Post-War British Drama* (London: Methuen, 1987) 8, that

"[Alison] is servicing the domestic scene and demonstrating to the audience in an immediate visual way [i.e., by ironing and by wearing one of Jimmy's shirts] that she is Jimmy's property." See also Anne Karpf's statement in *The Listener*, 15 April 1982: "The overwhelming impression now is one of rampant misogyny and pervasive sexism" (qtd. in Malcolm Page, ed., *File on Osborne* [London and New York: Methuen, 1988] 15).

44. See Kate Millett, *Sexual Politics* (Garden City, NY: Doubleday, 1970) 220–233. In these pages, Millett argues that a biologistic functionalism is reactionary and male chauvinist. She does not discuss the type of non-mechanistic, cybernetic functionalism I am dealing with here. For an influential ideological critique of the latter, see Anthony Wilden, *System and Structure: Essays in Communication and Exchange* (London: Tavistock, 1972) chapter 5, esp. p. 115.

THE ENTERTAINER AS A TEXT FOR PERFORMANCE

Robert Gordon

Early reviews and critical evaluations of *The Entertainer* suggest that the reception of the play's first production in April 1957 was coloured by two major facts: it was the first play of the controversial John Osborne to be staged at the Royal Court since the legendary success of *Look Back in Anger*, which had been running more or less continuously in London since May 1956, and it was the debut of the leader of the British stage, Sir Laurence Olivier, in a radical piece of contemporary theatre. In every respect, audience expectations were high (ten days after it was advertised, every evening performance of the initial four-week run was sold out), and it is not difficult to understand why reviewers were at the time more impressed by Olivier's performance as Archie Rice than by Osborne's skill as a writer for the stage.

Look Back in Anger had supposedly heralded a Royal Court "revolution" in the theatre that by April 1957 had not yet happened.[1] John Osborne was the great hope of the British theatre. Kenneth Tynan's famous encomium on the play not only rescued Osborne and the production from obscurity, but it no doubt shaped the expectations that the theatre-going public had of Osborne and his own sense of himself as a writer for the theatre.[2] Although in many respects *The Entertainer* is complementary to *Look Back in Anger*, Osborne appears deliberately to have conceived the later play in an antithetical relationship with the earlier one. Having given powerful voice to the dissatisfaction of the younger generation, he seems to have felt it necessary to understand the confusion and lack of idealism experienced by the middle-aged in contrast with the failed certainties of the prewar generation who were their elders.

In order to express the ethos of lower-middle-class society in the years between 1930 and 1957, Osborne embraced a very different dramaturgical form: *The Entertainer* stages a stylistic confrontation between the low-key naturalism of Terence Rattigan's *The Browning Version* (1948) and the overt theatricality of Noël Coward's *Red Peppers* (1936)[3]. Although this may have been a clever strategy to avoid the danger of repeating himself in the second of his plays to be seen in London, the theatricality that is so brilliantly exploited by Osborne was regarded by many at the time of its first performance as a gimmick intended to disguise the rather conventional nature of his dramaturgy.

Osborne has insisted that he did not write the role of Archie Rice with Olivier in mind, and that he had already written the whole of Act I before Olivier expressed an interest in reading the play.[4] There are different versions of the story of how Olivier came to show an interest in Osborne's work.[5] Whether or not Osborne had Olivier in mind when he first conceived the play, the production certainly exploited the London audience's familiarity with the actor's star persona in a powerful manner.

Fresh from his triumph in Peter Brook's horrifyingly effective *Titus Andronicus* at Stratford, Olivier was searching, as always, for the chance to do something startlingly different. To his audience, Olivier was the greatest heroic actor in the world, a master of impersonation who contrived to appear unrecognisable in each new role he played. For the last fifteen or so years he had almost exclusively played opposite his beautiful wife, Vivien Leigh, on stage. They were the Royal couple of the British theatre, film stars as well as stage actors. Even when, as in *Titus*, he played a villain, there was something glamorous in Olivier's persona. Toward the end of the Second World War, Olivier's virile performance in his successful film of Shakespeare's *Henry V* (1944) had associated him in the popular imagination with the mythical spirit of the Allied victory against the Nazis, British skill and heroism in defiance of an arrogant aggressor. His knighthood in 1947, his triumphant joint directorship of the Old Vic, and his films of *Hamlet* (1947) and *Richard III* (1954) enhanced his image as a pillar of the theatrical Establishment, which he was about to risk in assuming the role of a seedy music hall comedian.

In the event, the surprise impact of Olivier's Archie Rice proved irresistible. Whether or not he had him in mind when he first began to write, the casting of Olivier certainly was significant. Performance of a high cultural ritual traditionally exploited by the ruling class to celebrate English Establishment values (Shakespeare) was being replaced by the parody of an old-fashioned variety act (Olivier modelled Archie's performance style on that of the "cheeky chappie," Max Miller). The grotesque effect of Olivier's impersonation was partly derived from the spectacle of a great Shakespearean actor being reduced to the level of vulgarity that is a typical aspect of British popular entertainment. Osborne explored the notion that if Archie's debased patriotic show represents the sordid reality that is contemporary British society and culture, the more mundane, "kitchen-sink" reality of individual lives constitutes a debased form of domestic drama in which the actions and gestures of the characters may indeed be as cliched and devoid of expressive content as an out-of-date music hall routine.

It is this attempt to express domestic reality as a form of social performance that constitutes the source of *The Entertainer*'s originality as a play. Osborne has not attempted a Pirandellian discourse on the relationship between reality and illusion but a realistic play that rivals *The Iceman Cometh*, *A Streetcar Named Desire*, *Death of a Salesman*, and *Long Day's Journey into Night* in its depiction of the human capacity for self-delusion when confronted by the terrors of an unacceptable reality. The style of Archie's act ("Putting up a cheerful front") becomes emblematic of the family's (and Britain's) inability to face up to social changes brought about by history.

By casting Olivier in such a debased role, Osborne and George Devine were actually demonstrating to the Establishment how the mighty nation had fallen. The 1940s cinematic embodiment of Churchillian heroism is being made in 1957 to stand for the greed, duplicity, and compromise that was the reality into which the post-Churchill Conservative government were transforming the new Welfare State. *The Entertainer* is, for all that, far from being a piece of political theatre. While Osborne may well have overstated his ignorance of Brecht in response to John Russell Taylor's accusations that he had attempted "unsuccessfully" to utilise Brechtian techniques in structuring the action as a series of music hall "turns," his claim that he was directly influenced by his experience of the music hall accurately indicates that the device is not intended to distance the audience in order to prepare them to form objective social judgements on the characters' choices. In fact, the music hall setting provides both an emblem and a unifying atmosphere that the play elaborates through a complex and oblique interplay of text and subtext not always perceived by early critics, intent as they were on discovering a "state of the nation" drama of the sort Jimmy Porter might have written.[6]

> To show the ironic disparity between Archie's mind and the use he makes of it, Mr Osborne has hit on a stunningly original device. He sets out the programme like a variety bill, and switches abruptly from Archie at home, insulated by gin, to Archie on stage, ogling and mincing, joshing the conductor, doing the chin-up bit and braying with false effusiveness such aptly named numbers as "Why Should I Bother

to Care?" "We're all Out for Good Old Number One", and "Thank God We're Normal." In these passages, author, actor, and composer (John Addison) are all at peak form. A bitter hilarity fills the theatre, which becomes for a while England in little: "Don't clap too hard, lady, it's an old building."[7]

The majority of reviewers and critics commented on the overwhelming impact of Osborne's/Olivier's pastiche of the typical routines of a second-rate song-and-dance man, though they were less enthusiastic about the play as a whole.

Reviewing Max Wall's performance as Archie in 1975, Ronald Bryden asserted,

> The play, in fact, won't hang together and never did. It was always a loose assembly of episodes and attitudes spitted into a semblance of coherence on the gleaming spear of one great performance . . . ,[8]

echoing Kenneth Tynan's reservations about Osborne's failure to construct a coherent drama that might hold attention when Olivier was not onstage:

> With Sir Laurence in the saddle, miracles . . . come often. . . . When Archie is offstage, the action droops. His father is a bore and his children are ciphers: the most disquieting thing about the play is the author's failure to state the case of youth. There is a pacifist son who sings a Brechtian elegy for his dead brother, but does little else of moment. And there is Jean, Archie's daughter, a Suez baby who came of age at the Trafalgar Square rally but seems to have lost her political ardour with the passing of that old adrenalin glow. She is vaguely anti-Queen and goes in for loose generalities like "We've only got ourselves"; beyond that, *nada*. . . . Mr Osborne has planned a gigantic social mural and carried it out in a colour range too narrow for the job. Within that range he has written one of the great acting parts of our age.[9]

A comparison of the film that was made of *The Entertainer* with the text of the original play reveals just how clever Osborne was in exploiting the resources of the Royal Court Theatre to create a performance event that might not seem an anticlimax after the extraordinary success of *Look Back in Anger*. Leaving aside the question of whether or at what point in the play's gestation Osborne began to conceive the role of Archie as a vehicle for

Laurence Olivier, *The Entertainer* represents a remarkable advance in dramaturgical terms on the rather clumsy naturalistic form of the earlier play.

The screenplay of the film is a straightforward attempt to "open out" the play visually, intercutting segments of the original scenes in the seaside boardinghouse with other locations—short scenes in various pubs, backstage and outside of the variety theatre in which Archie's show is being staged, the promenade of the seaside town that Osborne evokes so atmospherically in the first stage direction of the playtext, the bathing beauty contest in which Archie meets the young woman whose parents he is trying to trick into investing money in his next show, and even a short lovemaking scene with the young woman in a caravan. Although one is grateful to possess even a partial record of Olivier's legendary stage performance, Tony Richardson's film version cannot bear comparison with the "new wave" of British films (e.g. *This Sporting Life, Saturday Night and Sunday Morning*) that Richardson and the "angry young writers" themselves helped to create.

Thirty years after it was made, the film's grainy black-and-white documentary-style realism seems rather a cliché, distinguished by certain moments of powerfully emotive acting from Olivier and from Brenda de Banzie (as Phoebe), which register, unfortunately, as jarringly theatrical moments in a somewhat contrived if low-key slice-of-life drama. Not even Olivier's performance in the film is much evidence of why *The Entertainer* caused such a stir at the Royal Court in April 1957. The film reduces the play to a British version of a Hollywood backstage melodrama, without the visual and vocal splendours of Cukor's *A Star Is Born* (1954) or the wit and style of Mankiewicz's *All About Eve* (1950).

The failure of *The Entertainer* as a film does, however, offer a key to understanding what makes the play so successful as a piece of theatre. Through the brilliant device by means of which the music hall in which Archie performs his act becomes a frame for the domestic action of the play, Osborne freed himself from the confines of the "box set"—in which context Jimmy Porter's exhilarating rhetorical tirades can seem rather artificial—and created a theatrical perspective in which mundane scenes of domestic squabbling are presented as a series of items on the variety bill at a tawdry music hall.[10] In this way, the banal details of domestic misery are subtly theatricalised, so what might appear as cliché in a straightforwardly naturalistic "kitchen-sink" drama of the 1950s achieves a resonance comparable to the ritualistic roll call of domestic horrors in a Strindberg play.

Osborne's dramatic strategy may be perceived from the opening scene in which, after an overture Archie's father, Billy Rice, enters on to a stage that has been furnished to suggest that a variety bill is in progress.[11]

> At the back a gauze. Behind it a part of the town. . . . Knee-high flats and a door frame will serve for a wall. . . . Also ordinary, tatty backcloth and draw-tabs. . . . The lighting is the kind you expect to see in the local Empire—everything bang-on, bright and hard, or a simple follow-spot. The scenes and interludes must, in fact, be lit as if they were simply turns on the bill. Furniture and props are as basic as they would be for a short sketch. . . .
>
> Music. The latest, the loudest, the worst. A gauzed front-cloth. On it are painted enormous naked young ladies, waving brightly coloured fans, and kicking out gaily. Written across it in large letters are the words "ROCK'N ROLL NEW'D LOOK".
>
> Behind the up-stage gauze, light picks out an old man. (11–12)[12]

Instead of beginning in the middle of a variety routine, the play presents an audience with a crudely theatricalised image of a real social environment: the provincial seaside town in which Archie's show is playing. The contrast between this rather dignified old man and the tasteless advertisement of a 1950s "nude show" introduces what is to become a leitmotif—the tension between a past world, nostalgically preserved in folk memory, and the grubby actuality of the present. After Billy has mimed walking up a stairway and entering an apartment "through the door-frame," he begins to sing the hymn "Rock of Ages" as he makes himself comfortable, pouring out a glass of beer and taking off his shoes in preparation for reading the newspaper. The overture and the stage setting have led the audience to expect some sort of comic sketch or musical routine, but in fact the actor playing Billy performs a rather elaborate piece of naturalistic stage business. Both the sleaziness of the environment and Billy's attitude toward it are economically presented, and the audience is primed to interpret the action as a kind of performance. In this context Billy's behaviour makes him representative of the older generation. He appears as a "character" whose values and attitudes are quite consciously portrayed as incongruous with the surroundings in which he finds himself.

The first appearance of Billy's granddaughter (Archie's daughter Jean), although conveyed by means of the same kind of detailed stage business as Billy's, also registers as domestic ritual because of the context of presentation. Osborne's telling stage direction, "*She has picked up her cue neatly*" (16), suggests that the social interaction in the play is being presented as in itself a piece of theatre. The attitudes of the younger generation are distinguished from the values of the older by means of a contrast between two acting styles. From the start of the action the audience is made critically aware that Billy's attitudes, no matter how confidently he holds them, represent the values of a past culture, while Jean's and her brother Frank's, no matter how tentative and confused, have the spontaneity that comes from being fully alive in the present moment.

Tynan and other critics have regarded Jean as an unsuccessfully realised character, perhaps because they were expecting a more obvious symbol of youthful protest in the mould of Jimmy Porter. It is interesting that Osborne chose to invest the speeches of the middle-aged failure, Archie Rice, with the bile that characterises Jimmy's rhetoric in *Look Back in Anger*, while his main representatives of youthful idealism in *The Entertainer* are the mild-mannered Jean and Frank, whose social and political attitudes are implied but never precisely articulated within the play. Jean is shown in the act of improvising her behaviour all through the play, never certain of the appropriate way of dealing with each new personal problem or political choice that faces her. Although the stage directions state that Frank "*has allowed himself to slip into the role of Archie's 'feed,'*" he is also described as "*impulsive, full of affection that spills over easily.*" In terms of the play's presentation of social role-playing, the young people have not become "characters" in a well-rehearsed drama: they are less set in routine patterns of behaviour and stock responses than their elders. The first scene between Billy and Jean is dominated by Billy's blunt if good-natured assertion of his prejudices. When he complains that the proprietor of the Cambridge pub has paid no attention to his complaints about the noise of the television, the audience is made aware that Jean's role has been merely to react to Billy's set speeches. The subtext of the scene is indicated by Billy noticing her failure to "cue" his performance properly as he becomes aware that she is not listening.

> Billy: . . . I don't know what's happening to everyone. I don't. Do you know?
> Jean: (*She isn't listening.*) No, Grandad I don't.
> Billy: It makes you sad—sometimes. . . . I haven't been able to go in there since, somehow. I got these in the off-licence over the way. (*He looks at her shrewdly.*) I suppose you've no right to expect people to listen to you. Just because you've had your life. It's all over for you. Why should anyone listen to you? (*Pause.*) Have you been drinking?
> Jean: Yes.
> Billy: I always know when a woman's been drinking. (22)

The lack of emotional connection between two characters who are in fact fond of each other introduces the major theme of people's inability to accept or properly to express their feelings. Although Jean says that she likes listening to Billy—a hint of the nostalgia that a number of characters express for the comforting certainties of the past—his memories of the pretty style in which Archie used to dress his children and the way he himself dressed Archie only serve to reinforce the emptiness of the present that is about to be directly dramatised. His words form a horribly ironic introduction to Archie Rice's turn:

> He was a pretty little boy. Funny how they all turn out. (*Pause, then softly, sincerely.*) I feel sorry for you people. You don't know what it's really like. You haven't lived, most of you. You've never known what it was like, you're all miserable really. You don't know what life can be like.
> *The light fades, a tatty backcloth descends.* (23)

This opening scene carefully prepares for the introduction of Archie in "Number Two," offering a few tantalising expository clues about the poor quality of his show and the small audiences attending it. Most significant is Billy's comment on the death of music hall:

> It was all over, finished, dead when I got out of it. . . . They don't want real people any more. . . . They don't want human beings. (18)

A key question posed by the play concerns the price of survival. Is Archie still a "real human being" or has his mechanical repetition of a tired routine reduced him to the level of an automaton?

The fascination of watching Olivier in this role derived not only from the pleasure of watching a brilliant impersonation of a third-rate comedian performing familiar-sounding songs, bad gags, and cliched tap routines, but also from the pathos created by Olivier's demonstration of Archie's heroic courage in attempting to go on performing an act that is "dying." The text provides an actor with an opportunity, on the one hand, to exploit the reactions of a theatre audience to the pastiche of an old-fashioned comedy routine with its built-in self-consciousness of being a performance and, on the other, to suggest the pain of an intelligent man forced to cope with such humiliation. The determined cheerfulness that characterised Olivier's performance of the "act," both on- and off-stage, only made the potential tragedy of the character more horrifying.

After this quiet expository scene, Archie's routine effects a surprising change of pace and tone, and puts members of a theatre audience on the spot, casting them in the role of a bored audience at a seaside variety show and making them contribute to Archie's failure as a performer (and that of the traditional type of music hall that he represents) as they invariably refuse to laugh at his bad jokes.

The song, "Why Should I Care," is at one and the same time a pastiche of a "Chin Up and Cheerio"[13] number and a darker, more cynical rationalisation of the selfish and escapist attitudes that actually motivate the behaviour of Archie and, by extension, his audience. Later in the play it becomes apparent that Archie's behaviour is entirely motivated by the idea of "looking out for good old Number One." His experience of the world has prevented him from having faith in any system of social values more coherent than that of the song:

> Why should I care?
> Why should I let it touch me!
> Why shouldn't I, sit down and try
> To let it pass over me?
> . . . .
> What's the use of despair,
> If they call you a square?
> You're a long time dead—
> Like my pal Fred,
> So why, oh, why should I bother to care? (24)

Sung quite slowly and with a studied nonchalance by Olivier, this was a poignant demonstration of Archie's inability as a performer to express anything but loneliness and despair. His performance of the song was deliberately flat, ironically missing the sense of reassurance that show business nostalgia is intended to provide. By exposing the emptiness of Archie's selfish creed of survival, the delivery challenged a Royal Court audience to declare faith in any other than the self-referential value system of show business. (A genuinely charming or more naive performance of the song might easily transform it into the conventionally optimistic celebration of the possibility of surviving against the odds, which is a typical ritual of popular show business escapism.)[14]

For a British audience in 1957 the force of the song lay in the vagueness of its political and social implication. When sung by Laurence Olivier a generation after his Shakespearean exhortation to an audience of servicemen and patriots,

> Once more unto the breach dear friends, once more;
> Or close the wall up with our English dead,

its ironic reference to the selfish materialism that had replaced the new idealism of the postwar Welfare State acquired further resonance through the comparison with wartime heroism implicit in the casting of Olivier. Contrary to the views of many early reviewers, it is just because Osborne avoids overt satire of specific political targets (which would, in any case, be out of keeping with the format of Archie's act) that audiences were, and in a slightly different way still are, challenged by the characters' struggles to discover or preserve an authentic form of existence in a world that has rendered idealism or the traditional values of community impossible.[15]

Carefully placed within this first routine is a stock misogynistic joke about marital infidelity, which ironically reflects the grim reality of Archie's unhappy marriage to Phoebe:

> My wife—my wife. Old Charlie knows her. A real road-mender's job she is—isn't she, Charlie? It's all right. I've taken his drill away from him now. I have. Haven't I, Charlie. He's the only boy soprano in the Musicians' Union. (24)

The cartoon-like world of sex-starved men and unsatisfied wives conjured up in the typical stand-up comedy turn does ironically mirror the misery of the Rices' domestic lives. The naturalistic depiction of one unhappy relationship achieves emblematic significance by being introduced through the grotesque music-hall image that represents the everyday unhappiness of lower-middle-class existence as a comic truism. The symbolic significance of Archie's comic self-presentation is given further point in the aside at the end of the song that closes "Number Two":

> So why should I bother to care?
> (Thank God I'm normal!)
> So why should I bother to care? (25)

The depressing environment depicted in the opening scene is ironically represented in Archie's song as a consequence of the need to hold on to respectability ("Thank God I'm normal") at the expense of one's true humanity. His own sad efforts at maintaining the flagging interest of an audience that has, in fact, paid to see the nude chorus girls exposes his vain attempt to be "a real human being" on stage, the kind of performer his father once was.[16]

"Number Three" introduces the audience to Archie's wife, Phoebe. It is significant that Archie does not enter the domestic environment until

"Number Five," thus restricting the character's function to one of choric commentator until that juncture. Consequently, an audience is unable to judge him as a character alongside Jean, Billy, and Phoebe until a third of the way through the play. Phoebe's behaviour on her first appearance adds much to the impression of the Rice family that is being built up:

> She is never still, she never listens—like most of the people in this house. Or, if she is obliged to sit and listen to anyone, she usually becomes abstracted and depressed. . . . (25)

Osborne effectively exploits the oblique dramaturgical method of naturalism to create a tension between overt behaviour and unexpressed subtext that reveals the true unhappiness of the Rice family. Phoebe's behaviour suggests an inarticulate escapist who is unable to express her feelings appropriately to those close to her. Brenda de Banzie's disturbing portrayal of Phoebe, fortunately preserved in the film version, puts one in mind of Mary Tyrone in *Long Day's Journey Into Night*, and it is a measure of Osborne's assurance as a dramatist that he is able to do justice to Phoebe's suffering without resorting to melodramatic scenes of direct recrimination between her and Archie.

Time and again the text implies the nature of the characters' feelings without overtly articulating them. This oblique dramaturgical method represents a definite advance on Osborne's approach in *Look Back in Anger*. The earlier play tends to move uneasily between detailed naturalistic presentation of characters expressing themselves in conversations that dramatise the nexus of relationships within a particular milieu, and virtuoso rhetorical tirades that effectively freeze the action to allow Jimmy Porter to comment upon the situation being presented. In *The Entertainer*, on the other hand, every speech is clearly motivated by the context in which it is delivered on stage in Archie's show or as part of a realistically conceived conversational situation.

Phoebe's continuous chatter creates a ritual of sociability that exposes her anxiety about being ignored and the fear of recognising her genuine despair. Her welcome to Jean is typical:

> Phoebe: Oh he [Archie] will be so pleased to see you. (*To Billy.*) Won't he? But why didn't you let us know? I'd have got you something prepared. . . . Oh, well it's lovely to see you. Isn't it, Dad? He's pleased. He doesn't have anyone much to talk to. Do you? I say you don't have much chance for a talk.

He's on his own here half the time. It's not my fault. He
won't come to the pictures with me. But you've got to go
somewhere as I say to him. You get bored stiff sitting in-
doors. He likes to listen to a play on the wireless sometimes.
You *like* a nice play. But I can't sit for long, I'd rather have a
spot of pictures.
Billy: I'm all right. (25–26)

Her drinking is introduced quite matter-of-factly. Her suggestion that she and Jean have a drink of gin appears innocuous in "Number Three," but the audience will eventually become aware that the members of the Rice family survive by being mildly inebriated for most of each day.

Phoebe: Let's open this, shall we? (*She indicates bottle on the table.*)
You shouldn't have brought gin. She's naughty, isn't she?
Billy: She ought to have more sense—spending her money.
Phoebe: Never mind, she's big hearted, that's the main thing. Hand
me a couple of glasses. You're going to have one with me,
aren't you? I don't want one on my own.
Jean: All right—just a small one. (26)

Phoebe's genteel manners and euphemistic manner of speaking are an elaborate strategy of evasion parallel to the "cheeky chappie" comic persona that Archie carries over into everyday life. Phoebe, Jean, and Billy never directly say what they mean in "Number Three," partly because they are unable to articulate complex attitudes and contradictory feelings and partly because neither Jean nor Billy wishes to risk a direct confrontation over their opposed political views. The arguments that do surface above the submerged tension of the scene establish the connection between their domestic unhappiness and the political malaise of a Britain that has lost its national and cultural identity.

Jean's closing lines have a drunken intensity, sarcastically implying that it is because Britons like the Rice family have allowed themselves to be duped by the reassuring platitudes of politicians that they have colluded in creating a value system based on selfish complacency that has effectively destroyed the possibility of idealism that may have existed in prewar society:

They're all looking after us. We're all right, all of us. Nothing to worry
about. We're all right. God save the Queen!
Blackout. Draw tabs. (31)

This naturalistic representation of a drunken gesture cues Archie's first gag in "Number Four":

> I've played in front of them all! "The Queen", "The Duke of Edinburgh", "The Prince of Wales", and the—what's the name of that other pub? Blimey, that went better first house. (31)

The way in which Archie's speech undermines Jean's sarcastic appeal to old idealism is parallel to his characteristic use of the cynical form of ridicule that he habitually extrapolates from his act and employs against his family in order to minimise their constant complaints about the sordid compromises of the present. "Number Four" reveals Archie at his worst, trying to ingratiate himself through the coy insinuations of his dirty jokes. Boasts about his sexual compulsiveness, presented as an attribute of the "normal" male, are inevitably accompanied by sneeringly euphemistic suggestions about the conductor's alleged homosexuality. The song that ends the turn gives spurious licence to the traditionally sexist values of Archie's patter: "We're All Out for Good Old Number One," accompanied by the unfurling of the Union Jack, equates the refusal of British politicians to give up their imperialist ambitions with the petty greed of individuals like Archie, alluding in 1957 unmistakably to the duplicity of the Eden government during the Suez crisis the previous year.

The abrupt switch to the domestic scene of "Number Five" contrasts the shabbiness of the present with a vision of an Edwardian past as remembered by Billy:

> They were graceful, they had mystery and dignity. Why when a woman got out of a cab, she descended. Descended. And you put your hand out to her to help her down. (33)

In Billy's mind the values of British imperialism in its heyday are associated with social grace and personal gallantry. In contrast to the assured manner of Billy's forthright criticism of the present day, the entrance of Archie into the domestic environment introduces an echo of the insecurity and evasiveness that an audience has already identified in Phoebe's behaviour:

> ... Whatever he [Archie] says to anybody is almost always very carefully "thrown away." Apparently absent minded, it is a comedian's technique, it absolves him from seeming committed to anyone or anything. (34)

The family's way of avoiding confrontation with reality is demonstrated most obviously in Archie's habit of substituting comic patter for conversation. Interestingly, when Archie is present Phoebe is able to drop her euphemistic babble and complain more directly. His arch habit of trivialising any serious issue provides a safety outlet, ensuring that the litany of complaints by Billy and Phoebe will never be taken too seriously.

> Billy: Your daughter went to that Trafalgar Square circus last Sunday, if you please!
> Archie: Oh really? Are you one of those who don't like the Prime Minister? I think I've grown rather fond of him. I think it was after he went to the West Indies to get Noel Coward to write a play for him. Still, perhaps only someone of my generation could understand that. Does he bring you out in spots?
> Phoebe: Oh, Christ, I wish I knew what was going to happen to us!
> Archie: I feel rather like that horrible dog downstairs. It brings me out in a rash every time I look at it. There are three things that do that to me, three things. Nuns, clergymen and dogs.
> Phoebe: I don't want to always have to work. I mean you want a bit of life before it's all over. It takes all the gilt off if you know you've got to go on and on till they carry you out in a box. (39–40)

The counterpoint of Archie's carefully acted insouciance and Phoebe's emotional outburst (she ends up in tears) is very powerful, theatrically illustrating Osborne's major theme of the gap between the expectations the lower-middle class have inherited and the depressing reality of their condition. Archie's avoidance of confrontation is not necessarily condemned here, but the intercutting of different speech modes (naturalistic emotional outburst and music-hall patter) expresses the contradiction between the image of a society inscribed in its cultural forms and the reality of an individual's lived experience of social existence. *The Entertainer* is arguably the first English play since the war to stage such a confrontation of personal identity and cultural form.[17]

Although Olivier presented Archie's relentless cheerfulness as irritating at times, at other times he managed to suggest that this quality expressed an heroic refusal to succumb to despair. This was made all the more poignant in the startling moments when he allowed Archie's comic mask to drop, conveying his terrible consciousness of his own failure. The end of Act I provides the first of a series of moments when the inability to perform the mechanical routine of self-denigration expresses the gulf between subject and persona:

> Archie: Did I ever tell you the greatest compliment I had paid to me. . . . Well, there I was walking along the front, to meet what I think we used to call a piece of crackling. Or perhaps it was a bit of fluff. No that was earlier. Anyway, I know I enjoyed it afterwards. But the point is I was walking along the front, all on my own, minding my own business, (*Pause*) and two nuns came towards me— (*Pause*) two nuns—
> *He trails off, looking very tired and old. He looks across at Jean and pushes the bottle at her.*
> Archie: Talk to me.
> Curtain (42)

From this point in the play, the recognition of Archie and Phoebe's fear of confronting the truth about themselves determines an audience's perspective on the action. The dishonesty of the social system is typified by the way in which the death of their son Mick in the Suez War is concealed from Archie and Phoebe until his body is flown home to England. The army's attempt to ameliorate the harshness of the true situation by allowing the family to live in a state of optimistic self-delusion since first learning that he has been taken prisoner is articulated through elaborate rituals of pretence that exploit the Rice family's unwillingness to face up to the truth. The habitual duplicity that characterises Establishment values is signified when Jean exposes the good manners of Archie's brother Bill as insincere playacting. Phoebe appears as a cheap snob, sentimentalising the gentlemanly Bill by mistaking his charming politeness for genuine affection.

> Jean: He's a barrister—that's why you like him so much. He's like that actor on the pictures who's always in a wig and gown in every other—
> Phoebe: I like him because he's a gentleman. (49)

Role-playing occurs as a motif a number of times in the last two acts of the play. The problem of knowing one's feelings and expressing them adequately is being explored from every aspect.

In a withering speech in "Number Six," Archie himself reduces the position of the Rice family to a situation in an outmoded and unconvincing play:

Archie: Why we have problems that nobody's ever heard of, we're characters out of something that nobody believes in. We're something that people make jokes about because we're so remote from ordinary, everyday experience. . . . All the time we're trying to draw someone's attention to our nasty, sordid, unlikely little problems. Like that poor, pathetic old thing there. Look at her. What has she got to do with people like you? People of intellect and sophistication. She's very drunk . . . and she's going to force us to listen to all sorts of dreary embarrassing things we've all heard a hundred times before. (54)

The self-reflexive quality of this speech in relation to the action of the play provides a further variation on the complex series of metadramatic games by means of which the domestic action is linked with Archie's stage performance. The speech is part of the strategy that self-consciously presents the life of the Rice family as stereotypical domestic drama. One of the most successful features of the writing is Osborne's employment of Archie's stage persona as the basis for his domestic behaviour: by turning every crisis in the life of the Rice family into a funny story or an excuse for a gag, Archie attempts to ignore the sadness of their existence. At this moment, however, he sees their situation as identical with one of the horrible jokes he regularly tells in his act. Stage cliché has become reality in an ironic inversion of the play's chief dramaturgical technique.

Clearly the play is not so much concerned to indict the specific viewpoint of one particular government or political party as to expose the ethos of British politics reflected in the experience and attitudes of the middle classes whose suburban respectable reticence was well-known to Osborne's audience through the "well-made plays" of the 1930s and 1940s.[18] What is striking about Osborne's revision of such drama is its refusal of the dignity to which the proverbial stoicism of such people had traditionally entitled them. As in *Look Back in Anger*, the revolutionary element of Osborne's dramaturgy is its directly confrontational quality. Although the play appropriately conveys the reticence typical of middle-class English behaviour—indeed this is its central theme—Archie's peculiar position as theatrical personality in a show-within-the-play licences him to act as a *raisonneur*, at times ironically attacking the same middle-class hypocrisy and evasiveness in others, of which he himself is guilty.

Later in "Number Six," when Phoebe reveals how she often lies awake listening to Archie having sex with a woman downstairs in the kitchen, he rounds on Frank and Jean, surprisingly, to accuse them of just such genteel evasiveness:

> Of course they know. They know what sort of a bastard I am, love. I think they know almost as well as you do. Well, almost as well. . . . (*To Frank and Jean.*) Now don't pretend you're not used to it. (56)

In "Number Six," Archie paradoxically comes closest to revealing his own feelings when he asks why the Rice family can't "be a little normal just for once, and pretend we're a happy, respectable, decent family" (58). Archie behaves here like the petit bourgeois whom he simultaneously celebrates and satirises in his onstage routines. (Olivier's louche manner and exaggeratedly checked suit deliberately contradicted the bourgeois values that Archie claims, in the words of "Thank God I'm Normal," to espouse.)

Having for once come close to expressing his true feelings, Archie immediately slips back into the habitual manner, making a racist remark about "the wogs" before asking the rest of the family to perform:

> Archie: And this is Mick's party. Phoebe, let's see you do your dance. (*This is thrown off in the usual casual, studied Archie manner.*) She dances jolly well, don't you, you poor old thing. I wonder if she'll make me cry tonight. We'll see. We'll see. Frank, sing us your song.
> Jean: I don't even know what I'm feeling. I don't even know if I do at all.
> Archie: Never mind, dear. I didn't know that for years either. You're a long time dead, Mrs Murphy, let's make it a party, Mick the soldier's coming back, let's just whoop it up! (58–59)

Although the idiom here evokes the confined and boring milieu of lower-middle-class suburbia, the feelings indicated below the surface of the text are complex and contradictory, allowing the actors playing Archie, Frank, and Jean to suggest powerful depths of emotion by demonstrating the characters' failure to put on a cheerful performance of polite sociability. Olivier, in particular, was able to employ his wonderful volatility as an actor, to move from a mood of blank despair to one of near hysteria. Jean's response suggests that the real feelings of each character run too deep for their expression in the conventional rhetoric available to the naturalistic play of domestic life, a restatement of one of the play's dominant themes.

This confusion of contradictory feelings is carried over into "Number Seven," which presents another segment of Archie's routine. Once more, he repeats his snide denial that he is homosexual ("You think I am, don't you? Well, I'm not. But he is!") as an introduction to another misogynistic joke about his wife that achieves added resonance by following so soon after his attack on the family's behaviour in "Number Six":

> Archie: Here, here! Did I tell you about the wife? Did I? My wife—not only is she stupid, but she's cold as well. Oh yes, cold. She may look sweet but she's a very cold woman, my wife. Very cold. Cold and stupid. She's what they call a moron glacee. (59)

The context transforms the stock misogyny into a powerful expression of the disgust that he feels for Phoebe. Archie's joke about being real hints at the depths of his personal anguish:

> Look at me—it's all real, you know. Me—all real, nothing shoddy. You don't think I'm real, do you? Well, I'm not. (*Stumbling.*) (59)

Having witnessed Archie's pretense at cheerfulness and normality in the domestic situation, the audience is now confronted with a complicated confession in the form of a comic turn. The song that he sings gradually implicates the theatre audience as "normal" members of the middle-class majority. The refrain, "Thank God I'm normal," gives way to "Thank God we're normal," and the appearance of the nude Britannia to the strains of "Land of Hope and Glory" represents the complete debasement of the British Imperialist dream that members of Archie's generation were brought up to believe in.

Olivier performed this song with a rasp in his voice and a sneering manner, as though the jaded theatricality of the performance was unintentionally overwhelming the lyric content of the song. An audience watched Olivier degrade the "cheeky chappie" Max Miller persona into a mask of bitter cynicism through which Archie's pretended burlesque of a jingoistic patriotic song appeared as a sinister lack of personal integrity.

"Number Eight" is a brilliantly constructed scene. Having already utterly demolished the myth of the cheerful music hall comedian that motivates Archie's act, the scene in which the family await Mick's return from Suez evokes nostalgic glimpses of the joy associated with a vanished popular culture. Frank introduces the motif by playfully singing a snatch of "The End of Me Old Cigar" (61–62), an Edwardian popular song. The pleasant banter of the Rice family has the ring of a comic music hall cross-talk routine, with all five characters engaging in the patter. When Frank is requested to sing, he chooses one of Billy's old numbers and introduces it by saying, "It's British . . . and very religious . . . so there's something in it for you all." He sings and dances a Kiplingesque ballad about the Boer War (the last Imperial war that Britain won).

Archie's parody of "The Girl I Love Is Up in the Gallery" (he substitutes "lavatory" for "gallery") in answer to Frank prompts Phoebe to remember a happy phase of her life with Archie ("He always used to sing that song, didn't you? It was his favourite, I think"), and is persuaded to sing a stanza of the song with its coy representation of romantic love (66). The character who has least connection with the professional stage expresses the pure joy associated with the popular culture of the music hall. Brenda de Banzie presented Phoebe as shy and utterly unaffected as she sang, transforming the mood of the scene with her deeply moving performance and succinctly expressing the difference between the music hall in its heyday and its travesty in the form of Archie's variety show.

At this moment, the play directly dramatises the social meaning of the death of Edwardian music hall. Although the presentation of Billy's prejudices clearly reveals the unpleasant aspects of the triumphal imperialism celebrated in the forms of popular culture, the metaphor is profoundly ambiguous: does the lament for the death of music hall signify regret for the end of Empire? "Number Eight" suggests a highly ambivalent attitude toward the relationship between present and past, emphasising not so much the politics of Empire as the impact of great political changes on ordinary people's lives. It is a play about a society's failure to create a culture that might offer its members any degree of authentic self-realisation. *The Entertainer* is perhaps the first English play since *Heartbreak House* (1916) to dramatise the idea that the political is personal.

Phoebe changes the mood of genuine nostalgia on stage to one of sombre realism when she informs Jean that her niece has offered Archie and herself a new start managing a hotel in Canada. This leads to Frank's attack on the "middle of the road" situation of postwar British society and on Archie for his infidelity with "that blonde bitch in the Cambridge." After Frank exits, singing "Rock of Ages," the hymn that Billy sang at the beginning of Act I,[19] Phoebe once more reads out a part of the letter in a half-hearted attempt to persuade Archie of the benefits of life in Canada. After she goes to bed, Archie confesses to Jean that it was the fact that her mother (his first wife) caught him in bed with Phoebe that caused the breakup of their marriage.

Archie's long speech is a kind of spoken aria, carefully balanced against the jokes and songs that have preceded it in the scene:

> *Archie is drunk, and he sings and orchestrates his speech as only a drunken man can, almost objectively and fastidiously, like a conductor controlling his own sound.* (70)

The writing has an almost expressionistic quality here, reminiscent of a monologue in a Tennessee Williams play or in late O'Neill. At the same time the speech is perfectly in keeping with the decorum of the particular situation. Typically, the confession is presented by Archie as a series of stories.

> Did I ever tell you the most moving thing that I ever heard? It was when I was in Canada . . . and one night I heard some negress singing in a bar. *Now you're going to smile at this*, you're going to smile your educated English head off. . . . But if ever I saw any hope or strength in the human race, it was in the face of that old fat negress getting up to sing about Jesus or something like that. . . . to see that old black whore singing her heart out to the whole world, you knew somehow in your heart that it didn't matter how much you kick people, the real people, how much you despise them, if they can stand up and make a pure, just natural noise like that, there's nothing wrong with them, only with everybody else. . . . There's nobody who can feel like that. I wish to God I could. . . . If I'd done one thing as good as that in my whole life, I'd have been all right. (70–71)

Not surprisingly, Archie's only direct expression of passion is a description of a performance. He can never be a great performer because he lacks the ability to feel passionately.

> You see this face, you see this face, this face can split open with warmth and humanity. It can sing, and tell the worst, unfunniest stories in the world to a great mob of dead, drab erks and it doesn't matter, it doesn't matter. It doesn't matter because—look at my eyes. I'm dead behind these eyes. I'm dead, just like the whole inert, shoddy lot out there. It doesn't matter because I don't feel a thing, and neither do they. We're just as dead as each other. (72)

The speech opens out to confront the theatre audience, challenging them to deny the charge of being dead behind the eyes. When a few minutes later

Frank rushes in, and in language that negates all his political principles blames the "wogs" for murdering Mick:

> They've killed Mick! Those bloody wogs—they've murdered him. Oh the rotten bastards! (73),

Archie can only respond by mimicking the negress's blues performance he described a few moments earlier:

> Archie: (*Slowly singing a blues.*) Oh, lord, I don't care where they bury my body, 'cos my soul's going to live with God! (73)

This moment of conscious performance at the end of Act II is complex and disturbing because it throws into question all the conventions that have been established in the scene for expressing subtextual emotions through various musical and theatrical forms. In one of the great moments of twentieth-century British theatre, Olivier collapsed against the proscenium arch before singing the lines slowly and huskily, implying not only Archie's deep shock, but also by his substitution of the negress's experience for his own, exposing Archie's inability to express his own personal grief honestly.

Act III constitutes a kind of coda. It has often been suggested by critics that "Number Nine," which is Frank's "battle hymn" in protest at Mick's death, is an unsatisfactory scene. Its reference to "those playing fields of Eton" is rather too overt, but I do not believe the conception of such a stylised scene to be a mistake.[20] Billy's death, apparently precipitated by having to appear as a commercial draw in Archie's new show, is appropriately announced by Archie as "Number Eleven." The use of an impressionistic collage of sound effects and stage props evokes typically nostalgic memories of the kind of performer Billy must have been, a powerful and economical way of informing the audience of his death. Archie's sentimental onstage valedictory tribute is entirely in character—ironically the only time in the play when Billy, as it were, enters the stage of the music hall upon which he had made such a success during his working life:

> Archie: Ladies and Gentlemen, Billy Rice will not appear tonight. Billy Rice will not appear again. I wish I could sing a song for him—in his place. A farewell. But, unfortunately, I can't. Nobody can. None of us, any way.
> *Exit.*

> Front Gauze. *Funeral cortège with Archie, Phoebe, Jean, Frank, Graham and Brother Bill. They gather round a coffin, C. stage, draping over it a Union Jack, Billy's hat, cane, and gloves. In the background, snatches of old songs, wisps of tunes, the stumble of a banjo. Fade to—*
> NUMBER TWELVE (83)

Instead of presenting a naturalistic scene in which each character's grief is articulated in words, "Number Eleven" requires the audience to imagine each character's feelings about Billy's death, a device fully consistent with the overall dramaturgical technique. "Number Twelve" is a tableau counterpointing two conversations taking place immediately after Billy's funeral. Both Jean and Archie reject the offers of escape made to them—a conventional marriage offered by Jean's fiancé, Graham, and a passage to Canada by Archie's brother, Bill. The implication is that each prefers the difficulties of an authentic existence rather than the ease of a dishonest compromise.

"Number Thirteen" reveals Archie struggling manfully through his act, which unravels into a somewhat surrealistic reflection on his own life in which the income-tax collector is waiting for him in the wings and the staff of the theatre are busy dismantling the set to close down the show before he actually finishes the act. The pathos of Olivier's quiet delivery of the final stanzas of "Why Should I Care" was devastating. He summoned up a tone of withering sarcasm to deliver his closing address to the audience:

> You've been a good audience. Very good. A very *good* audience. Let me know where you're working tomorrow night—and I'll come and see *YOU*. (89)

As he exits upstage escorted by Phoebe, who has been waiting for him onstage for a few seconds, the gap between onstage routine and offstage reality is closed. Phoebe walks into the routine as Archie finally relinquishes the role of comedian. The aggression toward the imaginary music-hall audience could have been Olivier's toward the Royal Court audience. In any event, the audience is left with a strong reminder of its responsibility for making the play. The play has been about its failure to achieve the community of response generated by a good night out at a local music hall.

NOTES

    1. The first plays by John Arden (*The Waters of Babylon*) and N.F. Simpson (*A Resounding Tinkle*) were given Sunday night productions without decor in October and December, 1957; Ann Jellicoe and Arnold Wesker were first produced at the

Court in 1958, Pinter's *The Birthday Party* at the Lyric, Hammersmith, and plays by Shelagh Delaney and Brendan Behan at Joan Littlewood's Theatre Royal, Stratford East, in 1958.

2. "*Look Back in Anger* presents post-war youth as it really is, with special emphasis on the non-U intelligentsia who live in bedsitters . . . to have done this at all would be a signal achievement; to have done it in a first play is a minor miracle. All the qualities are there, qualities one had despaired of ever seeing on the stage— the drift towards anarchy, the instinctive leftishness, the automatic rejection of 'official' attitudes, the surrealist sense of humour . . . the casual promiscuity, the sense of lacking a crusade worth fighting for . . . I agree that *Look Back in Anger* is likely to remain a minority taste. What matters, however, is the size of the minority. I estimate it at roughly 6,733,000, which is the number of people in this country between the ages of twenty and thirty. . . . I doubt if I could ever love anyone who did not wish to see *Look Back in Anger*. It is the best young play of its decade." Qtd. in Kenneth Tynan, *A View of the English Stage, 1944–1963* (London: Methuen, 1984): 176–78.

3. *Red Peppers* is one of a series of one-act plays by Noël Coward produced under the title *Tonight at 8.30*.

4. "I've never written anything for any actor ever because it's an impractical thing to do. And apart from anything else it gets in between you and what you're trying to create." "John Osborne," *Olivier*, ed. Logan Gourlay (London: Weidenfeld and Nicolson, 1973): 146.

5. By piecing together the conflicting versions of events given by Arthur Miller, Osborne, Olivier, and George Devine, Anthony Holden managed to create a plausible account of how Olivier came to play Archie Rice. See Anthony Holden, *Olivier* (London: Weidenfeld and Nicolson, 1988).

6. It is hard to believe, given the huge impact that the visit of the Berliner Ensemble made on members of the English Stage Company at the Royal Court during its visit to London in 1956, that Brecht could really have been, as Osborne has claimed, "little more than a name to me."

7. Kenneth Tynan, review of *The Entertainer*, *A View of the English Stage* (London: Methuen, 1984): 201–03.

8. Ronald Bryden, "*The Entertainer*," *Plays and Players* February 1975: 22–23.

9. Op. cit., 202–203.

10. In Tony Richardson's production, a big figure lit up on either side of the stage to tell us which "number" we were watching.

11. It is an interesting fact that the Royal Court, with its 455 seats in a proscenium arch arrangement of stalls and circle, is roughly the dimensions of the typical Edwardian music hall.

12. John Osborne, *The Entertainer* (London: Faber and Faber, 1990). All page references are to this edition.

13. Typical American equivalents are "Get Happy" and "When You're Smiling."

14. Cf. the delivery of Max Wall (1974) and Peter Bowles (1986).

15. The most obvious instance when a character actually offers an opinion on contemporary politics strikes me as somewhat gratuitous: when Billy complains in "Number One" that one cannot tell women from men anymore, Jean says "like the Government and the Opposition" (18). Ostensibly, this develops her characterisation as a left-wing opponent of the Establishment support for the imperialistic Suez campaign and the general debate in the play between Edwardian values and the new idealism of the postwar Welfare State. In performance it comes across as a spurious attempt at "contemporary relevance," unlike the discussions about Frank's pacifist stance against the Suez War or the intimations of Jean's growing opposition to the bourgeois conservatism of her fiancé, Graham.

16. See Olivier's comments on playing the routine "badly."

17. In this respect, *The Entertainer* is a forerunner of a major tradition of plays

that use the forms of popular culture to examine the state of the nation. Among the best-known are Charles Chilton and Joan Littlewood's *Oh, What a Lovely War!* (1963), Joe Orton's *Entertaining Mr Sloane* (1964), *Loot* (1966), *What the Butler Saw* (1969), Peter Barnes's *The Ruling Class* (1969), Peter Nichols's *Forget-me-not Lane* (1971), *Poppy* (1982), Charles Wood's *Dingo* (1967), *H* (1969), *Jingo* (1975), Trevor Griffiths's *Comedians* (1975), David Hare's *Teeth 'n' Smiles* (1975), Alan Bennett's *Habeas Corpus* (1973), Stephen Poliakoff's *City Sugar* (1975), Caryl Churchill's *Vinegar Tom* (1976), *Cloud Nine* (1979).

18. Many of the plays of J.B. Priestley and Terence Rattigan and most of Coward's plays and films, other than his high comedies of bohemian life, deal with middle-class life.

19. The series of hymns sung by Billy in the play constitute a motif through which traditional Christian values are set against the amorality of the modern creed of "looking out for number one" represented in Archie's songs. Frank's spontaneous echoing of Billy's Edwardian values is in contradiction to his liberal and pacifist politics and is one of the many ironies by means of which a complex and ambiguous image of 1950s British culture is elaborated.

20. It would have been more subtle to have Frank sing another Boer War song in which the criticism of twentieth-century jingoism and the class values that underpin it would be ironically implied.

LUTHER

THE MORBID GRANDEUR
OF CORPOREAL HISTORY

David Graver

Of all Osborne's plays *Luther* (1961) deserves particularly close attention because it has enjoyed significant popular and critical success and works with themes and forms unusual for Osborne.[1] In this play we can measure both the range of Osborne's expressive talents and his limits. *Luther* is one of only three historical dramas penned by Osborne and, by all accounts, the play in which he comes closest to the epic style of Bertolt Brecht. Unfortunately, if we judge the play by its ability to represent history or conform to a Brechtian dramaturgy, we must contradict several early assessments and declare the play a failure. Nevertheless, Osborne's shortcomings on these points reveal the strengths of his dramatic style as well as its limitations.

Luther traces the life of Martin Luther (1483–1546) from his youthful entry into an Augustinian monastery in 1506 to his settled, middle-aged family life in 1530. The play's twelve tableaux pick out key moments in Luther's life or in the world that shaped his life: (I,i) monastic rituals, (I,ii) preparation for first communion service, (I,iii) confrontation with father, (II,i) Tetzel selling indulgences, (II,ii) Luther as established scholar, (II,iii) sermon and Ninety-five Theses, (II,iv) Luther summoned before papal legate Cajetan, (II,v) Pope Leo issuing orders against Luther, (II,vi) Luther defying Rome, (III,i) Diet of Worms, (III,ii) Knight discussing Luther and Peasants' Revolt, (III,iii) reminiscences and new family.

It would be misleading to say the play traces the *development* of Luther's character through the strains of his religious training, the intellectual maneuvering in his disagreements with Rome, and the fiery conflicts of the Reformation, because through all these aspects of his life he seems to change very little.[2] By the end of the second scene Osborne has told us everything about Luther that seems to interest him. Subsequent vignettes just reiterate the points already established. Luther is described as a serious young man with a powerful intellect whose self-doubt leads him to doubt God's mercy and the efficacy of all human endeavor and induces dire physical ailments ranging from occasional epileptic fits to persistent constipation. Although reference is made in the play to Luther's intellectual gifts and interests, Osborne does not really portray Luther's intellectual powers. Luther rarely carries an argument very far in the words he actually speaks. He grumbles about the sale of indulgences and the authority of the Pope (issues that are given theatrical prominence in II,i and II,v) but only presents an argument against the adoration of relics (a marginal issue in the play). For the most part, where Osborne might have shown Luther constructing arguments, he settles on showing him posturing authoritatively or spouting invective. The play avoids a systematic treatment of intellectual issues to concentrate on the physical and emotional aspects of Luther's life. In the scene concerning the Ninety-five Theses, for instance, Osborne eschews a précis of these theses in favor of an account of Luther's constipation and how it is relieved when he realizes that faith is more important than good works. The sermon is certainly engaging and powerful, but it is more confession than argument. We do get snippets of Luther's theories—his stress on faith, his suspicion of any authority other than the Bible, his hatred of relics and indulgences—but these snippets are never linked into long, logical sequences. They are attached instead to the emotional and physical obsessions fixed in the first few scenes.[3]

The limitations on Luther's development are in part due to the limited research Osborne did before writing the play. A number of scholars have pointed out that all of his factual information concerning Luther, as well as his interpretation of Luther's motivations and obsessions and even some of the sixteenth-century art work he incorporates in the play, is drawn from Erik J. Erikson's *Young Man Luther*.[4] Osborne's reliance on this single source explains both his meticulous attention to the emotional life of the young monk and his scanty treatment of later moments in the reformer's life, particularly his involvement in the suppression of the Peasants' Revolt. Temperamentally, Osborne is clearly not suited to the writing of history plays. He lacks the motivation needed for the necessary research and an interest in how individuals make their mark on and are marked by the shifting shapes of social relations. It is a testimony to the strong interest in historical drama in Britain at the time that a playwright so unsuited to the medium should nevertheless feel compelled to try his hand. As Kenneth Tynan has pointed out, Osborne's interest in Luther may spring from a similarity in temperament the two men share (Tynan 314) rather than from any attraction to Luther's ideas or his impact upon religious doctrine or social relations. Osborne's approach to the representation of history is quite traditional in its focus on a great man, but his privileging of Luther over any extended consideration of his historical moment pushes the traditional notion of historical drama to a notable extreme.

The model of historical drama based on what Hegel has called "world historical characters" and what is exemplified in the history plays of Shakespeare, which revolve around the deeds of royalty, was, by the middle of the twentieth century, generally acknowledged as problematic and unconvincing. The contemporary understanding of the complex nature of society and the human psyche make it difficult to represent on the stage in traditional dramatic form an individual whose actions upon his surroundings change the world. Osborne is one of the last English playwrights to work with the traditional form of historical drama, but his approach to this form acknowledges and seeks to circumvent its shortcomings.[5]

To minimize the problematics of representing historical action on a scale in which individuals can act effectively, Osborne eschews a focus on agency for a focus on subjectivity. In the process, he inflates the historical subject. Rather than having characters make history (or, at least, participate in its development), Osborne's Luther embodies history. Rather than maneuvering effectively in the field of historical events, Luther's subjectivity expands to incorporate the movement of history.

Ironically, this attempt to salvage the conventional form of historical drama destroys that form as completely (if, perhaps, not quite so overtly) as more radical innovations. What *Luther* gains in the prominence of the central historical figure, it loses in the direct dramatic representation of that character's historical agency. *Luther* is not so much an historical *drama* in the Aristotelian or Hegelian sense of that term as a spectacle of history. Action gives way to display. The protagonist is not so much an agent as a subject of speculation in two senses. First, he is the theme upon which the eye and mind of playwright and audience dwell. Second, history becomes a picture held within Luther's mind's eye—his subjective consciousness forms within itself the image of history around which the play turns.

Osborne is not the only playwright to magnify subjectivity so that it can contain history, but his *Luther* is unique for the manner in which it collects history within a self of extraordinarily corporeal constitution. This play is not so much concerned with Luther's actions as it is concerned with Luther's body—particularly his physical body but also the body of his work. *Luther* uses the biography of its protagonist as a container within which to exhibit world historical moments that are attached to his life. We are not given a picture of Luther situated in a historical period but, rather, a historical period embodied in the mental and physical preoccupations of Luther.

Other characters in the play serve as little more than a frame or platform upon which to display Luther. Indeed, the rather wooden and crude way in which many encounters are reduced to obsessive reiterations of Luther's principle qualities is one of the more irritating weaknesses in the play. The attention to Luther would be worthwhile if it enlarged him into a vessel capable of containing significant portions of sixteenth-century history, but the aspects of Luther upon which Osborne focuses are lamentably narrow and static. Osborne seems to think that repetitive attention in itself produces a kind of grandeur. By all accounts the skills of the actors and designers at the Royal Court did produce a grand historical spectacle, but Osborne's play often contributes little more than a rudimentary scaffolding for the show.

Our first glimpse of Luther's father (I,i), for instance, tells us very little about either him or his son but does insist, with mind-numbing repetition, that Luther's decision to become a monk is somehow unusual and controversial. Osborne wants the father, Hans, to stand out as a stern and critical authority against whom Luther has rebelled, but he fails to make the father anything more than an eye that gazes upon Luther with one unvarying question:

> Hans: Do you know why? Lucas: Why? What made him do it? . . . What made him do it?
> Lucas: Let's go home.
> Hans: Why? That's what I can't understand. Why? Why?[6]

Rather than portray a situation that might lead the audience to wonder why Luther joins the friars, Osborne simply allows the father to tell us that we should wonder about this. Similarly, rather than demonstrate Luther's intellectual skills in dramatic scenes, we are simply told that these skills exist. The two scenes with Staupitz, the Vicar General of the Augustinian Order, (II,ii and III,iii) are not so much dialogue as directed voyeurism. Staupitz points out the aspects of Luther that Osborne wants the audience to note while Luther obligingly demonstrates these qualities.

> Staupitz: What's the matter with you? What are you making funny faces for?
> Martin: It's nothing, Father, just a—a slight discomfort.
> Staupitz: Slight discomfort? What are you holding your stomach for? Are you in pain?
> Martin: It's all right. It's gone now.
> Staupitz: I don't understand you. What's gone now? I've seen you

> grabbing at yourself like that before. What is it?
>
> Martin: I'm—constipated.
>
> Staupitz: Constipated? There's always something the matter with you, Brother Martin. If it's not the gripes, insomnia, or faith and works, it's boils or indigestion or some kind of bellyache you've got. (*Luther* 65–66)

The Knight's soliloquy (III,ii) is even more embarrassingly inept in its obsessive but vacuous attention to Luther. The Knight loses all attachment to the particularities of his time and place under Osborne's effort to articulate a vision of Luther that is both cynical and admiring. We learn a lot in this scene about Osborne's view of Luther but nothing about how a knight of the sixteenth century might fit Luther's proclamations and the events of the Peasants' Revolt into his world view. The Knight's comradely attitude toward the corpse of a peasant he has murdered and his casual but unclear denunciation of Luther do not make much sense, nor does his sudden intrusion upon the story along with his references to the Peasants' Revolt. The scene addresses an aspect of Luther's place in history that is never really presented in the play.

Given the sometimes awkward and often uninspired nature of the dialogue, it is odd that critics from Kenneth Tynan to Niloufer Harben have counted the play one of the best in its decade.[7] Tynan seems to have been distracted from the text's flaws by Albert Finney's extraordinary performance in the lead role and the "urgent and sinewy" style of Luther's oratory (Tynan 316). Harben seems more generally enamored of the way in which the play magnifies and elevates both the stature and detail of Luther's life (Harben 187–212). John Elsom has also noted Osborne's consummate skill in "crafting magnificent single roles," although he refrains from suggesting that this skill gives *Luther* an extraordinary aesthetic value. Elsom touches on one of the keys to Osborne's success when he notes that his plays helped revive the star system.[8]

What Osborne lacks in traditional dramatic skills he more than makes up for in traditional theatrical skills. His characters speak to and interact with one another awkwardly, but the central characters (such as Jimmy Porter in *Look Back in Anger* or Luther here) are virtuosos at declaiming and drawing attention to themselves. Although Osborne often fails at dialogue, he is a master of the soliloquy. Indeed, where Shakespeare, for instance, uses soliloquy predominantly for moments of introspection, Osborne finds an astonishing variety of dramatic and theatrical uses for the form. Luther's monologues can dig deep into his psyche to tug at knots of anxiety and despair rooted in half-remembered childhood traumas (I,ii); they can strike sharply and venomously at his enemies in the world (II,ii); or they can turn intellectual controversies into vivid physical realities (II,iii). In addition to Luther's many monologic performances, the play is enriched with the amusingly scandalous sales patter of Tetzel, the dealer in papal indulgences, Cajetan's intellectual and diplomatic lectures, and Pope Leo's incisive and strategic proclamations. The part of Luther is certainly a plum for any actor wishing to exhibit his skills, while the lesser roles also often provide moments at which to display oratorical virtuosity. The familiar skills the play demands of its participants make it appealing to producers and the quality of the speeches endear it to audiences despite the shortcomings of its dramatic situations.

Luther is, however, more than just an easy play with which to impress conventional audiences. One of the more unusual points of interest in it is Osborne's emphasis upon what might be called the materiality of personality. As many critics have pointed out, this play bears at least a superficial resemblance to the materialist theatrical style of Brecht. With direct audience address, an episodic structure in which each scene stands on its own, an interest in intellectual rather than sentimental issues, and a presentational rather than representational use of backdrops and accessories, Osborne clearly shows some debt to Brecht. His knowledge of Brechtian dramaturgy came from having played the part of Lin To in Brecht's *The Good Person of Setzuan* at the Royal Court in 1956 as well as having seen the Berliner Ensemble productions that toured to London in 1956 and the subsequent use of Brechtian staging techniques by English directors such as William Gaskill and Tony Richardson (director of *Luther*) and by designers such as Jocelyn Herbert, who designed the Royal Court production of *Luther*.

Although Osborne has never acknowledged the influence, *Luther* bears remarkable resemblances to Brecht's *Galileo* (1947–55).[9] Both plays pit the authority and power of the Catholic Church against one individual's reasoned arguments about truth. Both plays make reference to nascent capitalism and the first stirrings of reason freed from tradition. Luther and Galileo are both treated with a somewhat antiheroic, deflating realism that emphasizes the sensual nature of their lives as well as their ideas. Galileo takes great pleasure in his food and Luther devotes great attention to the unreliable functioning of his bowels. Even many individual scenes in *Luther* echo or respond to similar scenes in *Galileo*. Brecht shows the Pope weighed down with his ceremonial vestments, while Osborne shows the Pope lounging in a hunting outfit. In *Galileo* the common people take up the hero's discoveries in a subversive carnival celebration; in *Luther* the peasants take up the hero's ideas in their revolt. Both plays present these scenes as mimed sequences. Galileo condemns his own behavior in a soliloquy near the play's end. The knight condemns Luther's behavior in the penultimate scene. Both plays conclude with a meal scene (set sometime after the main action) in which the characters look back on the important events. Osborne even seems to take up Brecht's penchant for involving food and drink in key scenes, although Osborne's characters never enjoy their food as much as Brecht's do.

Although the similarities between *Luther* and *Galileo* are extensive, they are also superficial. Osborne's work remains far from the central concerns of a Brechtian dramaturgy. Brecht wants to display on stage the material social gests of a particular place and time. The Brechtian concept of the "gest" involves a clearly articulated theatrical gesture that sums up and presents for the audience's judgement a particular aspect of social relations. A gest displays both exploitation and the ideology that covers it up. It attaches the scene on stage to a particular historical moment and to the society that gives that moment its particularity. Osborne is more interested in quirks of personality than in social gests. He shows little curiosity concerning any aspect of the sixteenth century lying beyond his narrow conception of Luther's personal world. Rather than dramatize social relations, Osborne displays psychological anxieties. Where Brecht breaks from traditional notions of drama to construct political and moral arguments, Osborne does so to increase the theatrical impact of his central character. In moving as far from traditional dramatic structures as he does in this play, Osborne imparts an unusual material presence to the main character, but this is a materiality devoid of Brechtian social gest.

To make personality material, Osborne employs three apparently Brechtian strategies that have the un-Brechtian effect of obscuring the social contradictions of Reformation Europe. First, to prevent the narrative of Luther's life from taking precedence over his presence on stage, Osborne cuts his biography into discrete scenes, episodes only weakly connected and with little noticeable forward thrust. Thus, Luther stands before the audience more than he moves through his life. Second, to give historical weight to Luther's presence on stage, Osborne has his character quote copiously from the real Luther's works. The oratorical nature of these quotations and their consequent lack of a fully developed dramatic context cause the words to float before the audience, on display in themselves more than as agents in a dramatic interaction. Third, in an attempt to emphasize the power of Luther's presence independent of social conditions, Osborne dwells on the internal state of Luther's body more than on his position in society. Where one might expect doctrinal controversies to lead from the mind of the main character into the world, instead Osborne directs the energy of Luther's ideas into his body. Luther's struggle with constipation is stressed as much as his struggle with Catholic doctrine and, in fact, blends with it. Theological dilemmas freeze his bowels, and clear lines of argument release them. Thus, Luther's historical significance as manifested in his published works is turned away from the social field in which the works wrought their considerable influence and is forced into the convoluted confines of his intestines.

Luther's immediate surroundings, as delineated in the play, do little more than frame and highlight the effects his mental ruminations have upon his physical being. His body becomes a repository for both his emotional turmoil and the history of his age. Where Brecht makes history material, Osborne makes it corporeal. Social conflict is represented more vividly in the sweat on Luther's brow and the churning of his intestines than in the confrontations of personalities. Even when social issues do become the center of attention, they are quickly subordinated to Luther's fits and fatigue. Note, for instance, how his confession in I,i ends in convulsions and how Cajetan breaks off his debate with Luther because of the latter's delicate health. *Luther* is not so much the picture of an age as a catalogue of physical ailments and emotional anxiety illuminated by an aura of vague historical significance.

Osborne's corporeal history, like Brecht's materialist history, departs from the notion of history as the personal narrative of a great man. In the seamless fiats of personal narrative, the actions of the hero preclude any questioning of the turns history takes. When history is reduced to the actions of princes (or those with prince-like power), it becomes a story to be told rather than a set of changing conditions to be investigated. Osborne and Brecht both eliminate the seductive flow of narrative for the stark confrontations of tableaux. But where Brecht's materialist tableaux seek to unfold the functionings of social oppression, Osborne's corporeal tableaux seek only to confront us with the emotional and physical strains that accompany heroic action.

Rather than represent Luther's actions, Osborne displays his body, shaking on the verge of collapse due to the burden of the history it holds within. Osborne shows us a body that contains history rather than showing us history itself. The historical import Luther embodies, although hardly a full treatment of his age, is enough to put severe strains on the functioning of his internal organs, particularly his bowels. The distressing effects that history works upon Luther certainly make for a spectacular play, but not for a play that really investigates the workings of history. Where Brecht abandons traditional historical narrative in order to challenge it, Osborne abandons it in order to call it back as a presupposed and unexamined light in which to display the hero's body. Luther suffers from the demands of his place in history, but his sufferings are made spectacular and worthy of attention because of his place in history. Osborne obscures history with the body of his hero while allowing the obscured history to inflate the proportions of the hero's body.

In Osborne's corporeal history play, dramatic conflict gives way to reverie and tableaux of a rather morbid nature. The somatic obsessions of the play transform nostalgia into necrophilia and make history not so much an object of scrutiny as the contents of a reliquary. Since Luther does not act in the play so much as display himself, he lacks the motion necessary for life. Being reduced to an object of scrutiny illuminated by a nimbus of historical significance desiccates personality. Deprived of the moisture of movement through a living world, Luther becomes a mummified remembrance given only the semblance of animation by the rudimentary historical apparatus set up for his display. Osborne does not show Luther alive in his sociohistorical circumstances but offers instead images of what Luther was. The pettiness and banality of some of Luther's complaints and preoccupations really require the exoticizing distance of history to become worthy of attention, while the grander moments of Luther's life do not suffer unduly from being encased in museum glass, since all Osborne wants from history is a good show.

Osborne's rather static, schematic, inconsequential portrayal of the sixteenth century and its subordination to Luther's corporeal presence suggests that for Osborne history is essentially dead. Its power and attraction arise primarily from the way in which it can call to us from the grave, in this case, Luther's grave. Osborne's display of personages and events relies for its authority and grandeur upon the place of these personages and events in history just as the saint's reliquary relies upon the history of the saint for the authority and power of its contents. But, as with the reliquary, the poignancy of the display is tied to its morbidity, to its historical moment being past. One cherishes the saint's bones because the saint is no more; similarly, Luther's grandeur is tied to his existence having ended. *Luther*, like a reliquary, contains only the desiccated remains of history. The theatrical decoration of Luther's life, which the play accomplishes, makes it an object of veneration rather than a source of knowledge.

As a reliquary, *Luther* is often impressive. Osborne exploits well the exotic nature of the past. By abandoning the traditional dramatic project of representing the actions of a hero, he can concentrate on refining the image of Luther and the aspects of his age that his personality embraces. Although the history in this play is very superficial, the spectacle is rich and complex. Osborne's formidable skills at crafting soliloquies are matched by his sense of scenic splendor and theatrical business. The solemn monastic rituals of I,i and the casual magnificence of Pope Leo's hunting party (II,v) create a broad palate of fairly traditional theatrical scenes. To these colors Osborne adds more surreal tones borrowed from Bosch (I,ii and II,vi), as well as the more epic gestures (borrowed from Brecht and Piscator) of stylized tableaux, direct audience address, and images projected at the back of the scene (II,iv and III,i).

There is no denying the skill and magnificence of many of the scenes Osborne creates, but he might have listened more closely to the words he gives Luther in his sermon against relics:

> A man without Christ becomes his own shell. We are content with shells. . . . Your emptiness will be frothing over at the sight of a strand of Jesus' beard, at one of the nails driven into His hands, and at the remains of the loaf at the Last Supper. Shells for shells, empty things for empty men. (*Luther* 75)

Surely, a man unattached to a living historical context is ultimately just as empty as a man without Christ. Without the nourishment of a broad sociohistorical milieu, the history a hero like Luther contains must shrivel to an insignificant, embalmed remnant of itself. Although containing history may inflate Luther's theatrical proportions, it also leaves him epistemologically hollow. One can learn little from the dried-out historical references he contains. Is Osborne, perhaps, aware that he had created an empty spectacle for empty spectators?

In a way, Luther's lack of attachment to the complexities of his historical moment match well the lack of attachment that he feels toward his father and his God and that he creates between himself and the Catholic Church. Indeed, the play is always most convincing in its portrayal of severed ties. The friendship between Staupitz and Martin is flat and unimaginative, while the animosity between Martin and the Pope is vivid and surprising in the turns of its portrayal. This play obviously favors individualism over history just as *Look Back in Anger* favors Jimmy Porter's individualism over his relationships with his wife and friends. *Luther* carries the fury of Osborne's man alone onto the plain of history and shows that it can be just as devastating there as it is in a bedsit of 1950s England. Luther consumes his historical period as completely as Jimmy does his companions.

The isolation of Osborne's individualist heros has a special poignancy in *Luther* because it meshes well with the self-doubt under which Luther staggers. Luther is as alone on the stage as he feels himself to be in his heart. His encounters with others are infrequent and awkward. Only in the solitude of introspection or oratory, where he grapples with doubt and isolation, does his theatrical presence become impressively vivid. Insofar as *Luther* is a meditation on the dynamics of alienation and self-doubt, its lack of a well-articulated sociohistorical context and convincing dialogue is no handicap, and even an advantage in some scenes. But Luther's status as a world historical figure makes the meditation on self-doubt seem somewhat coy and inconsequential. Luther may doubt his own historical importance or the justice of his actions, but the audience cannot. The unusually strong emphasis on soliloquy in *Luther* helps isolate him from his surroundings, but Osborne cannot isolate him from the historical significance the audience attributes to him. Osborne's treatment of isolation in an historical context comes off significantly better in *A Patriot for Me* (1965). Although the formal isolation of the hero, Redl, is not nearly as radical as is the case for Luther, the less significant place Redl occupies in history makes it easier to appreciate his feelings of alienation and insignificance.

The best aspect of *Luther* is the surprising and spectacular delineation of the hero's isolation. The chief drawbacks of the play are the violence this isolation does to an understanding of how Luther actually played a part in history and the sometimes inconsistent or dishonest way in which Osborne wants to cut Luther off from history while nevertheless exploiting the nimbus of his historical significance to brighten the play's theatrical show.

NOTES

1. For a summary of the critical response, see Malcolm Page, ed., *Files on Osborne* (London: Methuen, 1988) 27–33. Particularly lavish praise of the play is offered by Kenneth Tynan, *A View of the English Stage* (St. Alban's: Paladin, 1976) 314–16, and by Niloufer Harben, *Twentieth-Century English History Plays* (Totowa, NJ: Barnes & Noble, 1988) 188–212.

2. Simon Trussler makes a similar point. See his *The Plays of John Osborne* (London: Gollancz, 1969) 988–99.

3. For examples of characters who do articulate and live by coherent arguments about morality and social realities, one might look to the plays of John Arden or Arnold Wesker, say, *Serjeant Musgrave's Dance, Armstrong's Last Good Night, Left-Handed Liberty*, or the "Wesker Trilogy."

4. Kenneth Tynan was one of the first to point out this source. See *A View of the English Stage* 314. The most thorough examination of Osborne's use of his source is provided by E.G. Rupp, "Luther and Mr. Osborne," *Cambridge Quarterly* 1 (1965–66) 28–42. Rupp's article is summarized by Arnold P. Hinchliffe in *John Osborne* (Boston: Twayne, 1984) 57. *Luther* is probably most impressive if viewed not as a play about Luther or the Reformation, but as a dramatic adaptation of Erikson's book. Osborne's skills at adaptation are very impressive even if his grasp of history is not.

5. Rattigan wrote two even more traditional historical dramas (*Adventure Story* and *Ross*). Bolt shows an interest in the lives of history's great men (*A Man for All Seasons, State of Revolution*), but the vast majority of post-1956 British historical drama either reduces the status of great men significantly and presents them as part of their age (Arden and D'Arcy, *The Island of the Mighty*; Barker, *Victory*; Bennett, *The Madness of George III*) or eliminates great men entirely in order to focus on the powers and plights of common folk or lesser historical figures (Storey, *Cromwell*; Bond, *Restoration*; Daniels, *The Gut Girls*). Osborne also turns to a lesser historical figure in *A Patriot for Me*.

6. John Osborne, *Luther* (New York: New American Library, 1961) 17.

7. Trussler is more critical of the play. John Russell Taylor also offers some criticisms, particularly of Osborne's poor skills at dialogue, but suggests that *Luther* is important for demonstrating Osborne's skills as a theatrical craftsman, his earlier plays being more inspired than well wrought. See Taylor's *Anger and After* (London: Methuen, 1969) 54–57.

8. See John Elsom, *Post-War British Theatre* (London: Routledge & Kegan Paul, 1979) 79.

9. There are several versions of Brecht's play in print. See, for instance, the 1952 English version by Charles Laughton: Bertolt Brecht, *Galileo* (New York: Grove, 1966).

FROM OUT OF THE SHADOW OF NICOL WILLIAMSON

INADMISSIBLE EVIDENCE

Mark Hawkins-Dady

John Osborne's public profile and dramatic reputation lay in something of an uneasy relationship by the early 1990s. With the appearance of his second volume of memoirs, accompanied by interviews and public appearances, the author's past life and current views had become increasingly widely aired, drawing criticism for what was perceived as Osborne's misogyny, organic misanthropy, and unrighteous anger. These perceptions threatened to define the plays, too. Yet, as *dramatist*, Osborne has seemed to share with Arnold Wesker a niche as a figure of the late 1950s/early 1960s, known still to be "here," but remaining somehow "invisible." It was in such a context that London's National Theatre mounted its 1993 revival of Osborne's 1964 play, *Inadmissible Evidence*, which, intriguingly, was directed by one of Britain's leading women directors, Di Trevis. In terms of Osborne's *oeuvre*, this revival would be, implicitly, a test of Simon Trussler's assertion (one echoed by other critics) that *Inadmissible Evidence* was "the likeliest of his plays to retain an audience in the living theatre."[1] In terms of the stage-history and reputation of the play itself, it would also unavoidably be an attempt to wrest the play and its gigantic central role from the hold on it by actor Nicol Williamson, star of the 1964 premiere, the 1978 Royal Court Theatre revival (directed by Osborne), and the film version—an association of actor with play as strong as Olivier's with *The Entertainer*.

The stylistic challenge for director and cast in the post-Williamson theatre was to locate the right theatrical conventions to realise a play frequently viewed as untidy and sprawling, and that varies from an opening dream sequence, through the apparent stage naturalism of office life, to moments of expressionistic vision as characters move into self-reflective "arias" in the second act. Osborne instituted no discernible rewrites for the production, and in not making any textual cuts Di Trevis thus also took on board the multitude of period references to figures, institutions, and events of the 1960s, and thus also had to create a sense of period while trying to speak to an audience of the 1990s.

Despite these challenges, the scope for *widely* differing readings of the play-text, however, is not huge. That the two acts chart stages in the professional, social, spiritual, and physical decline and isolation of Bill Maitland, a middle-aged, adulterous, hard-drinking London solicitor, is undeniable. But, within that field of certainty, the exact nature of his decline, the degree to which it has wider social or metaphorical significance, and the extent to which the central character's malaise earns sympathy or antipathy are all debatable. The interpretive crux lies ultimately in the attitude taken toward the play's title. In a court of law, "inadmissible evidence" can cover any information that is attempted to be brought into play, but which is deemed irrelevant or contrary to the rules of court. Essentially, the concept is a neutral one. But the play's structure, as a case study of a man in his environment, purposely creates innumerable conflicts between strictly legal, causal, and rational motivations on the one hand, and the jumbled, inchoate, self-induced, and societal (the theoretically "inadmissible") on the other, and challenges all who confront the play, from director to audience, to judge which are the more profoundly relevant and to what extent moral judgement is appropriate thereafter.

The play opens with stage directions calling for "*an air of floating inertia before three actors come to some sort of life out of the blur of a dream*" in "*the bones and dead objects of a Solicitor's office,*" "*a site of oppression and polemic,*" to enact Maitland's reverie of being in the dock on the vague charge of "having unlawfully and wickedly published and made known, a wicked, bawdy and scandalous object."[2] The accusation remains unspecific, but Maitland's dream persona feels the need to define and explain not only past and present sexual and legal indiscretions, but his very existence. The stream-of-consciousness monologue that follows, punctuated by almost-caricatured legal points of order from the judge and defending-turned-prosecuting counsel, is a jumbled self-assessment that has its realistic justification in the nature of the scene[3] as the illogic of a dream, but, more important, has its psychological and ambiental justification in its emphasis on what Osborne stresses as the inherent "*ambiguity*" of reality and recall (63). As such, the scene prefigures much of the "real" world of the play, and plants in the mind of spectator or reader a number of "time-bombs" that explode at later points.

In this scene, Maitland's speeches establish, almost promiscuously, the 1960s context, replete with scathing references to the "white heat" of Harold Wilson's technological revolution, and Maitland's sense of not belonging in such a world. Personal exposition is given—it is learned that Maitland is thirty-nine; has been working in the legal profession for twenty-five years; has inherited a managing clerk called Hudson; regards himself as "tolerably bright" but "finally, that is to say, irredeemably mediocre" (17); is in his second marriage; and is losing his capacity for retaining events in his memory and for making decisions. Most important, he admits to having "depended almost entirely on other people's efforts" and "always knew in my own heart that only that it was that kept me alive and functioning at all" (19). His conclusion is a self-perception of entrapment: "I can't escape it, I can't forget it. And I can't begin again" (20). Thus the dream, Maitland's *"prison of embryonic helplessness"* (20), introduces both the key elements of the central character's present state and the essential concept of *judgement*, real and imagined, by self and others.

With the initial dimming of the house lights, the National Theatre introduced this scene with the concluding cacophonous crescendo from the end of the Beatles' "A Day in the Life"—a sly evocation of the super-fashionable youth culture that Maitland is at odds with, as well as an expressionistic confusion of sound paralleling Maitland's confusion in his sleepy mental processes. The final chord of the song, with its ominous finality, closed the scene, as the dock and judge's chair withdrew out of sight. Trevor Eve's twitching mannerisms and bewildered delivery of his lines conveyed a combined resentment at being, unaccountably, on trial with the unstoppable urge to confess. His speech mode was erratic, rambling, and unpunctuated, then suddenly highly articulated and emphatically precise, expelled mostly at speed.

The dream scene is, in fact, a semi-comic précis of the play as a whole. Almost all the essential dimensions of Maitland's character are introduced, but Osborne is still playing with his audience in this first phase of the presentation. At this stage, the effect of the scene in performance was not *quite* Kafkaesque (a description applied by some of the first-night critics), but more like a *comic* nightmare—Maitland's mental prison was yet *"embryonic"* and was new to the audience; the character's anxiety was yet untested in the context of a "real," non-dream world, his confusion severe but also humorous, and the audience could afford to laugh at his self-deprecation. Only with the poignant, exhausted last statement of irrevocability did the scene begin to suggest the true awfulness and inevitability of a downward trajectory.

It is tempting to think of the play then progressing clearly from the introductory dream sequence into the stage-naturalism of its second phase, the office life of the first act. Yet Osborne allows few opportunities to flesh out fully the professional world. Once the opening sequence dissolves into the interior of Maitland's office, managing clerk Hudson and assistant Jones (whom Maitland's dream cast as judge and prosecutor respectively) are found in a brief, matter-of-fact, expository conversation—that Trussler rightly dismisses as "striving for banality" but failing to be "convincingly trivial."[4] But this tone gives way to a sequence of interaction between characters that *always* has Maitland at its centre, involved in a succession of duologues with other individuals in person or by phone. Osborne does not allow us ever to see, for example, the secretary Shirley talk to the telephonist Joy; Joy never speaks to Hudson or Jones; Bill's wife, Anna, is telephoned, evoked, discussed, but never appears in person. Thus, while the veneer of office life is in place, a fully realized milieu is abandoned in order to have Maitland emphatically at the epicentre of a world that is then shown going through its convulsions of diminishment.

Scenically, the National Theatre production went to some elaborate lengths to reinforce this centrality by having Maitland's office, at once refuge and prison, on a front raised stage as his inner sanctum, but with the outer office, inhabited by his staff, as effectively the physical interface with the invading or threatening outside world, visible in the rear behind huge sliding walls of black gauze. These gauzes, when lit from behind revealed the quiet activity of office life behind, and when lit frontally became opaque to concentrate attention on the inner sanctum. Several critics felt the play would have achieved greater intensity in the National's studio space, the Cottesloe, rather than on the sizeable proscenium stage of the Lyttleton. Yet, if Maitland were seen to *fill* his world in a smaller space, it is doubtful whether his final isolation and sense of separateness would be as fully apparent as it was to be on the larger stage.

Maitland's office was furnished in a manner that was both realistic and metaphoric. Its slightly shabby mixture of leather and polished wood conveyed neatly the ambience of an Edwardian London gentleman's club (an ambience often associated with the legal profession); but more specifically, its lack of 1960s modernity (save the telephone and intercom) suggested the retreat of a man out of step with the times. Within this environment, Maitland is allowed, via the intercom and the telephonist Joy, to block or receive communication with others, maintaining control, as far as he can, over his world.

Trevor Eve's Maitland reemerged from the bewildering dream world into the office in a tetchy but surprisingly ebullient mood ("chipper," as two critics described him). Osborne has Maitland, in the rest of this act, elaborate upon his dream-diatribes against the state of Britain, the suburban consumerist masses whom he despises (along with his junior clerk Jones, whom he sees as their intruder in his midst), and the hypocrisy of the legal profession—all punctuated by the occasional responses from Hudson (Roger Sloman achieved a subtle balance of quiet independence and acquiescent indulgence in his relationship with Maitland in the role). The production emphasised a comic lightness of touch here in the humour derived from Maitland's refusal to bow to social and professional conventions. It is true that even at this stage he is embroiled in a battle to keep abreast of the daily routine through sheer rhetorical energy, endless glasses of water, and headache pills; but in production, this was a Maitland awakened from the guilt and reproach of his inner consciousness to play his deliberately audacious role as devil-may-care womaniser and reactionary-rebel provocateur in the "real" world, almost relishing his contrast with the family man Hudson ("you.... Wives and angels. Me: mistresses and devils"); the young, dull, but ambitious Jones; and the ingénue, Joy (40).

Yet Osborne places ambushes for Maitland and for the audience, as the developing pattern of rebuffs and withdrawals (both real and imagined), that chart Maitland's decline, becomes more evident. This pattern is initiated by Maitland's apparently inconsequential inability to hail a taxi for work ("the first time I've never got one," he comments indignantly), followed soon after by his mystification as to why the caretaker "turned his back on me" (21, 28). The encroaching personal paranoia is accompanied by a generalised professional one because "some clattering brute of a computer" will obviate the need for solicitors (29). The rebuffs continue during the act: Anna puts the phone down on him; Shirley resigns abruptly, ostensibly because of her pregnancy (although this production emphasised her description of the tawdriness of her sexual history with Maitland); Hudson is considering a job offer from the rival firm Piffards; and, most cuttingly of all (and more palpably in the concreteness of production), Maitland's client, Mrs. Garnsey, sums up her adulterous husband as a character unnervingly evocative of the Maitland that is emerging: "nothing really works for him. Not at the office, not his friends, not even his girls.... everyone's drawing away from him" (55). That Bill acknowledges the relevance of her words is suggested in Osborne's stage directions: "*Bill gets up to comfort her but is paralysed*" (55), and at the National Theatre the awkward absence of response from Maitland adequately conveyed his frozen discomfort.

Eve's performance carefully graded these moments of realization, from the vague irritation at not getting a taxi, through his slow but forced recognition of Shirley's complex mixture of thwarted love and personal humiliation, to the apparently gentlest yet most profound confrontation with his own self occasioned by Mrs. Garnsey's words. His superficial jauntiness and quick wit were under constant attack from the signs of physical and mental exhaustion—headaches, searches for his pills, constant demands for water, a rasping dry cough, memory failures, his visible contortions of expression conveying his slow struggle to absorb the facts of the other characters' lives—so that his available energy was very much that of effort rather than organic. Yet Osborne imbues Maitland with the power of at least one profound and revealing self-recognition; when Hudson complements his quick mind, he responds: "I have a very small, sluggish, slow moving brain. I just run it through quickly, at the wrong speed like a piece of film and it darts and flickers, but it perceives little and it retains nothing" (40). The depth of this self-perception makes the comment paradoxical; but the truth of it—his inability to think anything through to resolution—is at the root of the character and a fundamental reason for the play's apparently repetitive or reiterative structure: Maitland can be made aware enough of the dimensions of his problems so that they remain constantly in play in his conversation, but he remains incapable of locating any solutions, and the anxieties simply revolve and intensify. As John Gross noted in *The Sunday Telegraph*, the play's "swollen and tundra-like stretches are simply the faithful expression of an underlying, inescapable self-absorption."[5]

Eve also provided strong motivational links in the sequence of events, by showing the extent to which Maitland's reactions to rebuff or shock are automatic, addictive attempts to shore up his sense of self-worth by other means. Compensation for rejection was seen to be an instinctive reaching out to either a material prop (glass of water, telephone, pill) or a human one. Eve amply exploited Osborne's text to suggest the almost arbitrary quality to these attempts in their timing and fitting clumsiness. After his pessimistic dissection of the legal profession, and immediately following the truncated phone call with Anna, Maitland makes his offer of a partnership to Hudson. More complexly, Mrs. Garnsey's evocation of a Maitland parallel of personal and social inadequacy became the immediate cause, in performance, for Maitland's advances to the as-yet unjaded Joy. Sex is clearly a drug for Maitland—as Hudson pointedly observes, "some people seem to use things like sex, for instance, as . . . a place of escape, instead of objects . . . in themselves" (35).

The first act, on the page but especially in performance, entertains and outrages with the overwhelming exuberant solipsism of the central character, with the tone darkening as the act progresses and the reality of Maitland's own decline and his inability to affect others' lives in other than a negative fashion becomes more palpable. While the dramatic conventions of the act after the dream sequence are largely those of naturalistic interaction, the second act—the next day in the office—moves into territory in which naturalism falters as Osborne's interest moves to portray the workings of failed human relationships both within the individual mind and in the society at large.

To an extent, Act II mirrors Act I with a dreamlike opening developing into another office day. The stage directions specify that Maitland should be seen emerging into consciousness, having slept in his office following a post-dinner-party row with his wife the previous evening. With a spotlight highlighting a single telephone in the centre of the stage, the production noted Osborne's stress on the symbolic significance of the telephone as, variously, lifeline, intruder, and inquisitor, which is *"stalked, abused, taken for granted, feared"* (63). The production had the office setting emerge on its inner stage from the rear, to the aural accompaniment of a warped, drawn-out telephone ring: a parallel device to the play's opening Beatles song, suggesting Maitland's struggling from sleep on the expressionistic level, and the struggle for communication on the more symbolic.

In this opening sequence, Trevor Eve's Maitland popped his headache pills, rushed offstage to throw them up, took more, spat into his handkerchief and into the filing cabinet, and scrutinized his seemingly broken thumb. Act I had gone some considerable way to stressing an animalism in Maitland's character—he scratched his crotch when musing on Joy's physical attributes and made a ridiculously crass attempt to comfort Shirley by groping her breast, which came over as cheap opportunism. If his expressions of lust in Act I were evidence of some physical vigour, then even that dissipated during Act II, as his real ailments and imagined ones merged to present the image of a man halfway to the physical state of Beckett's Krapp.

Before others arrive at the office, Maitland has long rambling monologues with mistress, then wife; to the first he confesses his sense of alienation and dissolving identity the previous evening: "I'm frightened. . . . It was as if I only existed because of her [Anna], because she allowed me to, but if she turned off the switch. . . . I'd have been dead. . . . They would have passed me by like a blank hoarding or a tombstone" (62). It is now Maitland's turn to echo Mrs. Garnsey's vocabulary: just as Maitland's hypochondria is intertwined with his real physical ailments, there is ambiguity here as to how much of his self-absorption consists of appropriation of others' anxieties and ways of expressing them. Osborne stresses that for Maitland, at this point, *"most of all"* there is *"the fear of being cut off, of no sound from either end"* of the phone (63). During the scene, Eve staggered around, picked up phones, dropped them, dialed and redialed, and at one point comically yet credibly mistook his whisky bottle for the phone, speaking into its neck. Since Maitland's needs, notably with Liz, are almost entirely confessional, a failure actually to be *exchanging* words with her would not necessarily be noticed by him: the character's solipsism constantly creates the paradox that his fear of losing contact is balanced by his inability to notice when the other person is no longer there or listening. The comic touches of the scene thus had a disturbing edge, since they toyed with Maitland's increasingly fragile grasp of the reality of his world.

In this second day at the office, Maitland's professional and social isolation assumes further concrete forms: Hudson confirms Shirley's definitive departure, and later Jones confirms the loss of Mrs. Garnsey as a client. Joy's arrival, however, establishes for the audience that she and Maitland did indeed have a sexual encounter the previous evening, although one interrupted by Anna's arrival. Joy admits to nymphomania and Maitland reassures her that "for a woman to make that admission is no shame" (72). But the one-line joke has a serious undertone—for a moment Maitland, as a requirer of self-affirming sex, seems to have found a female parallel; yet the reassurance fades. Joy's morality is conventionally hypocritical: she needs verbal redefinition of the sex to justify itself in terms of statements of love, but to this Maitland cannot respond.

Osborne has both Hudson and Jones out of the office during the rest of this act, thereby pushing Maitland into the position of having to deal with all the day's clients. Four encounters—three with clients and one with his daughter Jane—provide opportunities to investigate the context for Maitland's relationship troubles and his inability to find a role for himself in the modern world, and—important in a play often thought of purely in terms of the central character—to illustrate a much more general failure of human relationships.

Osborne specifies that the two female clients, Mrs. Tonks and Mrs. Anderson, should be played by the same actress who played Mrs. Garnsey. What may, at first, seem like merely an economy of casting reveals itself, in performance, to be a technique primarily to identify the audience's perspective with Maitland's—women may wear different clothes, have different accents, and inhabit different social strata, yet they are all, to him, "other": they are representatives of the gender that has been his obsession and stumbling block. Yet by undercutting their individuality of personality in this way, Osborne also insists upon their symbolic status as representatives of the unhappy married woman's situation. All three female clients in the play are filing for divorce and thus, in their statements, have to dredge through the circumstances of their suits—that is the naturalistic premise for their monologues. But their testimonies also become hooks on which Maitland hangs his own trawl through his past and its intertwining with the present from the male point of view. The clients' names evoke, for Maitland, former girlfriends, and he supplements the muddled thumbnail sketch of his pre-marriage youth given in the dream sequence with these impressionistic, rhetorical anecdotes about them, anecdotes that also speak more broadly of a previous era: the overwhelming impression from these reminiscences is one of nostalgic fondness for a youth that Maitland cannot "reassemble," as he puts it, combined with a sense of the obstacles and inhibitions encountered in postwar, pre-1960s sexual relations.

Mrs. Tonks's testimony is constantly challenged and undercut by Maitland's reading of her husband's version, although an initial ambiguity, in performance, as to whether Maitland is voicing his own thoughts or not, seems intentional on Osborne's part: Maitland's sense of gender divisions and his own marital failings give him an instinctive sympathy for the erring husband's view (as evident in his Act I banter with Hudson). But the overwhelming effect, in the theatre, was of a brutally crude reduction of the complexity of the case, and of the awfulness of a legal system that redefines the grey *"ambiguity of reality"* of relationships as the polarised exaggerations of plaintiff and defendant (63).

Mrs. Tonks's individuality, already tenuous in Maitland's perception, is yet clearer to him than that of his next client, Mrs. Anderson. The naturalistic exterior of the Mrs. Tonks scene gives way here to a double interior monologue. As Mrs. Anderson moves away from her straightforward reading of her petition to evoke her upbringing and marital problems, Maitland speculates on the subject of death, which has entered his conversation previously, and moves into imagined future scenarios concerning his own and Anna's death. His own death, and the numbers of those at his funeral, represents for him the supreme test of how truly alienated he is or is not from those around him. Anna's death, on the other hand, would force him into the status of single man again, challenging him with a new freedom. The tone of these musings, in Eve's performance, was part playful, an experiment in imagination. Maitland posited for himself a new life, sensuously relishing the unusual pleasures of independence, from buying a new suit ("something a bit too sharp for someone my age and size") to "reading a new novel perhaps, by some woman perhaps" (86, 87). In contrast, if the brutality and indecent intrusion of divorce proceedings dominate in the Tonks scene, the portrait of a marriage breakdown given here by Mrs. Anderson is one of a man and woman struggling not with each other but with their yearning and inability to communicate. In a poignant passage, the effect of which was deepened in performance, Mrs. Anderson sums up a situation in which both participants are mystified victims:

> He slept in another room for a few weeks, but he used to cry quite often and kept me awake. We would both cry sometimes. He offered to leave me alone. I told him I would leave him if that's what he wanted. I still wanted some happiness for him. (85–86)

The juxtaposition of the Anderson/Maitland monologues here could produce substantially different effects, depending on the stress of a particular performance: Maitland's scenarios could, if performed with more jocularity than they were here, emphasise Maitland's callous self-indulgence when compared with the despair felt by the likes of Mrs. Anderson—characters who possess neither inner fortitude nor the ability to live on their wits. But Trevor Eve's meandering into and out of the worlds of the clients interwove Maitland's imagination with their stories so that they became interrelated: the women spoke not only for themselves, but also for their gender, for their social strata, and for the women of Maitland's life; and Maitland's musings on love ("it has to be heaved and dropped into the pool after you . . . and then you have to duck down below the surface and bring it up") and death ("wasn't it [sex] just another effort. . . . some way of fighting off what's going to happen to you") reflected not only on the unresolved questions of his own life but on the fundamental questions his clients did not face (84, 85). Maitland behaves not so much as a legal adviser but as a self-interested confessor, learning about others' lives insofar as they mirror or prompt reflections on his own, but nevertheless drawing their lives into the central dilemmas of the play.

The final client scene concerns Maples, Maitland's only male client, up on a charge of indecency. His story is as pathetic as those that precede him, but importantly, he is allowed to pursue his monologue—of his childhood, his unenthusiastic marriage to Hilda, his snatched homosexual comforts behind the Midland Bank—with almost no interruption from Maitland, either in the form of naturalistic intervention or flight of imagination. Clearly, part of Osborne's aim is to include both homosexual (then illegal) and heterosexual relationships in his portrayal of a broad cross section of human relationships essentially indefinable within the legal system, as well as to challenge society's definition, in 1964, of homosexual acts as illegal. But in production, Maples was also seen to form a curious counterbalance to Maitland as a male outsider trapped in an unhappy marriage. Whereas the female clients represent, in Maitland's imagination, rough counterparts to

Anna, Liz, previous girlfriends, or women at large, Maples's account here increasingly absorbed Maitland's rarely won attention. It was not that he was, in terms of naturalistic motivation, becoming *less* self-centred, but that the homosexual outsider offered him parallel images of male isolation, an understanding of society's hypocrisy, and a semisecret life of sexual and emotional indiscretions. Interestingly, Osborne hints at this parallelism by suggesting some behavioural similarities: "*He gives his evidence, like Bill himself, mostly at speed, more polemic than reflection*" (92).

The Maples scene has often puzzled critics because of its seemingly tangential quality, and it has often been interpreted purely as a gesture against the illiberal homosexual laws of the period. This production located a place for it at the centre of the play's concerns and within Maitland's solipsistic vision. But perplexingly, Osborne specifies that the actor playing Jones should act Maples. Why? Osborne suggests in the stage directions that "*Maples has some of Jones's unattractiveness but with other elements. In place of his puny arrogance and closed mind, there is a quick-witted, improvising nature, not without courage. His flashes of fear are like bursts of creative energy, in contrast to Jones's whining fixity and confidence*" (91). The trick here seems to be on both Maitland and the audience in that we are invited to identify Maples as a Jones-type before he rebels against that type: in production, his initially comic gaucheness gave way to a form of self-expression that was refreshingly open and honest, gaining both the audience's serious attention and Maitland's fascination.

The patter of Maitland's behaviour establishes, with psychological accuracy, the human tendency to carry over emotions and frustrations from one event or circumstance into another apparently unrelated one—the gap between slow absorption and response. Thus Maitland's daughter Jane, who has been summoned apparently because he wishes to explain his absence from her birthday party to her, becomes the repository into which Maitland pours the accumulated frustrations of his life and, more immediately, those of the lives of the clients he has just seen. The stage directions highlight this scene by separating it from preceding and subsequent action by lighting fades, and this separation both allows Maitland to be captured in mid-flow of the most sustained piece of rhetorical invective in the play, and makes this "purple passage" the most poignant and theatrically disturbing scene of the play. Eve's Maitland shouted, goaded, bullied, insulted, pleaded, in a wholesale verbal assault on his daughter, whose only response was to retain her outer self-composure, despite being, as a classic Osbornesque contradiction suggests, "*cool, distressed, scared*" (101–02). Inasmuch as the play portrays a society, with the previous scenes revealing the wreckage of relationships among mature adults, this scene portrays Maitland's clash with the younger generation and his confrontation with the era's *Zeitgeist* as he perceives it. His bitter envy of 1960s carelessness and carefreeness contrasts with his own experiences of growing up in postwar Britain, before the "permissive" age, caught between the still-embryonic rebellions of a developing youth culture and his inheritance of existing social norms, particularly regarding marriage. Maitland's seemingly contradictory morality is deeply rooted in a culture that espouses norms and regards transgression as sin, and Maitland's own self-reproach stems from a consciousness of his transgression. His chief accusation against Jane is that she, as a representative of her generation, lacks a sense of sin and is thus free of morality and self-reproach. Just as Maitland and Maples have married young but badly, because, well, it was expected, the younger generation has unburdened itself of such obligations and responsibilities in favour of a self-contained amorality.

It would be possible—and possibly tempting considering Osborne's reputation as a misogynist—to perform this scene as a wholesale demolition by a man in a situation of power over a defenceless young woman. But more important that Maitland's misogynistic tendencies—which are viewed, in the context of the play, as an aspect of a pre-1960s world where women were mothers, girlfriends, wives, secretaries, mistresses, but never friends, equals, or colleagues—are the intrinsic ironies of the scene. Maitland's assault reveals as much his weaknesses as his aggression, his daughter's silence as much her quiet confidence as her passiveness. Osborne's skill at constructing a scene that at once shows his central character at his most wistfully romantic and vulnerable *and* at his most sadistically aggressive is a theatrical *tour de force*, stunningly eloquent in the psychological realism of Maitland's contradictions. Eve's portrayal (which had become considerably more sophisticated on second viewing) did not hesitate to allow all the character's contradictions to stand, moving, in an instant, between gentle lyricism and vicious sarcasm. At his most aggressive, he spat his accusations out, prowling around the stationary Jane like an interrogator; at his tenderest, he embraced her from behind and swayed his body with hers as he imagined taking her out on dinner dances like some "rather grand married couple, a bit casual but with lots and lots of signals for one another" (102). His final words, "Go on now," can simply be read as his impatient dismissal of his daughter after subjecting her to the tirade (107). However, through his vocal inflection, Eve's Maitland linked the words directly to his earlier comment that "God said . . . Be fruitful and multiply and replenish the earth. And *subdue* it. It seems to me . . . you are on your way at last, all, to doing all four of them" (107). Thus his final comment was not so much brutish dismissal as prophetic release of Jane from both the responsibilities and the anxious disabilities of his world and that of his generation to fulfil what he sees as the destiny of hers—a vision of the freedom of youth that he interprets as the opposite to his own entrapment.

For the audience as well as for the characters this was a tautly strung and emotionally draining scene, representing both something of a climax and an extinguishing in terms of the vigour of the central character. The Maitland of the final phase of the play has little opportunity for rhetorical abandon, and little of the witty and vicious cut and thrust of the first act. The ambiguous "little worm of energy" he tells Jane he possesses (107), with its connotations as both a positive, life-giving force and as a parasitic sapper of his mind, was, in production, shown to have given way to a fatalistic vacuum of will. In a rare overt directorial intervention, Di Trevis avoided the obvious return after the lighting fade to the naturalistic veneer of the office setting, evidently seeing this last phase more as a stylistic counterpart to the original dream sequence. Thus the production stripped away the elements of scenic naturalism by pulling back and shutting off the office set behind the huge gauze sliding screens, and had an exhausted and puppet-like Maitland seated centre stage, in a pool of light—a stark contrast to the animalistic prowling and twitchiness of previous scenes. If the Jane/Maitland scene represents the fullest expression of Maitland's alienation from his society, then the last scenes, in production, were intended to aim for psychological realism as Maitland grapples, in a more fundamental way, with his sense of isolation and the barriers to human love in general—a level that is more existential than specifically social.

The professional world is now dealt with deftly by Osborne. Joy is going home (there's "not much to stay for, is there?" [107]), and it is learned from her that Hudson has "apparently" accepted Piffards' job offer; Winters, the lawyer whom Maitland believes is also deserting his circle, remains uncontactable; and Jones believes the Law Society is now investigating Maitland's practice. There is a last feeble attempt by Maitland at emotional compensation, as Joy's departure for the day prompts him to tempt her to a drink and a "chat" (presumably sex, although the enfeeblement of the Maitland of the production may have meant it literally); but by now Joy has joined the exodus from Maitland's life, declaring "I think they're all right. I don't like you either" (108). Maitland's professional collapse is completed by her departure and indications of uncertainty as to whether she'll ever return.

Osborne plays a surprising card now in having Liz enter the scene. The play thus far has suggested that Liz would remain, like Anna, strictly offstage, at the end of a telephone line. But her introduction allows another perspective on Maitland to be offered to counter an audience's direct absorption or rejection of his own solipsism. While Joy has, in the course of the play, given Maitland a chance to shore up his sense of potency sexually, his ability still to make a "conquest," it is to Liz that his most urgent appeals for emotional support have been directed, notably after his unprecedented "rebuff" by Winters (although whether this rebuff is in Maitland's mind is one of Osborne's ambiguities). In production, the power structure of the Maitland/Jane scene was completely reversed here: the passive Maitland assumed the role of recalcitrant patient, even child, while Liz wrested the roles of provoker and conversational challenger from him.

The encounter ends with Liz apparently walking out on the relationship, although the scene contains a highly complex mesh of attitudes toward love and relationships. By this stage Maitland has reached near-complete resignation to the impossibility of success in any aspect of life. It is not so much defeat in the war to establish a proper role in the professional, social, and personal lives of those who constitute his environment, as a surrender to the confusion and constant paradox of battle. In one of the most eloquent and succinct metaphors of the play, in performance thrown out almost casually, Maitland remarks:

> Do you know what a client said to me today? . . . She said when I go out to the shops, I go to the ones furthest away so that I can be out of the house and away from him longer. Then I get angry when the shopping is so heavy, and I can't carry it on my own. (106–07)

Although couched in the language of the everyday, the significance drawn by Maitland is fundamental and universal: we are trapped in a cycle of unhappy and contradictory desires for both independence and support. He is berated by Liz for his guilt ("a real peasant's pleasure" [107]), and for his lack of courage and fibre in attempting resolution of the demands he has had of himself and of/from others, most particularly in terms of herself and Anna. Yet the dialogue here always has Maitland affirming impossibility, for his perception of this paradox kills what remains of his will. Gone is even the day-to-day arrogance and indignation characterising earlier scenes, as his responses testify to his capitulation to irresolution.

Specifically, the scene concerns love. Several times Maitland seems to affirm his love for Liz—Trevor Eve's characterisation made these confirmations unabashedly sincere, untraced with irony. Yet equally palpable for Maitland is the impossibility of realizing love in the context of any actual relationship. And while this scene, in psychological terms, concerns a further stage of breakdown, the client scenes have confirmed that Maitland's malaise may be *in extremis,* but is not, ultimately, unique: the dilemma of how to realize love when set against social pressures, the burdens of upbringing, the inadequacies of the law, and sheer human contrariness is not ultimately the dilemma of an unbalanced mind. In this latter sense Maitland, perhaps surprisingly, emerges from the play as a thwarted idealist and purist. Just as he criticises Hudson for his easy legal objectivity ("morally—or emotionally—do as you like" [40]), and Jane for her sublime amorality, his misanthropy and self-loathing becomes a response to the elusiveness of the kind of profound and moral human experience he finds himself incapable of achieving. The realization of his incapability has vitiated the "worm" of energy, even the vitriolic kind, that has been the source of his *modus vivendi.*

The National Theatre production's style, at this point, was, nevertheless, somewhat at odds with the still largely naturalistic form of the dialogue: the metaphysical resonances existed still under the veneer of conversation about business travel, domestic arrangements, and specifics of the Maitland/Liz relationship. Yet the directorial approach, from Liz's departure, with Maitland now the sole figure on stage, justified itself in the Beckettian image of a man suspended in a form of spatial and temporal purgatory. The source within the text was probably the passage from Maitland's earlier phone call to Anna: "I'll be like something in a capsule in space, weightless, unable to touch anything or do anything, like a groping baby in a removed, putrefying womb" (64). His last words, according to the stage directions, are spoken into the telephone. Here they became semi-coherent rhetorical questions and statements to which there were no adequate answers. In psychological terms, it was regression to an almost catatonic state, a realistic representation behaviourally, and in social terms a self-removal from the "real world." What does Maitland await? "The Law Society or someone" (115). But by now, the oft-mentioned Law Society has assumed greater proportions as an almost God-like metaphor for judgement.

Thus the production took its cue from Maitland's earlier musings on death and isolation to emphasise the existential, universal nature of Maitland as a symbol of man awaiting judgement, as much moral as social. And the production's very final image found an ironic visual correlative for the text's implications. The opaque black gauze was lit from behind to reveal an entire jury, representative of both the cast of Maitland's life and society at large. But this was not so much an invitation to make judgement on Maitland as to assess the very viability of the act of judgement itself. The challenge to the audience was to disentangle the "admissible" from the "inadmissible" evidence given, for the play had offered a multilayered account of its central character. It is clear, even from the opening dream sequence, that Maitland fatalistically expects to be judged, at some time or another, and the play illustrates his consequent inability to modify his way of life. Yet the conclusion challenges the audience to be wiser than Maitland. Inevitably, the self-indulgence of the central character will always alienate some sections of an audience, who will regard the play as amounting to little more than "a sob for a cad" (as critic Nicholas De Jongh described it in the *Evening Standard*). Yet, while refusing to iron out the ambiguities of the text and the central character, the National Theatre production created the overriding sense that *any* moral judgement of Maitland could only be made with extreme caution. While this production showed Osborne as a writer whose presentation of the circularity of despair evoked Beckett in theme and aspects of technique, he also showed himself as being rigorously naturalistic in the philosophical sense in its perception and demonstration of human beings defined by the myriad jostling circumstances of their environment, history, and expectations—circumstances that one dismisses as "inadmissible" at great risk of a failure to comprehend.

In responding to the first night of this production, most reviewers summarised their preconceptions about the play's subject and structure, and several common viewpoints emerged. The play was generally perceived as:

1. a play very much reflecting its time, concentrating on the social realism of 1960s Labour-ruled Britain.
2. a satire on the inadequacy of divorce laws of the 1960s.
3. a play that was too long for its subject matter, its attack blunted by overwritten rhetoric, an ill-thought-out juxtaposition of dramatic conventions, and tangential, extraneous scenes (notably the Maples scene).
4. a play whose previous stage success was indistinguishable from the histrionic assault on the central role by Nicol Williamson. The implication, and sometimes the explicit view, was that it was largely Williamson's extraordinary all-devouring dynamic as Maitland that had rescued and given coherence to an otherwise sprawling series of scenes.

As regards the first observation, the play's historical context of 1960s Britain in fact proved surprisingly elastic. The social and personal disjunctions between generations, between an increasingly technological society and those who feel redundant within it, between society's accepted forms of relationships and "pure" feelings and desires—all remain problematic in today's society. It is the parameters that have changed, not the essential nature of the problems. There was one exception—Maitland's casual sexism with Joy and Shirley, which today would qualify as blatant sexual harassment, may have been more acceptable in the early 1960s. Trevor Eve's lascivious gestures and dismissiveness of intellectual abilities on the part of Joy or Shirley were, if anything, highlighted in performance, as aspects of his general animalism, at times drawing audible hisses of discontent from the audience. Di Trevis, rather than simplistically understating these aspects of the character or using them to define Maitland negatively, simply made them prominent enough to go into the melting pot of Maitland's character as one of the pieces of "evidence" to be taken into account, and linked his sexism to the earlier era in which Maitland learned his social and professional manners.

The programme for the production concentrated on giving background information to the play's era and to the divorce laws of the time. Undeniably, the situation in Britain has changed: in 1964 divorce by mutual consent was not an option—one partner had to admit or be accused of adultery or some other wrongdoing. Yet those critics who found the play thus dated were less sensitive to the general underlying principle that any legal system is bound to be reductive and inadequate in dealing with human relationships. Maitland, as a solicitor, is not only a practitioner in the law—the device enables Osborne to have him (and the audience) encounter and assimilate other stories of desperate lives, including that of the parallel male outsider, Maples. While homosexual relations may now be legal, few would argue that it is now therefore easy to live an open and accepted homosexual lifestyle. Osborne's presentation of the law at work within society is broader and more fundamental than the 1960s setting might suggest.

Perhaps the most widely stated criticism of this production, though, was its lack of a Nicol Williamson. Most of the reviewers had seen Williamson as Maitland, and the extent to which that portrayal had ingrained itself as synonymous with Osborne's character was widely evident. Reviewers yearned for his "electrifying performance" (Neil Smith in *What's On*), his "demonic energy" (John Gross, *The Sunday Telegraph*), his "poisonous misery" (John Peter, *The Sunday Times*), his "crumpled despair" (Steve Grant, *Time Out*), and his "whiff of spreading, yeasty rot" (Paul Taylor, *The Independent*). So strong was the ghost of Williamson that Robert Butler, in *The Independent on Sunday*, felt the production needed "to gain a Williamson or lose an hour," and that Neil Smith felt that "bereft of his [Williamson's] magnetism, the play's weaknesses become chasms." Sheridan Morley expressed this kind of view most strongly, in *The Spectator*:

Without such voltage, *Inadmissible Evidence* really doesn't work at all: a desperately overlong, sloppily conceived and rambling legal nightmare, it was hauled off the page and driven into lifelike drama by Williamson's blazingly electric and mesmeric talent to abuse. . . . About that production I can remember nothing but him.

While undoubtedly Trevor Eve's performance was not in the same mould as Williamson's (and, while it also received many plaudits on opening night, doubtless lacked the surety it was to develop as the run progressed), such comments reflect rather more on the preconceptions of the reviewers, historically conditioned to perceive Osborne's play purely as an occasion for a Romantic identification of mercurial, self-destructive actor with self-destructive role to the diminishment of any other value in the play or its production. Evidently, the role of Maitland does demand a rare stage authority and presence. But it was the strength and originality of Di Trevis's production that neither she nor Eve attempted to reproduce the volcanic Romantic disintegration characterising the Williamson productions, but went back to basics to rethink the balance of styles in Osborne's dramatic structure, its distribution of roles, the relations of scenes, and their expressive requirements for an audience in the 1990s. The most exploratory reviewers (including some, such as Michael Billington, who *had* seen Williamson perform) felt impelled to reexamine the dimensions of the play and to note how much of it is a "dream-play" and "a journey into a head in terminal disarray" (Michael Billington in *The Guardian*), how much of it transgressed the norms of stage naturalism and the period setting in its compressed case study of decline, and how much the frame of reference had to include not only 1960s divorce laws but also the psychology of depression and despair, and the literary ambiences of Kafka and Beckett.

The National Theatre's production certainly had its faults, most notably that its emotional drawing back to present the evidence, which reminded some reviewers of Brecht, led occasionally to a mismatch of dramatic style with theatrical convention. The opening dream sequence required a much greater, more surreal and bravura theatrical expression; the central client scenes likewise needed greater directorial intervention to create a suitably expressionistic atmosphere (Billington noted that Osborne's own 1978 production had wisely dimmed the lights at certain points here); and the final Beckettian presentation of human beings in pools of light was introduced at too early a stage, being fully appropriate only for Maitland's last speech. In these respects, what is perhaps this director's instinctive theatrical minimalism inhibited full realization of the text's theatrical potential. But this production restored a specificity and balance to Osborne's play. Maitland was no longer a histrionic meteor flashing over a half-sketched naturalistic world. He was a recognisably mediocre human being in successive stages of collapse and isolation, viewed progressively in four stages: a premonitory dream, a largely naturalistic scene illustrating his professional world, a deeper exploration of the social and psychological avenues, to a final confrontation and surrender to the basic, unresolvable human dilemmas of (in)dependence, love, and death. Maitland's characteristics ceased to be Romantically organic, but acquired a context in his past, present, and his expectation of judgement. And while the centrality and self-obsession of Maitland will always be a dominating theatrical impression in any good performance, this production restored the other characters to prominent positions in the dramatic structure—not as mere satellites circling the central star, but as the necessary constituents of his social and professional context, as the personifications of his lost youth and freedom, isolation, marital failure, and who all have a *mutually* affecting contact with Maitland (most notably, the embryonic stories of failure of Maitland's clients suggested, in production, that their authors too might have embarked on journeys of decline).

The production's chief virtue, and chief claim to reestablishing Osborne's text, was then its reintegration of the character of Maitland into the contexts for his decline provided in the play as a whole, with the result that he emerged as a heightened but *representative* human being, embroiled in a recognisable disintegration, rather than a uniquely dysfunctioning individual. If the production did not fully achieve all that it suggested, it certainly went a long way toward justifying Trussler's contention about its stageworthiness and providing an argument as to why *Inadmissible Evidence* has been regarded by many as some kind of a masterpiece, if a strangely unquantifiable one. One looks forward with much interest to the next major revival, now that the play has crept from under the shadow of the great Nicol Williamson.

NOTES

    1. Simon Trussler, *The Plays of John Osborne* (London: Victor Gollancz, 1969) 120.

    2. John Osborne, *Inadmissible Evidence* (London: Faber and Faber, 1964) 9. This quotation and subsequent quotations, cited parenthetically, are from the 1978 reprint of *Inadmissible Evidence*.

    3. There are no scene divisions as such in the play. The term "scene" is used throughout this essay to refer loosely to the more or less self-contained units of action that are evident in reading or watching the play.

    4. Trussler, 125–26.

    5. The major reviews of the National Theatre production are usefully

anthologised in the issue of *London Theatre Record* for 4–17 June 1993. This and all subsequent quotations from reviews are from the *Record*.

Seduced by Meritocracy

Class and Sexuality in *A Patriot for Me*

Robert F. Gross

I

How fearful are all things around me! Like some thief who treads forbidden ground, fearful I enter each apartment of this well-known house [. . .] what must be my life? Ever to speak a language foreign to my heart, hourly to add to the number of my crimes to conceal 'em. (Lillo, II,i, 1–4, 8–10)

Long before there was Alfred Redl, there was George Barnwell. More than two centuries before John Osborne's *A Patriot for Me*, George Lillo's *The London Merchant* enjoyed incredible popular success, great literary influence, and became one of the founding texts of English bourgeois tragedy. Osborne's play, by comparison, is a work of limited appeal, virtually no influence, and is generally viewed as the unsatisfying work of an important writer in decline.[1] Rather than a founding text, it comes as a late manifestation of the tradition of bourgeois tragedy, a form that has grown increasingly problematic as the twentieth century has worn on, enduring the attacks of the avant-garde, the many critical pronouncements of its obsolescence, and the pressures of a rapidly changing world, yet surviving as a genre on the verge of the twenty-first century. The very fact that *A Patriot for Me* could be written and performed in the 1960s testifies to the surprising tenacity of the middle-class values celebrated, and already problematized, in Lillo's play of 1731.[2] At the same time, Osborne's play pushes the aporias of bourgeois tragedy to the verge of incoherence, making it one of his most fascinating, if less theatrically rewarding, plays.

On the surface, the plots of *A Patriot for Me* and *The London Merchant* seem similar. Each tells the story of a talented, hard-working young man, marked for success in a world of male homosocial enterprise. His promise is cut short, however, as he falls prey to lust. Lust leads to acts of betrayal against the homosocial order, and the talented young man is destroyed as a result.

The agents that awaken the protagonist's sexual desire, however, differ markedly in the two works. In Lillo, young George Barnwell falls under the spell of Millwood, who seduces him and then uses her sexual allure to compel him to commit theft and murder. The closest equivalent to Millwood in *A Patriot for Me* is Countess Sophia Delyanoff, a Russian spy who briefly becomes Redl's lover, and reports on him to her superiors. Sophia, however, by no means controls the fate of Redl. Indeed, her hold on Redl is very weak. She admits to Colonel Oblensky that her seduction of Redl was a waste of time, as far as espionage is concerned:

> Oblensky: What's your assessment of Redl?
> Countess: Ambitious. Secretive. Violent. Vain. Extravagant. I expect you know as much as I do. You don't have to sleep with him to find that out.
> Oblensky: Precisely. It doesn't seem to have added much to our total knowledge. (119)

Like Millwood, the Countess seduces and betrays. Unlike Millwood, she is totally without influence on the protagonist or the progress of the plot. She is a Millwood without power, a red herring in the plot. The Countess, like Hilde the prostitute, only exists as a marker for the heterosexuality of the male characters; since Redl is homosexual, they can only have negative significance, as people to whom Redl is *not* attracted.[3]

Women are reduced to shadowy presences throughout *A Patriot for Me*. Their function is best seen through an incident at the Baron von Epp's drag ball. Jaroslav Kunz announces that he has brought a woman to this all-male event. Her presence, he explains, is meant to liven up the party, since all the drag queens must now be viewed with suspicion, since one of them is an "impostor." The Baron is thrilled at this innovation. "Marvelous!" he exclaims, "We'll unmask her. I'll offer a prize to the man who strips her" (134). The woman is reduced to an object of sport among the men, and an object of violent sport at that. Rather than exposing a male transvestite to be a man, the object is to expose the woman. In the homosexual world of the drag ball and, I would argue, throughout *A Patriot for Me*, women, having lost their power to be Millwoods, are rendered powerless.

There is yet another level of deception in Kunz's stratagem, however, but here Osborne is the trickster. Neither Osborne's stage directions nor the cast list that accompanies the printed version of the play bear out Kunz's assertion that there is a woman at the ball. The spectator, misled by Kunz, will look in vain for a woman on stage, and may well misidentify one of the transvestites as a woman. If Kunz's stratagem serves to make the characters at the ball more suspicious, it also serves to make the audience more credulous. For the audience, Kunz's woman is as much a red herring as the Countess's power to betray Redl to the enemy.

Superficially, the difference between Barnwell and Redl is one of sexual preference. While Barnwell puts himself at peril by moving outside the "mercantile monastery" (Hammer, "Economy" 84) of Thoroughgood's homosocial realm to encounter Millwood, Redl finds himself sexually attracted to other men within the homosocial realm of the Austro-Hungarian army. With this conflation of homosociality and homosexuality, the male establishment grows increasingly unstable; one cannot flee from lust to the illusory protection of a monastery. In Osborne's variation on *The London Merchant*, George Barnwell lusts after the other apprentices.

II

Where are you, Redl, you're always disappearing? (159)

Act I of *A Patriot for Me* takes the form of a coming-out narrative in which Redl, and the audience, become increasingly aware of Redl's sexual preference as we move from oblique hints to a fully-consummated homosexual encounter. A coming-out narrative works by constituting its protagonist's homosexuality as a secret, and then disclosing it. There are two kinds of forces at work in the constitution of the secret: psychological resistances to self-understanding on the part of the protagonist, and social opposition to homosexuality in the protagonist's world. Without these resistances, there is no secret. Osborne establishes both kinds of resistance. The nature of Redl's psychological resistances remain shadowy, (as Hayman observes, "all through Act One he's less than half-aware of what he feels" [58]), but Osborne dramatizes the effects of those resistances. We are told that he is not contemplating marriage (91), he is rarely seen at the local house of prostitution (92), and, when he engages the services of a prostitute, he faints (97). His liaison with the Countess Delyanoff is fraught with anxiety (112–118). When asked why men marry, he responds, "Children, property" (111), as if he could not imagine that the wife herself might be a motivation.

At the same time, Redl's lack of enthusiasm for heterosexuality is accompanied by a fierce homophobia. When a young man cruises Redl in a café and says to him, "I know what *you're* looking for" (123), Redl flies into a rage, yelling and physically accosting the young man. It is at this moment, in the penultimate scene of the first act, that Redl is "outed." Before he is able to put his desire into words, it is articulated by someone else, someone who has the mysterious ability to read Redl's sexual orientation. This outing is vehemently resisted by Redl, but only for a few moments of stage time. A mere five lines after the Young Man's revelation, we see Redl in bed with a young soldier, having just had sex with him. Redl's relaxed posture and musing, "Why did I wait—so long" (123), stand in pronounced juxtaposition to the anxiety that surrounded his scenes with Hilde and the Countess. The rapid transition from the Young Man's articulation of Redl's sexual identity to Redl's sexual capitulation dramatizes a sudden, almost dizzying, movement from self-delusion to self-acceptance.

If the nature of Redl's resistances are left shadowy, the social resistances to homosexuality are made crystal clear in Act I. The first scene of the play shows Redl seconding August Siczynski in a duel. The provocation for the duel was his being called "Fräulein Rothschild" (83) by an aristocratic officer, Ludwig von Kupfer. Siczynski explains that he did not object to the surname, but to the imputation of effeminacy. This attempt to defend his masculinity, however, has fatal consequences, and Redl is seen cradling Siczynski's dead body as the scene ends. In the following scene, Redl is asked to account for his part in the Siczynski–von Kupfer duel. As the questioning goes on, it is clear that the duel, although officially not allowed, is less of a problem than his association with Siczynski, who had run up huge debts without a woman to justify the expenditures. Not until Redl implicitly repudiates his dead comrade, explaining "I don't think he was ever in his right element" (91), is the matter closed. In the first scene, imputations of homosexuality lead to a loss of life; in the second, they threaten a career. These two scenes together establish life in the Austro-Hungarian military as highly homophobic, and provide a sense of menace against which Redl's coming-out story can unfold.

Although scenes 3–9 do little to reinforce the homophobia dramatized in the first two scenes, it returns with increased ferocity in scene 10, the final scene of the first act. There, Redl's first homosexual encounter (with Paul, a young soldier) immediately leads to him being beaten and robbed. As the curtain falls, Paul explains to the bloodied Redl, "Don't be too upset, love. You'll get used to it" (124). Osborne thus depicts a homosexual lifestyle as a life of inevitable victimization. Paul is a male Millwood, seductive and traitorous. By the end of the first act, the sense of peril that accompanies coming out in the world of the play is extreme.

The second act, however, quickly dissipates the peril through an extravagant drag ball. While the first act was largely built around two-person scenes, this act is dominated by this heavily populated scene, laden with spectacle. There are ten characters who make their first appearance in this scene, plus Redl, Judge-Advocate Kunz, Steinbauer (Siczynski's other second in the duel), and von Kupfer, who we were led to infer in the first scene of the play was a homophobe. Beyond these attendees, Osborne describes at length five different kinds of costumes worn by guests at the ball, leading us to assume that the event is very well-attended indeed.

This scene sharply undercuts the sense of menace established in the first act. Osborne moves from one homosexual man being robbed and beaten by five assailants to a vast and opulent display of a male homosexual culture, including a baron, a judge, and higher-ups in the military. One moment Redl seemed isolated and outnumbered; now he seems part of an insular crowd. It seemed before that his position might be in jeopardy due to his sexual orientation; now one wonders if there are any straight men in the Austro-Hungarian Empire. The size of this scene and the degree of spectacle in it gives the "secret" homosexual culture of Vienna a theatrical impact far beyond any other culture presented in the play. Although the scene begins with the baron reminding Redl that the ball is conducted secretly, the general ambience and action of the scene is one of openness: Redl and Stefan are both admitted, despite the fact they are inappropriately dressed, and Kunz is able to bring a woman to the ball without her being immediately evicted. These notes of casualness lessen the mood of secrecy. The lighthearted, comic tone that predominates also serves to minimize tension. Although the ball contains repeated references to homophobic institutions that oppress the homosexuals, such as the Roman Catholic Church and the medical profession, they are merely objects of ridicule, and the sense of threat is minimized, by their absence, by their seeming ineffectuality, and by their comic treatment. By the time the scene is over, it is hard to believe that Redl is in any danger whatsoever.

The mood and language of the drag ball also contrast strongly with that which preceded it. No longer the clipped, elliptical exchanges of Act I, but a whirl of repartée, jokes, sexual innuendo, and camp. When Hirst defines *A Patriot for Me* as comedy of manners, saying that it "takes an issue basic to the comedy of manners—the conflict between passion and the strict code of behavior society forces on the individual—and gives it precise definition in relation to the problems of the homosexual" (86), he seems to be more influenced by the drag ball than the death of Siczynski and the beating of Redl. The conflict between passion and a strict code of behavior, after all, is not in itself comic; one need think only of Phaedra, Gonza the Lancer, or The Lady of the Camellias. The conflict is only comic when it can be resolved through means that are neither violent nor deeply painful. The fact that Hirst is able to define *A Patriot for Me* as comedy gives evidence of the extent to which the second act succeeds in erasing the sense of extreme homophobia established earlier.

This new, comic construction of male homosexuality continues in the scenes after the drag ball. It manifests itself in the use of wit and comic invective, some of which Hirst proclaims equal to Congreve at his best (86). Most important, it surfaces in an epigrammatic redefinition of homosexuality and homophobia. Oblensky explains to Redl:

> You're a romantic. You lust after the indescribable, describe it, to yourself at least, and it becomes unspeakable (161).

In this definition, the external forces that serve to oppress homosexual men in *A Patriot for Me* cease to exist, and the closet is constructed solely by the subjectivity of the male homosexual. In the light of such a definition, Redl's fear for his position, the violence he was subjected to, and the blackmail that forces him to betray his country, all disappear. It becomes completely a matter of his own self-loathing. From Oblensky's point of view, Redl alone is responsible for his oppression.

Osborne does nothing to repudiate Oblensky's statement. Neither Redl nor any other character comes up with an argument against it. Redl's response to it is weak, "You sound like a drunken Russian Oscar Wilde" (161), and the reference to Wilde further reinforces the force of the statement. Oblensky's epigram, with its use of paradox and symmetry, not only has a Wildean ring to it, but the use of the word "unspeakable" echoes Wilde's famous description of an English fox hunt, "the unspeakable in full pursuit of the uneatable" (Wilde, *Plays* 87). Osborne appropriates the style and figure of Wilde from gay culture to give rhetorical weight to an argument that denies the oppression of homosexuals.

Furthermore, Osborne makes Redl behave at the drag ball in a fashion that lends credibility to Oblensky's analysis of Redl. Early in the scene, Redl appears relaxed and playful in this environment, which one would think would be a welcome relief from his closeted isolation in Act I. Suddenly, however, he responds to the campy display of one of the guests by striking him, and abruptly leaving. This outburst parallels earlier moments of violence in the play, such as the Siczynski–von Kupfer duel, Redl's attack on the young man in the café, and the beating of Redl; it is yet another instance of violence against homosexual men. After Redl's coming-out and suffering in Act I the outburst comes as an unpleasant surprise. In the comic society that Osborne has created in the scene, the violence makes Redl appear aberrant. It is a disconcerting about-face for Redl, from the isolated homosexual in a homophobic environment in Act I to the isolated homophobe in a homosexual environment in Act II. Either way, Redl seems to be odd man out. The effect of him being ill at ease in both environments begins to make the audience suspect that the problem is in Redl himself, and not in the world. Like Oblensky, Osborne tends to dismiss the social forces that construct the closet and turns to purely psychological forces to explain its origin.

III

Osborne, in his statements outside his plays, seems not to be very sympathetic to homosexuals (he always calls them "poufs") but then the same could be said about his comments on women and he has married several of them. (Hinchliffe 82)

In Act III of *A Patriot for Me*, Osborne advances a semiotics of male homosexuality that obliterates the idea of the closet altogether. According to this theory, the Russians need not set out elaborate surveillance mechanisms to identify homosexual men. Even the guest list to the Baron's ball would be a redundancy, since, according to Osborne, gay men come to bear the sign of their sexual preference on their bodies, in a way that anyone can read. This sign is first mentioned by the Countess: "Alfred: every one of *you* ends up, as well you know, with a bottom quite different, much plumper and far wider than any ordinary man" (153). This is later reiterated to Redl by Victor: "In the bottom, that's where we all go and you can't mistake it. *Everyone'll see it!*" (164). Male homosexuality is equated with passivity in anal intercourse, and it is that passivity that inevitably marks the gay man, as clearly as Hester Prynne's scarlet letter. In Osborne's play, the male homosexual body is identified by a sign that stems from a chain of images all too familiar in the Western discourses on sexuality: to be a male homosexual is to be sexually penetrated, is to be passive, is to be female, is to be degraded. Homophobia and sexism reveal a close interdependency here, as the man's "shame" is to be associated with any cultural practices that are identified with women. Osborne takes the terms of this ideological system one step further. For him, the homosexual closet turns out to be a futile refuge, since the male homosexual's body itself will inevitably become a sign for all to read. Just as in one of the founding texts of homosexual modernism, *The*

Portrait of Dorian Gray, the body inevitably comes to bear the traces of its actions upon itself. But, whereas the profligate's body becomes aged and decayed in Wilde's novel, the male homosexual body in Osborne's play becomes feminized, as the buttocks grow wider than those of "any ordinary man" (153).

The drag ball must be interpreted in the light of the homophobia and sexism manifested in the references to homosexual men's buttocks. There is in this scene none of the Bakhtinian carnivalesque, none of the gender-bending so extolled by some postmodern critics. Instead, the event is repeatedly defined by elements that are hostile to women. Three of the six groups that Osborne describes in attendance at the ball use drag as an exercise in grotesquerie: men in evening dress with heavy makeup—"more frightening than any of the others—with middle-aged, decadent faces, painted like whores" (128); men who hate women and wear drag only to make them appear odious (128); and the ones who "go out of their way to turn themselves into absolute grotesques" (127). There is no celebration of the "feminine" in these three categories, only misogyny. Of the remaining categories, one rejects drag altogether, and the other two do not travesty images of women maliciously, but, even in these two final categories, the element constituted as "feminine" is given no positive value of its own, but is seen as inviting a comic response, as a form of camp. This camp effect can be intended by the character, as when a singer opens the act by parodying the role of Susanna in *Le Nozze di Figaro*, or it can be unintended, as when Baron von Epp, in full drag, defines the elements that he believes make up a "man" (133). Whether conscious or unconscious, the invocation of codes culturally related to women undercut the authenticity speech acts, whether singing Mozart, or talking about masculinity, and render them camp. In this misogynistic milieu, the presence of a woman invites violence and humiliation, as the Baron looks forward to having the woman who has infiltrated his drag ball stripped naked.

The cumulative effect of the drag ball, Oblensky's definition of homosexual self-oppression and the semiotics of the male homosexual buttocks, is to completely undercut the notion of the closet, and with it, both the coming-out plot and the blackmail plot, since both of these plots rest on the premise that homosexuality can be kept secret. By destroying the category of the secret, Osborne renders his story of Alfred Redl incomprehensible.

It is at this point in the plot that *A Patriot for Me* lurches into incoherence. The protagonist's story demands that homosexuality can be kept secret. If it cannot be, neither the coming-out or blackmail plots make any sense. At the same time, Osborne introduces the notions that: (a) homosexuality need not be closeted in the Austro-Hungarian elite (the drag ball), and that (b) every male homosexual is inevitably recognizable as such. Both notions undermine the validity of Redl's story. We are left with a strange contradiction: a construction of homosexuality that is, by turns, a carefully kept secret and common knowledge.

IV

There are no secrets better kept than the secrets everybody guesses. (Shaw 331)

One possible approach to explaining this contradiction would be to invoke the category of the "open secret."[4] The open secret is a paradoxical construction that allows the person holding the secret to have an illusion of having a distinct subjectivity, which resists the forces of social construction around it. At the same time, for the secret to have any social force, it must already be known. As D.A. Miller elegantly express the notion, "I have had to intimate my secret, if only *not to tell it*; and, conversely, in theatrically continuing to keep my secret, I have already *given it away*" (194).

Using the idea of the "open secret" as an interpretative device, we can begin to generate the following reading, which accounts for some of the text's incoherence. Through most of the first act of *A Patriot for Me*, Redl is a person with a secret. He does not offer any information about himself; he tends to retreat behind his official position. When pushed, he expresses a preference for solitude over the vulnerability of interpersonal relationships:

> Countess: If you leave me, you'll be alone.
> Redl: That's what I want, to be left alone.
> Countess: You'll always be alone.
> Redl: Good. Splendid. (117)

His rage at the young man in the café is a response to discovering that his secret is an open one. Once he learns that his secret is known, his defenses crumble; he has sex with a young soldier, he is attacked by men who somehow know his secret as well, he enters a ballroom filled with people who know and share his "secret." No longer in sole possession of a secret that he believed insured his individuality, he behaves aberrantly, lashes out violently at one of the guests, and leaves the ball. But he is unable to regain his sense of self; he is even told that his secret can be read by anyone. In desperation, he becomes a spy, if only to have a new secret. When that is found out, he sees no recourse but to commit suicide. End of play.

An investigation of the forces working upon Redl further supports this reading of the play. As the son of a railway employee, Redl is rising in the military due to his personal talents, not his family or connections. Early in the play, Möhl explains that the "modern army" (87) will operate on individual merit:

> No one's going to be passed over, every man'll have his chance to prove himself, show what he can do, given half the chance. (87)

Osborne later reiterates this point through the voice of General Conrad von Hötzendorf:

> The army's like nothing else. It goes beyond religion. It serves everyone and everyone serves it, even Hungarians and Jews. It conscripts, but it calls the best men out, men who'd never otherwise have been called on. (106)

This styling of the army as a self-proclaimed meritocracy has more to do with Great Britain in the '50s and '60s than the Austro-Hungarian Empire at the turn of the century. The development of Britain's Welfare State, along with increased opportunities in education, led to the promulgation of the myth that class barriers were no longer insurmountable (Segal 69, 80). Although this myth was far from universally accepted (Marwick 158–166), the discourse surrounding the growth of meritocracy proliferated throughout the period, as can be seen in Michael Young's 1958 satire, *The Rise of the Meritocracy, 1870–2033*. Sinfield has observed that it was a young, educated, upwardly mobile theatergoer who characterized Osborne's audience at the Royal Court Theatre, an audience that tended to sympathize with attacks on the established middle class (178–79). Such an audience would be particularly sensitive to the tensions, complexities, and hypocrisies of meritocracy in contemporary Britain.

As Osborne portrays it, the Austro-Hungarian military has two major shortcomings. The first is that it remains largely an aristocratic system, despite the token presence of Redl. Möhl, despite his support of Redl and his belief in merit, admits that class privilege still plays a great role in the military (87, 109). Osborne dramatizes the persistence of privilege in the story of aristocratic von Kupfer, whose position in the military is not in the least threatened by his killing Siczynski in a duel or his attending the Baron's drag ball. All that is *officially* seen of von Kupfer is his family background. Redl, on the other hand, is minutely observed; Möhl wants to know everything about him, including his talents, his professional accomplishments, and his private life. Merit can only be established through scrutiny; therefore, the person who attempts to rise in the meritocracy must forfeit all privacy. There is no difference between what Möhl, as a representative of the Austro-Hungarian military, wants to know about Redl, and what Russian Intelligence wants to know. Redl's open secret, then, is a desperate defense against a system that offers him rewards, but also subjects him to a system of surveillance that robs him of any interior, private space. As the Countess tries to explain to Redl, "You can't have your kind of competitive success *and* seclusion" (117). Osborne had criticized the invasion of privacy by the mass media in his 1962 *Under Plain Cover*; here it is the government itself that is involved in surveillance.

This personal, open secret of Redl's, however, is only part of a larger open secret in his society. The larger secret is that the ostensibly homosocial and heterosexual order of the military elite is, in reality, largely homosexual. The duel between Siczynski and von Kupfer, which we are originally led to construe as a confrontation between a homosexual and a homophobe, collapses when we see von Kupfer at the Baron's ball. In Acts II and III of *A Patriot for Me*, there is minimal tension between homosociality and homosexuality. This permeation of a supposedly heterosexual realm with a homosexual presence parallels perhaps the most famous open secret in gay literature, the fabled brothel La Féria in Jean Genet's *Querelle*. This heterosexual house of prostitution is fabled because sailors can play dice with the male brothelkeeper, Nono, and, if they lose, can be penetrated by him. It is this homosexual presence that makes the place a legendary open secret:

> On board there never is anybody who would know exactly what La Féria really is, nor do they precisely know the rules of the game which has given it such a reputation, but no one, not even the greenest recruit, dare ask for an explanation; each and ev'ry sea-farin' man will have it understood he knows what it is all about. Thus the establishment at Brest appears ever in a fabulous light, and the sailors, as they approach that port, secretly dream of that house of ill-repute which they'll mention only as a laughing matter. (Genet 6)

This erasing of the boundaries between homosociality and homosexuality is, of course, not limited to Genet and Osborne. It is a common strategy of male homosexual pornography, which takes traditionally all-male societies, such as sailors, cowboys, and truck drivers, and reconfigures them for fantasies of sexual abundance. But, while Genet retains the sexual charge found in this literature, Osborne moralistically condemns the presence of homosexuality in the elite. The Countess, Oblensky, and finally Redl himself verbally attack homosexuality, sometimes condemning it for its effeminacy: "you're like a guild of housewives" (152); "Dear Mother of God, you're like a woman" (164), thus reiterating the same sexist stereotyping that Osborne used to portray male homosexuals at the drag ball. No defense is offered. For, in *A Patriot for Me*, male homosexuality is marked in two different ways: as a secret that the aspiring hero tries to keep for himself against the hypocritical powers of the meritocracy, it is valued positively; as a sign of the decadence of the Establishment, it meets with disdain. Redl and the Establishment may share the same open secret, but Osborne is only sympathetic to one of them.

Osborne's divided feelings toward the open secret, however, wreak havoc with his narrative, because he wants both to defend secrecy and expose it, too. He builds up the secret in Act I, dissolves it in the first scene of Act II, only to ask us to accept the strength of the secret again in the last scene of Act III because he needs Redl's sexuality to become a secret again if Redl is to be blackmailed by the Russians. Although an analysis of the play based on the idea of the open secret may make sense on a thematic level, it fails to make the play cohere on the level of plot. My earlier summary of the plot, told from the point of view of the open secret (see earlier) was inaccurate on one, very important, narrative incident: Osborne does not show Redl becoming a spy in order to have a new secret, but in order to keep his sexual exploits from being known. Osborne wants the closet to be both transparent and opaque: he tries to unite a melodrama about blackmail with a satire about decadence, but the two dramatic impulses remain at odds with each other. The melodrama insists that the secret is important; the satire dismisses it as trivial. By trivializing the secret, Osborne robs the melodrama of both its force and the sense of compelling psychological motivation that it is built on. Why then, are Osborne's feelings about male homosexuality so deeply divided in this play that they destroy his ability to create a coherent narrative?

V

Men like Philby, Burgess and Maclean were deadly to British society because we have not had to deal with such people for a long time. That Englishmen of seemingly commonplace aspect might be secretly in bond to an alien and all-justifying ideology was something which had been forgotten since the religious conflicts of the sixteenth century. The Elizabethans would have been less surprised by the phenomenon. (Page 297)

The particular identification of decadence, treason, the Establishment and male homosexuality manifested in *A Patriot for Me* can be better understood by reference to the scandals surrounding the defection of Soviet agents Guy Burgess and Donald Maclean in 1951, and Kim Philby in 1963. It did not surprise people that there were Soviet spies, but that these spies were men of privilege, who may well have been protected within their elite circle, and allowed to escape when they risked detection. The case served to sharpen public awareness of an aristocratic circle, whose primary loyalty was to itself and not to the country. Indeed, the term frequently used in the '50s and '60s to refer to a real but often unofficial power elite, "the Establishment," was first introduced into general use in a *Spectator* article on Burgess and Maclean (Hewison 166). In John Le Carré's introduction to Page's *The Philby Conspiracy* (which postdates the premiere of *A Patriot for Me*, but is contemporaneous in its attitudes), Le Carré asserts that the Philby case proves that the Establishment exists:

> In the unequal duel between Kim Philby and the British Secret Service, a new dimension is added to the relationship between the privileged Englishman and the institution which he collectively comprises. Let anyone who derides the notion of the Establishment read this book. (1)

No longer the shabby, alienated outsiders of Graham Greene's espionage fiction, the spy becomes the ultimate insider, whose success leads the reader to question the institution that shelters the spy, and the treachery of the double agent suggests the treachery of the Establishment.

In discussions of the Philby affair, the secret allegiances of the Establishment were primarily presented as allegiances of class, but they were secondarily presented as allegiances of sexual preference. The upper classes had been represented as feminized as far back as the Victorian period (Sedgwick 146-160, 174-175), and male homosexuality had been viewed as a class-specific marker for them in 1930s Oxford (Kermode 24-25, 64). The popular view of Maclean and Burgess's homosexuality was colored by these traditions and played an important part in discussions of the Philby affair. In an attempt to relate all three spies through a common sexual preference, there was persistent speculation that there had been a sexual component to Burgess's relationship with the apparently heterosexual Philby (Page 72). To the Communist and Establishment conspiracies was added a homosexual one, usually less openly addressed, but hovering, shadowlike, behind the other two conspiracies.

The grounds for identifying double agents with homosexual men found some support in the homosexuality of Burgess and Maclean, but ultimately relied more on a series of mythic resemblances than any historical examples. In the '50s and '60s, both the spy and the homosexual were seen as closeted creatures, people who put incredible effort into developing a misleading appearance. Notice how Le Carré's description of Philby can easily be transformed into the description of a homosexual "passing" as straight:

> Effortlessly he played the parts which the Establishment could recognise—for was he not born and trained into the Establishment? Effortlessly he copied its attitudes, caught its diffident stammer, its hesitant arrogance; effortlessly he took its place in its nameless hegemony. (Page 5)

As secretive creatures, both spies and homosexuals were portrayed as having a secret loyalty to their own kind, rather than to society at large. In 1965, Claud Cockburn portrayed the Leftist homosexual of the '30s (the college and young professional years of Maclean, Burgess, and Philby) as a *poseur*, for whom political involvement meant nothing when compared to amorous involvement:

> Just as one thought that he was going to sit down and write an article for a magazine, or go to Spain, it turned out he was getting his boy friend out of the hands of the police. This was a number one priority. Homosexuality had a sort of prestige value that took precedence over politics, and the end of the world, and everything else. (Cockburn 52)

For Cockburn, the homosexual is linked to his own kind in a trivial, apolitical bond that inverts any sensible or responsible hierarchy of values. The fact that a person is motivated to get their lover out of jail is presented as sheer folly. Cockburn adds to the familiar stereotype of the male homosexual as a person dedicated to triviality, the suggestion of a perverse brotherhood with its own bizarre priorities.

This mythical association of male homosexuality with conspiracy found a less sinister, but no less telling, expression in a joke that was at least contemporaneous with *A Patriot for Me*, and may have circulated for years before. As a character in S.N. Behrman's comedy of 1964, *But for Whom Charlie*, tells it:

the international homosexual set, to which an Oxford wit has applied the generic appellation: the Homintern. (Behrman 83)

The "Oxford Wit" is most probably W.H. Auden, who uses the term in an essay published the same year (99).[5] Underneath the linguistic playfulness, however, lies a set of associations very similar to that of Cold War homophobes: an identification of a Communist network dedicated to subverting democracy (Comintern) and a male homosexual network, equally elusive and subversive.

As with all closeted creatures, however, spies and closeted homosexuals share the risk of being found out. As early as 1950, before the defection of Burgess and Maclean, a United States Senate committee issued a report, entitled *Employment of Homosexuals and Other Sex Perverts in Government*, which argued that homosexuals both lacked the emotional stability for government work and were exceptionally susceptible to blackmail by foreign agents. The only historical evidence it was able to muster for this appalling argument was the case of Alfred Redl (D'Emilio 228).

It may well be this new-found notoriety of Redl's, coupled with the Cold War's fascination with espionage literature, that led to the first biography of Alfred Redl in English, Robert B. Asprey's *The Panther's Feast*. This 1959 volume, which served as Osborne's major source for his play (Goldstone 242), is an odd assortment of research and imagination, complete with lurid sex scenes, invented conversations and moralizing, and unencumbered by any specific citations. *The Panther's Feast* shows how completely male homosexuality could be equated with the emotional makeup of the double agent in Cold War literature. The conflation of those two elements begins with the book's title, which is taken from Oscar Wilde's *De Profundis*:

> People thought it dreadful of me to have entertained at dinner the evil things of life, and to have found pleasure in their company. But then, from the point of view through which I, as an artist, approach them they were delightfully suggestive and stimulating. It was like feasting with panthers; the danger was half the excitement. (Wilde, *De Profundis* 185).

Appropriating Wilde's description of his lifestyle, Asprey is able to make it point in two directions; the exciting dangers lived by both the homosexual and the double agent. Or rather, pointing in one direction, for Asprey finds them identical. His Redl is an unnatural creature who is capable of manipulating a child until she unwittingly betrays her father to military intelligence

(164–166); whose case of syphilis is the occasion for lengthy descriptions of his symptoms and treatment (62–69); whose cynicism may go unnoticed by Redl's fellow officers but which repels their more innately sensitive wives (207–209; 222); who had a "voracious appetite for sensation that could never be realized" (180) and a "force of will so great as almost to defy human imagination" (172). The actions of this Austro-Hungarian Iago, Asprey explains, were not the product of neurosis but of unremitting vice: "His evil was ever present in his thoughts" (180). As both double agent and homosexual, he is portrayed as a heartless master of appearances who is able to keep *two* secrets with surprising, and terrifying, success (45). Asprey's demonization of Redl is yet another example of the figure of the Pervert, whose history has been so brilliantly traced by Jonathan Dollimore in *Sexual Dissidence*.[6] Asprey, however, does not make any link between Redl and a corrupt Establishment or establish any parallels between Redl and Burgess. Those connections are made by Osborne.[7]

In trying to reconcile the two stories, however, Osborne runs into some irreconcilable dissimilarities. The story of the historical Alfred Redl, in which his homosexuality is a carefully guarded secret, and which makes him vulnerable to the Russian intelligence network, does not square with the Burgess/Maclean story of a corrupt Establishment, in which homosexuality is accepted as a matter of course. Nor does Redl's rise in the meritocracy sit well with the privileged status of the Philby circle; their true equivalent in *A Patriot for Me* is von Kupfer, not Redl. For a writer with Osborne's strong sense of class identification, the stories of Redl and the British spies can never be made one.

Osborne's tendency to interpret male homosexuality as a function of class identification can be seen in two contrasting dramatic portraits in two other of his plays from the 1960s. In *Inadmissible Evidence*, Maples, who works in his father-in-law's drapery business, is presented with dignity and sympathy (Gross, 48–51). He is the victim of police entrapment, he, like Redl, is subjected to surveillance. In *The Blood of the Bambergs*, the German prince is presented farcically and is little more than the butt of some tired jokes. The sexual orientation is the same in both cases, but the class is different, and that, for Osborne, makes all the difference.

It is in the light of this strong sense of class identification that one should interpret Redl's sudden outburst of violence at Baron von Epp's. Redl, the son of a railway worker, and his lover, Stefan, the son of a chef, make no attempt to fit into the extravagant and transvestite world of the ball. They come in their military uniforms, which testify to their status in the meritocracy, and the Baron is surprised that they were admitted (128). By so doing, they separate themselves from the aristocracy and the lower-class male prostitutes who are supported by it. Visually, Redl and Stefan stand apart from the effeminacy of the ball by the "masculinity" of their costumes. When Ferdy makes fun of the "masculine" notion of exercise, and performs a ballet step, Redl strikes him and leaves. Read this way, Redl, although homosexual, is resisting the effeminacy of the class that seeks to assimilate him. In this context, it is important to note that Osborne chooses not to make use of a detail in Asprey, that Redl owned women's garments (Asprey 210). For Osborne, it is necessary to distance his hero from transvestism, which serves for the playwright as a marker for the decadence of the Establishment.

It is at this point that the similarity between *A Patriot for Me* and *The London Merchant* reasserts itself. In Lillo's play, George Barnwell is seduced out of the Thoroughgood's masculine world of mercantilism and frugality into Millwood's female world of sensuality and extravagance (Hammer, "Economy" 84). Redl undergoes the same seduction, from linguistic simplicity to extravagant tirades, from celibacy to sexual excess, and from solvency to debt. Although the first act of *A Patriot for Me* may resemble a coming-out story, an analysis of the whole play reveals that it tells the story of the destruction of a promising young man by a corrupt status quo:

> By the time the play ends, it is very clear how much the society Osborne presents, particularly the elitist officer corps, can fatally jeopardize, if not fatally corrupt, human worth, and how difficult it is to resist this temptation. (Goldstone 122)

Redl belongs, like George Barnwell, to the countless literary descendants of the Prodigal Son, and the Austro-Hungarian elite (even more than Millwood, who defends her actions brilliantly) is yet one more literary manifestation of the World, the Flesh, and the Devil.

Osborne presents the process of corruption, however, far less clearly than Lillo. While Lillo thoroughly dramatizes the two realms that vie for Barnwell, the masculine, working-class background of Redl and Stefan is only hinted at. Redl is identified with, but dramatically estranged from, his class origins. As a result, it is much easier for the critic in the library to come to an understanding of this play than for an audience in the theatre; Osborne is so lost in his own ambivalences toward class and sexuality that he is unable to give them a satisfactory form. As Hayman has rightly concluded, "what the play as a whole lacks is a vantage point" (Hayman 60).

Despite its aesthetic confusion, however, *A Patriot for Me* remains valuable as a cultural document. It registers the tension between two opposed constructions of homosexuality that not only shaped discussions in the '50s and '60s, but which continue to this day. On the one hand, male homosexuality is viewed as effeminate decadence, which is to be morally opposed. On the other hand, it is seen, just like heterosexuality, as a fundamental constituent of selfhood, authenticity, and individual expression that must resist social control. These two views, one based in Judeo-Christian thought, the other in Romanticism, continue to play their part in contemporary discussions of sexuality. Despite all the things one can say against *A Patriot for Me*, one cannot say that its confusions are a thing of the past. Unfortunately.

NOTES

1. See, for example, Gale, "Osborne's revelation of his main theme is so distended that the audience feels they are caught in the midst of a film co-directed by Antonioni and Fellini in which no one is quite sure what is going on" (6), and Ferrar, "a very deliberate, stiff and finally pompous play" (35).

2. My reading of *The London Merchant* is indebted throughout to Stephanie Barbé Hammer's work on the play. See her "Economy and Extravagance: Criminal Origin and the War of the Words in *The London Merchant*" and *The Sublime Crime: Fascination, Failure and Form*.

3. Throughout the essay, I will be using the term "homosexual" rather than "gay" to refer to characters and situations in *A Patriot for Me*. As my reading of the play unfolds, I think it will become clear that this play does not present sexual desire between men with any of the positive political identity associated with the gay movement. This play does not oppose homophobia, as a gay play would; indeed, it provides grounds for its continuation.

4. For a fascinating discussion of this phenomenon, especially as it applies to *David Copperfield*, see Miller 192-220.

5. See also Pequigney 79-80.

6. See Dollimore 103-278.

7. After the production and publication of *A Patriot for Me*, however, Page compares Philby and Redl, yet without elaborating much on the comparison (Page 169).

WORKS CITED

Asprey, Robert B. *The Panther's Feast*. New York: G.P. Putnam's Sons, 1959.
Auden, W.H. "Shakespeare's Sonnets." In *Forewords and Afterwords*. Selected by Edward Mendelsohn. New York: Random House, 1973. 88-108.
Behrman, S.N. *But for Whom Charlie*. New York: Samuel French, 1964.
Cockburn, Claud. "A Conversation with Claud Cockburn." *Review* 11-12 (1965): 52.
D'Emilio, John. "The Homosexual Menace: The Politics of Sexuality in Cold War America." *Passion and Power: Sexuality in History*. Eds. Kathy Peiss and Christina Simmons. Philadelphia: Temple UP, 1989. 226-240.
Dollimore, Jonathan. *Sexual Dissidence: Augustine to Wilde, Freud to Foucault*. Oxford: Oxford UP, 1991.
Ferrar, Harold. *John Osborne*. New York: Columbia UP, 1973.
Gale, Steven. "John Osborne: Look Forward in Fear." In *Essays in Contemporary British Drama*. Eds. Hedwig Bock and Albert Wertheim. Munich: Max Hueber Verlag, 1981. 5-30.
Genet, Jean. *Querelle*. Trans. Anselm Hollo. New York: Grove Press, 1974.
Goldstone, Herbert. *Coping with Vulnerability: The Achievement of John Osborne*. Lanham, MD.: UP of America, 1962.

Gross, Robert F. *Words Heard and Overheard: The Main Text in Contemporary Drama.* New York: Garland, 1990.

Hammer, Stephanie Barbé. "Economy and Extravagance: Criminal Origin and the War of the Words in *The London Merchant.*" *Essays in Theatre* 8, no. 2 (May 1990): 81–94.

———. *The Sublime Crime: Fascination, Failure and Form.* Carbondale: Southern Illinois UP, 1992.

Hayman, Ronald. *John Osborne.* London: Heinemann, 1968.

Hewison, Robert. *In Anger: British Culture in the Cold War: 1945–1960.* New York: Oxford UP, 1981.

Hinchliffe, Arnold P. *John Osborne.* Boston: Twayne Publishers, 1984.

Hirst, David L. *Comedy of Manners.* London: Methuen, 1979.

Kermode, Frank. *History and Value: The Clarendon and Northcliffe Lectures, 1987.* Oxford: Oxford UP, 1988.

Lillo, George, *The London Merchant.* In *Plays of the Restoration and Eighteenth Century.* Eds. Douglas MacMillan and Howard Mumford Jones. New York: Henry Holt & Co., 1931. 616–45.

Marwick, Arthur. *British Society Since 1945.* New York: Penguin Books, 1982.

Miller, D.A. *The Novel and the Police.* Berkeley: U of California P, 1988.

Osborne, John. *A Patriot for Me.* In *Four Plays.* New York: Dodd, Mead & Co., 1973. 71–170.

Page, Bruce, David Leitch, and Phillip Knightley. *The Philby Conspiracy.* Intro. John Le Carré. Garden City, NY: Doubleday, 1968.

Pequigney, Joseph. *Such Is My Love: A Study of Shakespeare's Sonnets.* Chicago: U of Chicago P, 1985.

Sedgwick, Eve Kosofsky. *Between Men: English Literature and Male Homosocial Desire.* New York: Columbia UP, 1985.

Segal, Lynne. "Look Back in Anger: Men in the '50s." In *Male Order: Unwrapping Masculinity.* Eds. Rowena Chapman and Jonathan Rutherford. London: Lawrence and Wishart, 1988. 68–96.

Shaw, George Bernard. *Mrs Warren's Profession.* In *The Bodley Head Bernard Shaw: Collected Plays with Their Prefaces.* Ed. Dan H. Laurence. Vol. 1. London: Bodley Head, 1970.

Sinfield, Alan. "The Theatre and Its Audience." In *Society and Literature.* Ed. Alan Sinfield. New York: Holmes and Meier, 1983. 173–197.

Wilde, Oscar. *A Woman of No Importance.* In *Plays.* Baltimore, MD: Penguin Books, 1968. 73–146.

———. *De Profundis and Other Writings.* Intro. Hesketh Pearson. New York: Penguin Books, 1973.

"Honey, I Blew Up the Ego"

John Osborne's *Déjàvu*

Sheila Stowell

Does the theatre world need another look back in anger? John Osborne evidently thought so. "A bit of a parlour game," his self-styled *Look Back II* "started as a technical exercise" that eventually mushroomed into the full-length *Déjàvu*,[1] a three-act translation of an angry young man of 1956 into an angry old one of 1992. And if, as Osborne confesses, he was prompted by a type of literary curiosity ("after all, one does wonder what happens to Nora in *The Doll's House* after she slams the door"), the resulting work's pedigree lies not so much with the myth-making expansiveness of a work like *Oedipus at Colonus* as with formulaic Hollywood sequels whose unashamed raison d'etre is to make more money than their predecessors. Jimmy Riddle in his *Time Out* review (10 June 1992) notes the coincidental appearance of Robert Altman's film *The Player*, in which "a writer hopelessly pitches an idea about a remake of *The Graduate* thirty years on with the central characters still played by Hoffman, Ross and Bancroft," with the debut at London's Comedy Theatre of Osborne's old "new" play.[2] Still, it is difficult to dismiss *Déjàvu* merely as a cynical box-office ploy by a playwright whose later work for the theatre has been characterized as a string of "unmitigated disasters" (*Sunday Times* 7 June 1992). Indeed, if this had been Osborne's primary objective, it was a miscalculation on a colossal scale. As early as second night "the Comedy Theatre was at best half full" (*Scotsman* 13 June 1992), and less than a month later the play was fighting the prospect of an early close (*Standard* 3 July 1992). Certainly, the evening I saw it midway through what turned out to be a somewhat less than three-month run, the theatre management had sealed off the balcony, ushering balcony ticket holders into the stalls to make the house "feel" full.

But if the play failed to realize its box-office hopes, its status as a sequel to one of the most celebrated works of modern theatre ensures for it a degree of notoriety, raising at the same time a number of questions about the nature of dramatic reprise. As its very title suggests—its elided French proclaiming Osborne's contempt for all things foreign—*Déjàvu* has been both seen and not seen before. According to the play's now aged Jimmy Porter, déjà vu describes the sensation of a recall that is in fact illusory, "a *recherché* experience which could not have ever possibly taken place" (20). Thus Osborne toys with audience expectations: what we are asked to witness in *Déjàvu* both is and is not—because we did not see "rightly" the first time—*Look Back in Anger*. Set once again on a Sunday in the Midlands, we look "anew" at "*two armchairs, right and left respectively, [in which] J.P. and Cliff are seated. All that we can see of them is two pairs of legs, sprawled way out beyond the spread of newspapers which hide the rest of them from sight*" (2).

Jimmy, however, over the course of thirty-six years, has been transformed into "J.P.", a name designed to confer mythic status in the face of likely audience resistance. The single attic room has also undergone an (upper-) middle-class metamorphosis into a fifteen-room "*minor gentleman's residence*," courtesy, we are led to believe, of a legacy from Alison's father. Of the earlier play's iconic properties, Alison's stuffed squirrel has departed, but Jimmy's scruffy teddy bear survives. Alison, too, still irons stage left, and while her clothes are different—"the cherry red shirt of Jimmy's" has been replaced by a t-shirt bearing the legend "I AM SCUM"—she has at first glance not changed. She has remained young and pregnant, Jimmy's daughter, we soon learn, instead of his wife. But if Jimmy's target of "class privilege" has been superseded by what J.P. derisively calls "yoof culture," it remains to be played out on a woman's body. True to the action of the earlier play, Alison is, like her mother before her, literally driven away, the Edwardian Colonel of *Look Back in Anger* replaced behind the wheel by the trendy Rev. Ron, self-appointed "spokesperson" for youth. Not to be forgotten, young Helena (this time round a friend of daughter Alison) makes her appearance only to be seduced again, rather improbably one would have thought, by an old man whose moody eroticism lay wholly with his youth. J.P. even suffers another death in the Tanner family—last time Hugh's mum, this time Hugh himself.

To frame this contrived series of reactions, Osborne adopts what he himself had earlier characterized as the "formal, rather old-fashioned" three-act structure that had molded the action of *Look Back in Anger*.[3] As Cliff and J.P. lament metatheatrically, in Osborne's third act, the demise of third acts in general, their conversation neatly points Osborne's conservative, some would say reactionary, remembrance of things past. Yet the demands of an "old-fashioned" form had served a very different function in *Look Back in*

Anger. There they operated as formal and symbolic constraints upon the angry outpourings that heralded Jimmy Porter as the "first spokesman in the London theatre" for a younger generation disillusioned with the failure of the postwar Labour government to deliver "a brave new world" (Tynan, *Observer* 13 May 1956; Russell Taylor 41). Ironically, Osborne had been abetted by the efforts of the Lord Chamberlain's office, which lent its power to censor to keep Osborne's fulminations in check. The fact that much had to be left unsaid—the Examiner's dictates, for example, extended to the deletion of "brothel," "pubic hair," "bull," and "short-arsed" (Lord Chamberlain's Correspondence 1956/9832)—underscored Jimmy's inability to break free, rhetorically or physically, of a social order he could neither join nor flee. By contrast, nothing restrains "the aging J.P. [who] merely proves that, in less shockable times, the unspeakable is all too easily spoken" (*Independent* 12 June 1992). Unleashed, the vituperative tongue of J.P. Senior points up the paradox that when everything is said, nothing is.

Yet *Déjàvu*'s most startling departure from *Look Back in Anger* lies in Osborne's effort to pry Jimmy Porter free of youth and antiheroic disaffection in order to raise him up new born as a hero of "gentle susceptibilities, constantly goaded by a brutal and coercive world" (vii). It is, according to the play's director, Tony Palmer, "an essential difference between the two plays: ... where Jimmy Porter was an anti-hero, J.P. has become a hero" (*Independent* 10 June 1992). What we witness, however, is more a dramatic attempt on Osborne's part to reclaim Jimmy as his own creation. The enemy here is a critical intelligentsia, *Déjàvu* a creator's document presenting in definitive form the meaning of Jimmy Porter. According to Osborne, "wearisome theories about J.P.'s sadism, anti-feminism, even closet homosexuality ... [had been] peddled to gullible students by dubious and partisan 'academics.' They continue to proliferate and perpetuate themselves among those who should know better" (vii). Osborne's response is to put Jimmy, now J.P., back on stage to speak for "himself." Word of "an American academic ... who thinks Shakespeare's a pretty ordinary writer" provokes J.P./J.O. into commiseration with "W.S.": "Poor old W.S. How they hate him. Dumb bruins and pushy professors in soft jobs, guzzling in the armpits of a god. It must be irksome" (16).

Clearly the team of Osborne and Porter, dissatisfied with their niche as harbinger to the new drama of the 1950s, have more ambitious goals. And it is here that the overlap between author and character, and the resulting loss of perspective, becomes an aesthetic liability. In spite of *Déjàvu*'s opening *Hamlet* gambit ("What ho, Barnardo!"), the figures Osborne uses to argue a Shakespeare connection are comic rather than tragic. In the introduction to the play's published text we are assured by Osborne that "J.P. is a comic character. He generates energy but, also, like, say, Malvolio or Falstaff, an inescapable melancholy" (vii). Director Palmer has made the triangle explicit: J.P. "is a very humble man at the end, that's why it's so moving. John is like that too. J.P. has a life-enhancing Falstaffian quality—he was a coward, a braggart, a liar, totally unscrupulous, a drunk, with an inheritance, like J.P. And just like Falstaff, J.P. can stop the play dead in its tracks and say, 'What is honour?'" (*Independent* 10 June 1992).

Yet despite such claims, the lineage is spurious. Falstaff, after all, faces formidable opponents. *His* set-piece on honour, for example, is poised against the exuberant heroism of Hotspur ("yoof culture"), as well as the weary pragmatism of Henry IV. Falstaff is, moreover, continually bested by Hal in the vaudeville routines in which he appears at his most genial. Nor is he given the last word. *1 Henry IV* ends with Hal's decision to conceal Falstaff's battlefield cowardice, while *2 Henry IV* concludes with the old knight's banishment and Hal's coronation. We may feel through both parts that Falstaff picks at some very unpleasant scabs on the body politic, but in the end his is not the sole, nor even the controlling, view. J.P., in sharp contrast, has no foils worthy of the name. Cliff, Alison, and Helena are all sham characters, without a decent defense between them. As John Gross has noted in the *Sunday Telegraph*, "There is no real dramatic conflict with Cliff and the other characters. They put up a certain amount of token resistance, but Jimmy always has the last word" (14 June 1992). It is not that their positions are indefensible. It is merely that J.O., the author, protects J.P., the character, from having to engage them at a serious level. Indeed, stage directions in the published text ensure J.P. a privileged invincibility denied Falstaff. In describing the "exchange" that closes Act I, scene i, Osborne actually specifies that

> it must be controlled so that both Cliff and Alison may repeatedly undercut J.P.'s more lyrical flights without diminishing him, still allowing him to remain intact. It requires a delicate delivery from the actors and, above all, the overriding force of irony, to carry him through the snares of ridicule. (49)

The result is an extended monologue masquerading as drama, "in essence, one long speech" (*Sunday Times* 14 June 1992), a "monodrama for one furious tongue" (*Evening Standard* 11 June 1992). As Sheridan Morley observes, "Time and again we are brought up against a monologue without a play" (*International Herald Tribune* 17 June 1992). *Déjàvu* may be viewed as the playwright's attempt to resituate Jimmy Porter in a literary/dramatic tradition that pushes back beyond the 1950s to the Elizabethan and Jacobean eras. Yet J.P. as he is now set before us, with his coddled attacks against *inter alia*, Australians, feminists, the Lower Middle Classes, ethnic culture, homosexuals, "political correctness," AIDS sufferers, abused children, the homeless and the handicapped have less to do with Falstaffian subversiveness than with the televised fulminations of those '60s codgers for the status quo, Alf Garnett and Archie Bunker.

In attempting to reassert the "true" meaning of Jimmy Porter and *Look Back in Anger*, Osborne allows J.P. a set speech in which to clear up the problem, "What's he angry about?" He begins by pronouncing, in true Osbornian fashion, the question itself to be wrong:

> Anger is not *about* . . . It is mourning the unknown, the loss of what went before without you, it's the love another time but not this might have sprung on you, and greatest loss of all, the deprivation of what, even as a child, seemed to be irrevocably your own, your country, your birthplace, that, at least, is as tangible as death. (36)

The passage, in its very virtuosity, gives the game away. By raising and replying to the critical dilemma most closely associated with Jimmy Porter, Osborne assumes an audience for whom both question and response will have resonances well beyond the confines of *Déjàvu*. Certainly, the reviewer for *Plays & Players* concluded that "Anyone not familiar with Osborne's earlier play would feel excluded by the stream of injoky allusions to it" (July 1992). The play's director might insist that references to the earlier work "are irrelevant . . . [and] don't affect one's understanding and enjoyment of the play," maintaining that "the play stands absolutely four-square on its own feet" (*Independent* 10 June 1992). Yet this jibes oddly with a play whose 'hero' radiates an awareness of his own "legendary status as a fictional character" (*Independent* 12 June 1992). As Michael Billington observes in a positive *Guardian* review, "Osborne deliberately echoes phrases and situations from the original play as if Jimmy is aware of his own status as a character" (11 June 1992). The result, Billington concludes, is "a post-modernist play in which Osborne seems to imply that he has been haunted by his own creation."

Indeed, seen in these terms the play may be defined not so much as a sequel as a freewheeling docudrama on the life and times of John Osborne. Certainly, much has been made of John Osborne's complex relationship with J.P. In fact, for many critics the playwright is barely distinguishable from his character. According to Emma Lilly, it's "hard to see where John Osborne ends and JP begins" (*Good Times* 18 June 1992), while in Vera Lustig's eyes "it's easy to identify JP with JO" (*Plays & Players* July 1992). Charles Spencer insists that while "Osborne may deny that he is Jimmy Porter . . . both playwright and character speak with the same unmistakable voice" (*Daily Telegraph* 11 June 1992), and Ian Shuttleworth concludes that although "Peter Egan and his fellows strive valiantly to persuade us that there may be more to it than simply that JP = JO, . . . director Tony Palmer doesn't believe it and Osborne sure as hell doesn't" (*City Limits* 18–25 June 1992). Peter Egan, got up to play J.P. as an uncanny Osborne look-alike—the play programme insisted upon the similarity by juxtaposing photographs of Osborne and Egan's J.P.—does try to draw some distance between the character and his author: "If I was to say that there was an awful lot of John Osborne in Jimmy Porter I might be doing John a disservice . . . or if I was to say there's very little I might also be doing him a disservice." Yet even Egan, baffled in the end by the unnerving overlap between producer and product, lamely offers by way of explanation that "any writer is going to be writing what he feels" (*Plays & Players* July 1992).

For director Palmer, there is no equivocation. In his eyes "Jimmy Porter is John Osborne" (*Independent* 10 June 1992). This is particularly suggestive given that Palmer, making his theatrical debut with *Déjàvu*, has been most closely associated with the genre of fictionalized film biography.[4] In fact, this "documentary-maker," as he was described in the *Sunday Times*, was picked by Osborne on the basis of "a strong hunch" (7 June 1992). The result, at least in terms of the Comedy Theatre staging, was to cement the play's significance as docudrama. Although Osborne continues to express irritation with the widely held view that his characters speak for him ("People who make that assumption don't understand the creative process. There was a lot of Falstaff in Shakespeare but Shakespeare wasn't Falstaff"—*Guardian* 11 June 1992), his hand-picked specialist in documentaries connived in the production of a play replete with autobiographical references. J.P.'s attacks upon daughter Alison, for example, mirror Osborne's "lurid rejection . . . in the national press" of his twenty-seven-year-old daughter, Nolan, "who seems to have committed the crime of being young" (*Time Out* 10 June 1992), while J.P.'s verbal assaults upon his ex-wives generate their own sense of déjà vu for those who have read the first two installments of Osborne's much-publicized autobiography. In his ungracious swipe at the Royal Court Theatre, so significant a player in the debut of *Look Back in Anger* and now characterized as "BO, pot and bargain breaks at the gay sweatshop" (54), one hears Osborne's reaction to that theatre's refusal to stage *Déjàvu*. More generally, the play has been viewed as a mere staged reading of selections from Osborne's collected journalism:[5] "There are many times when the play strikes you as a series of tacked-together magazine columns in his splenetic, reactionary mode" (*Independent* 12 June 1992). Morley puts it more gently, concluding that Osborne "seems to have become a journalist rather than a dramatist, and while welcoming him to our ranks it is more difficult to welcome him there in a theatre at $30 a ticket" (*International Herald Tribune* 17 June 1992).

There seems little doubt that the identification of Osborne's voice with that of his "narcissistic alter ego" (*Times Literary Supplement* 19 June 1992) is so close that the play might well "have been called *John Osborne is Unwell*" (*Independent* 12 June 1992). For some this did not present a problem. Billington, for example, one of the play's staunchest defenders, was prepared, in judging *Déjàvu*, to throw out "the standards of a conventional play" in order to praise the work of a writer unique in the way he "allows his soul to show": "The spellbinding result could be summed up as Osborne Agonistes" (*Country Life* 25 June 1992). The *Observer*'s Michael Coveney also praised Osborne as "a great dramatist rather than a *Spectator*-ish pamphleteer," in the process recycling Kenneth Tynan's praise of *Look Back in Anger* as "the best young play of its decade" by proposing that *Déjàvu* "could well be the best old one of this" (14 June 1992). Malcolm Rutherford of the *Financial Times* took the unusual step of writing a second review of the play to pump up his original praise (15 June 1992), and while John Gross for the *Sunday Telegraph* judged the play only semi-successful, he maintained that "even the worst things have their documentary interest" (14 June 1992). Yet if the major newspapers were by and large supportive, neither the alternative, trade, nor intellectual papers (the latter one of Osborne's particular targets) were prepared to be so accommodating. Peter Kemp, writing for the *Times Literary Supplement*, found himself resenting the play's "incoherent stridency," "juvenile nastiness," and "leaky-eyed sentimentality about its hero" (19 June 1992). Looking beyond the play itself, Vera Lustig writing for *Plays & Players*, asserted that "the world is brutal and coercive precisely because we give house room to characters like JP/JO and their hangers-on" (July 1992). Indeed, for one *City Limits* reviewer, Tynan's 1950s boosterism itself became a target. Selecting, as Coveney had done, a phrase from Tynan's original *Look Back in Anger* review—"I doubt if I could love anyone who did not wish to see *Look Back in Anger*"— Ian Shuttleworth concluded, "I do not think I could love anyone who believed their time would more profitably be spent watching *Déjàvu* than lying in a darkened room masturbating" (18 June 1992). Yet the closed system of *Déjàvu* allows no room for dialogue off stage or on. To push dissent beyond the limits Osborne prescribes for Cliff or Alison makes one a humorless "prig" or a straw-spokesperson for "political correctness." Under the circumstances, one is left to lament J.O./J.P.'s failure to heed the music produced after that "Gatling gun of the guitar" he so despises "had mastered the world" (80). Either Pete Townshend's "I Hope I Die Before I Get Old" or Bob Dylan's "Don't Look Back" might have given some pause for thought. So, incidentally, might Hal's second thoughts on Falstaff: "I know thee not, old man, fall to thy prayers / How ill white hairs become a fool and jester." But because any criticism is deemed a victory in the self-aggrandizing agon of J.P./J.O.'s making, one is left, in the end, wondering whether the best tactic is to imitate the silence of Alison in *Look Back I*. It is surely our best chance of forestalling a trilogy.

NOTES

1. Osborne stated in an interview with Lesley White that "*Déjàvu* was slower, harder work than usual." *Look Back in Anger* was completed in just fourteen days (*Sunday Times* 7 June 1992:6).

2. An anticipated premiere in Liverpool in 1991 failed to materialize after Peter O'Toole walked off the set. He insisted that the play was too long and wanted cuts; Osborne responded that "old Gloria O'Swanson" wasn't up to the demands of the role. In a programme note for the production, Osborne complained that "*Déjàvu* has had a bizarre and bumpy ride in reaching the stage. Distinguished producers and some famous 'stars' have pledged their lives to it and then, finally, treacherously, reneged. I used to defend the members of my profession from those who dislike and distrust its 'Luvvy' superficiality, cupidity and vanity. Now I'm not so sure."

3. Osborne repeats the observation in his *Déjàvu* programme notes, elaborating that "it was an ironic line, lightly thrown away. But, for years, know-alls held it up as some kind of disastrous slip of the tongue in the dock."

4. Osborne and Palmer met when the latter was directing a film on Handel Osborne had scripted.

5. The game "Who Would You Rather?" that kicks off Act II, scene ii, for example, first surfaced in one of Osborne's columns for the *Spectator*.

WORKS CITED

Osborne, John. *Déjàvu*. London: Faber and Faber, 1991.
Taylor, John Russell. *Anger and After*. London: Methuen, 1962. Rpt. London: Methuen, 1988.

JOHN OSBORNE, SUMMER 1993

Kimball King

For more than a decade John Osborne has worked hard and effectively on two important autobiographical volumes, *A Better Class of Person* (1981) and *Almost a Gentleman* (1991). He has written a television adaptation of the former volume as well as several other television plays, including *You're Not Watching Me, Mummy* (1980), *Very Like a Whale* (also 1980), and *God Rot Tunbridge Wells* (1985). He has also contributed reviews, letters to the editor, and essays on subjects ranging from playwright Joe Orton's literary reputation to his anguish over Laurence Olivier's death to his disappointment with policy decisions of the Royal National Theatre. Osborne's intellectual involvement in contemporary British culture has never waned, but because he was known first and foremost as the playwright who transformed modern British theatre with his production of *Look Back in Anger* at the Royal Court in 1956, his announcement that he had written a new stage play in 1991 was curiously greeted as a resurgence of productivity, a "comeback." That the new work, *Déjàvu*, recalled Osborne's most famous play by sharing his semiautobiographical protagonist, Jimmy Porter, now thirty-five years older, suggested a kind of closure to the author's career and tacitly encouraged critics to compare the twenty-six-year-old and sixty-year-old playwright as well as his dramatic spokesperson. Thus a revaluation of Osborne's career has taken place, and this volume attests to the world's interest in a major writer's canon.

Claire Armistead, in a largely unfavorable commentary on Osborne's *Déjàvu*, falls, along with others, into a persistent critical trap: she fails to distinguish between an autobiographical protagonist and the author himself. Quoting from *Déjàvu*, Armistead indicts Osborne with self-confessed testimony of the now middle-aged Jimmy Porter: "I am still after thirty years a churlish, grating note, a spokesman for no one but myself, unable to be coherent about my despair" (25). Armistead implies that the playwright's concerns are equally idiosyncratic, self-serving, and irrelevant. What she fails to point out is that any author unable to perceive his own failings would not have chosen to create so complex a protagonist, one who is alternately bullying, misogynistic, self-indulgent, but consistently astute.

Neither is Osborne what Armistead calls "a soap box reactionary" (25). Many critics have left the impression that the young revolutionary idealist has grown into a conservative defender of the old Order—as if confessing his love of Turkish cigarettes were an act of political bad faith. He continuously satirizes animal-rights groups and trendy charities, and the increasing influence of the lower middle class, but he does so because he considers certain popular liberal causes a distraction from genuine political and social reform. The young Jimmy Porter, we recall, would embarrass his wife, Alison, by crashing parties of his in-laws' friends. Never being asked to leave despite his frequently boorish behavior confirmed Jimmy's perception that the upper middle classes closed ranks and maintained order through hypocrisy. In other words, young Jimmy and young Osborne shared contempt for the posturings of privileged people. No doubt the Osborne of this decade is repelled by what he believes to be the self-righteous ardor of contemporary social activists. But he is not necessarily repelled by their particular causes, which can, he realizes, be used to distract followers from fundamental systemic changes.

In the minds of many, champagne is an elitist drink, associated with the decadence and excesses of the old aristocracy. Osborne is repeatedly referred to in interviews and conversations as a lover of champagne, and one recalls that the young Jimmy Porter expressed a preference for it. The subtext of all Osborne champagne stories is that sparkling wine is not a suitable socialist beverage. To accept that stereotype is to accept the dictates of a class system that denies certain privileges to its less exalted segments. Osborne's living in a Regency house in Shropshire, Osborne's staying in the expensive Cadogan Hotel (which he told me he selected because it was Oscar Wilde's favorite hotel), his membership in the Garrick Club (a very traditional haven for theatre people), and his wardrobe of tweeds and cardigans are considered indulgent choices for a dedicated reformer. We must challenge the assumption that certain traditional tastes imply a recalcitrance of mind.

My original intention for this volume was to arrange a meeting with Osborne so that he and I would discuss the wide range of his achievement, determine the most urgent statements articulated in his plays, and explore both the historical and political possibilities of the theatre in the transformation of English society. Although we planned to get together several times, we were thwarted by certain contingencies of our mutual schedule—my university schedule and Britain travel dates, his illness on one occasion, production problems with *Déjàvu* in 1992, and his frustrations with the National Theatre's 1993 revival of *Inadmissible Evidence*. Osborne has an aversion to using the telephone and prefers to correspond by notes—always prompt, legible, and courteous. He has alluded in these notes to his frustrations with the National Theatre, his puzzlement over the bad press he often receives in England, as well as a brief mention of health problems and occasional financial worries. His selling of the original manuscript of *Look Back in Anger* at auction was noted in London tabloids and suggests a persistent need for money. Even the most successful playwrights (the American Neil Simon excepted) are far from rich.

Our correspondence has confirmed my opinion of Osborne as a basically kind, frank, unaffected person, but one who feels he has been betrayed by some people he trusted and is, hence, cautious.

The qualities that made Jimmy Porter, and by extension his creator, a hero to post–World War II Britons still define the sixtyish John Osborne today: a scathing wit, an impatience with hypocrisy and double-talk, and a willingness to express his feelings in a society that values the suppression of them.

Osborne confessed to Lesley White that "I know I'm thought to be something of a monster" (7). I think White's summation of Osborne's recent life is more perceptive than most interviewer's. She entitles her piece "More in Sorrow Than in Anger," and correctly, I believe, underscores the elegiac quality of his recent writing and public commentary, noting that he is a man "mildly disappointed by life but perfectly resigned to its cruel jokes—like making him a star at twenty-six and not returning his calls a couple of decades later" (6).

The appearance of the Osborne autobiographies, the completion of *Déjàvu*, and possibly even Osborne's disapproving pronouncements about the state of the arts in England may have influenced the Royal National Theatre's decision to revive *Inadmissible Evidence* in June of 1993. Written in the 1960s, the play had not been produced in a major London theatre for more than a decade. Many critics believe it to be one of Osborne's finest plays, and its powerful depiction of a self-destructive protagonist in midlife crisis may have been an inspiration for Simon Gray's *Butley* in 1971 and/or *Melon* in 1987, and a host of modern "breakdown plays."

I was scheduled to meet Osborne at the Cadogan Hotel when *Inadmissible Evidence* first opened at the Lyttleton. In preparation for our talk together I witnessed the play in previews. The play seemed longer to me than when I had read it years before and first sensed its potential, and I was slightly distracted by the stage lighting—which alternately seemed capriciously bright or gloomy. Nevertheless, I believed in protagonist Bill Maitland's anguish as Trevor Eve interpreted him and was touched by Lynn Farleigh's portrayal of three different women who seek legal advice from Maitland about impending divorce problems. Before I could see Osborne, he had quarreled with the National Theatre, refused to accept cuts in the three hour and twenty minute production, and had, according to his own words, been "banned" from the National Theatre. He apologized to me for the "execrable production" and lamented his being treated "so shabbily." In spite of the playwright's disappointments, reviews of the play were, for the most part, favorable. Michael Billington claimed "the play moves one profoundly." While expressing reservations about its rambling structure, he acknowledged that "Bill Maitland is unequivocally a tragic hero" ("Evidence of Anger" 5, "Cri de Coeur" 25).

It is somewhat surprising that the National Theatre had expected Osborne to be malleable with the *Inadmissable Evidence* production, considering that Peter O'Toole had so recently refused to continue as the aging Porter in *Déjàvu* because O'Toole and the playwright were unable to agree on cutting certain speeches. Capitulation to popular demands for brevity and disrespect for the "integrity" of the modern artist have consistently dismayed Osborne. What some suggest is an "ego problem" and what Philip Howard has described as his being "morbidly thin-skinned at the faintest whiff of criticism" (16) may be the inevitable result of a personal belief that compromise, especially when it has commercial advantages, is unethical.

A complicating factor of another kind is that Osborne is known to have suffered from bouts of depression. As recently as his sixtieth birthday, when his wife, Helen Dawson, arranged a celebration for eighty-four people at the Garrick Club, he appeared to have been so distraught by the impending gathering that she canceled the event at the last minute. Surely he has always had instinctive insights into a mind tormented by self-doubt, an almost paranoid sense of betrayal, and disillusion with contemporary society, qualities that informed very early works like *The Entertainer* and *Look Back in Anger*.

Persistent myths about Osborne past sixty are that the playwright has abandoned his youthful socialistic idealism by living so comfortably that fame and affluence have caused him to reject his humble origins and that his views on society are reactionary and intractable. Yet none of these myths bear close scrutiny. The young Osborne railed against a class system that locked people into unfulfilling lives and perpetuated privilege for mindless well-born people like Alison's shallow brother, who reappears in *Déjàvu* with a knighthood but who has been forever branded by Porter's description of him as "The Platitude from Outer Space." Much of Osborne's original anger was directed at England's compromised power and influence following World War II. Bitter disappointment over the impending Suez crisis in 1956, the rapidly progressing loss of Empire, and the Americanization of the West were palpable influences on the mood of the playwright and theatre audiences. Osborne's more recent concern that the Europeanization of the West with the common market and Maastricht agreement have replaced some of his distrust of America; but his concern that England may be subsumed into an anonymous commercial entity is unchanged.

Lynn Barber quoted Osborne as saying in a 1991 interview that "I'm absolutely besotted with this country and always have been" (10). It is his deep loyalty to England that prompts him to criticize his countrymen so impatiently. Jimmy Porter complained of Alison's hypocrisy in refusing to express her anger at betrayal—he considered such middle-class stoicism debilitating. When Osborne is wounded, he retaliates or shrieks with pain. Thus, those who consider his comments about the suicide of his fourth wife, Jill Bennett, to have been what Anthony Page widely referred to as an "Inadmissible Epitaph" (12–13), or his unsympathetic portrait in *Almost a Gentleman* of his third wife, the recently deceased journalist/author Penelope Gilliatt, as being indiscreet, might listen to what Billington said recently with reference to *Déjàvu*: that "there are some hurts so profound that they can never be healed with swift and noiseless time" ("Cri de Coeur" 25).

Reviewing Osborne's second volume of autobiography, John Carey disapproved of Osborne's contempt for the lower middle classes, implying that the well-known author was trying to distance himself from his origins: "Given the emphasis he lays on his lower-middle-class background (in the autobiography) it is odd . . . that his snobbery should hone in so persistently on middle-class targets" (1).

Carey, who nevertheless describes the volume as "a classic autobiography by a major writer" (1), missed the opportunity to point out that it is not their inherent inferiority that causes Osborne to mock people who share his social background but their inability to see how their euphemisms, affectations, and misdirected sense of propriety have been imposed upon them by a behavioral code they never question. Similarly, readers of *A Better Class of Person* who were shocked by Osborne's portrayal of his mother's horrifying (to them) behavior overlook the author's practical, and realistic, explanation. She probably would never read the book, and "she was flattered by all the attention" (Grove 7). Nellie Beatrice Osborne was molded by the times in which she lived, and her standards were the result of generations of enforced social stratification and ignorance.

Although *Déjàvu* is Osborne's latest play, it is by no means his final one. It had to be written to place *Look Back in Anger* in context and to conclude a legend. Critics are again free to explore the complex and often experimental treatments of urgent topics in plays like *The Hotel in Amsterdam*, *A Patriot for Me*, *Luther*, and *West of Suez*. Claire Armistead's and Peter Kemp's rather negative evaluations of *Déjàvu* are minority opinions. Michael Billington and Benedict Nightingale have contributed more balanced critical essays and will, I believe, prevail. Kemp appears to have been impervious to Jimmy Porter's outcries in both the 1956 and 1992 plays, describing the young and old Jimmy Porter as "the stand-up chronic complainer," thus alluding to Osborne's *The Entertainer*, as well as to *Look Back in Anger* and *Déjàvu*. Kemp maintains that the latter play could be dubbed "Hark Back in Archness," and that the heart of Osborne's theatrical repertoire is "the aggrieved monologue" (18). Kemp's and Armistead's viewpoints have been effectively countered by Nightingale's review of the Faber text of *Déjàvu* that was published before the play's London opening and that Nightingale claims left him "longing to hear its sandblaster rhetoric come roaring over the footlights" (12). Joining Nightingale in his admiration of Osborne's latest play, Billington, who clearly understands Osborne's historical significance to British theatre, notes the playwright still has "a gift for language that scorches the senses" and that has "an elegiac quality" to its "parodic wit." Perceptively he notes that *Déjàvu* is "a deeply self-referential work about the pleasure and penalty of creating a dramatic myth" ("Cri de Coeur" 25). History may already have conferred upon *Look Back in Anger* the distinction of being the most influential British play of the twentieth century, but Osborne retains the capacity to break new ground and to enrage and delight audiences for decades to come.

WORKS CITED

Armistead, Claire. "Return of the Churlish Mysogynist." *Guardian* 11 June 1992, Features: 25.
Barber, Lynn. "Bad Behaviour." *Independent on Sunday* 2 February 1992, Review Supplement: 8–10.
Billington, Michael. "*Cri de Coeur* of an Eloquent Misfit." *Guardian* 11 June 1992: 25.
———. "Evidence of Anger." *Guardian* 18 June 1993, sec. 4: 5.
Carey, John. "Almost a Gentleman." *Sunday Times* 3 November 1991, sec. 7: 1.
Grove, Valerie. "No Mistake, The View Is Still Unmellowed." *Sunday Times* 30 July 1989: B7a.
Howard, Philip. "Angry Old Codgers." *Times* 10 June 1992: 16c.
Howell, Georgina. "Look Back in Candour." *Sunday Times* 13 October 1991, sec. 4: 1a.
Kemp, Peter. "Tantrums and Teddy Bears." *Times Literary Supplement* 19 June 1992: 18.

Nightingale, Benedict. "Come Back, Jimmy; All Is Unforgiven." *Times* 15 June 1992: 12.
Page, Anthony. "Inadmissible Epitaph." *Guardian Supplement* 6 June 1992: 12–13.
White, Lesley. "More in Sorrow Than in Anger." *Sunday Times* 7 June 1992: 6–7.

THE ANGRY YOUNG MAN WHO STAYED THAT WAY

John Mortimer

When the playwright John Osborne died late last month in England, it seemed that only moments before he had shaken the British theatre to its foundations. John Mortimer, the novelist and playwright, remembers those days.

On Christmas Eve died John Osborne, an unexpected Christian. At 65, his voice of perpetual protest, sometimes magnificent, often vitriolic, occasionally intolerable, always dramatic, was silent. With it vanished the amused, often quite gentle charm, which was only known to his friends. His singular achievement was to have created a total revolution in the British theater.

The 1950's were a pretty dull time in England. The excitement of the war, and the Labor victory that followed it, had drained away. The theater was a place for respectful revivals. There were almost no new playwrights. And then, in 1956, an unemployed young actor, living on a barge in the Thames, saw an advertisement in The Stage asking for new plays for the Royal Court (Shaw's old theatre), which had been taken over by George Devine. John Osborne sent in "Look Back in Anger," and we are still reaping the benefits of its extraordinary success.

Strangely enough, "Look Back in Anger" was, in shape, a conventional well-made play of the sort that might have been constructed by Noël Coward or Terence Rattigan. What made it different was that Jimmy Porter, the play's antihero, was the first young voice to cry out for a new generation that had forgotten the war, mistrusted the welfare state and mocked its established rulers with boredom, anger and disgust.

The age of respect was over. It was a time of protest, of processions

---

Originally published in *The New York Times* for January 8, 1995. Reprinted by permission of John Mortimer and ADVANPRESS LTD 1995.

to Downing Street and sitting down in Trafalgar Square. It was the first play that got a laugh out of the Royal Family, and the work gave birth to a long line of sullen young men, often from the north of England, racked with mysterious longings and ill-defined resentment. But better news for us than all that, "Look Back in Anger" burst open the gates to a flood of new British playwrights. Now we could find fresh voices the way the American theater had already done with Tennessee Williams and Arthur Miller.

It didn't happen immediately. The first night was not a success, and the critics were unenthusiastic. "You didn't expect them to *like* it, did you?" the director, Tony Richardson, asked the discouraged author. But that Sunday, Kenneth Tynan, the most influential of the younger critics, wrote a rave review in which he protested that he couldn't love anyone who didn't like "Look Back in Anger." The play became a huge success, not only because it spoke for a new generation but because it was true and touching and written with marvelous theatrical panache. Theater managers, searching for further hits, allowed us all to write plays. John Osborne had masterminded the attack, and the playwrights' army of occupation followed. The age of revivals was over. A new and memorable period in the British theater began.

When Osborne announced that he was writing a new play, George Devine hoped that there would be "a part for Laurence." Osborne said, "Laurence who?" But he and Olivier produced a rare piece of stage magic. "The Entertainer" comes from Osborne's best-loved tradition, the British music hall, which reached its height at the end of the last century as a great popular art with brave, sexy and, for that period, outrageous performers.

Archie Rice is the last gasp of that tradition, dead behind the eyes but still prepared to stand up before a thin and unsympathetic audience and "have a go." At one moment of great grief, Archie, played by Olivier, burst out singing in the deep, tragic tones of Bessie Smith and collapsed slowly at the side of the stage. There has been no more effective moment in the theater since.

In "Luther," Osborne had Albert Finney struggling with his conscience and his constipation and managed, as a British critic said, to get a West End audience fascinated by the problem of salvation through faith.

The plays after "Inadmissible Evidence" (this time the burned-out case was a lawyer out of love with the law) and "A Patriot for Me" may have been less satisfactory, but John Osborne remained a great dramatic writer. He wrote, in books and articles, as well as for the theater, long, angry monologues, often casting himself after the angry young man as a crusty old blimp. The targets changed, the enemy was no longer the establishment, the culturally pretentious, or the girls with nice daddies in country houses who set out to snare and smother men. Now the great fusillade of words was aimed at the young, backpackers, gay-rights activists, trendy priests and all those who would turn the world gray in the name of political correctness.

All he said was calculated to grab the attention of the audience and keep it listening, as when he made the terminally politically incorrect boast, "I have been blessed with God's two greatest gifts, to be born English and heterosexual." Did he mean all he said, or were his speeches theatrical in the sense that they hovered above reality? Does it matter? In the end we all need a sense of outrage to keep us alive.

He wrote a brilliant volume of autobiography, "A Better Class of Person," an unforgettable account of the suffocating values of lower-middle-class English life with a mother whom he turned with great dramatic effect into the villain of the piece. "I am ashamed of her," he wrote, "as a part of myself that can't be cut out." Later he found fault with an actress who played his mother in a television version of the book, as he thought she looked far too sympathetic. Englishmen aren't meant to criticize their mothers, but the book, and its sequel, "Almost a Gentleman," struck a chord with many readers.

After his first success, Osborne wrote "A Letter of Hate" to the Tribune magazine in which he damned England and his countrymen. In fact, he was as English as Dr. Johnson or Chesterton. He had no sympathy with politicians who "proclaim 'I believe in Britain,' meaning that what they believe in is a Tory Britain, and that if you suggest that there are a whole lot of things about Britain that stink, then you are a cad." At his most discontented he said he regarded the idea of exile from his native land as chilling a prospect as the bang of a prison door closing on him.

Cantankerous, pugnacious, unfair, Osborne was capable of great eccentricity. He wrote to the distinguished Times of London critic Benedict Nightingale on behalf of his own invention, the British Playwrights' Mafia: "It's safer for your health to avoid downtown Chichester." He once said that critics were like corrupt police or faulty sewers and should be regularly exposed. His war with them wasn't entirely selfish. When one of them gave me a not entirely friendly notice he rang up the offender and offered to punch him in the nose, a threat which, to my huge relief, was not carried out.

The man who was so often angry in public ended his life in a huge country house near the Welsh border with Helen Dawson, his fifth and most devoted wife; who had, strangely enough, been an excellent dramatic critic.

It was said that Osborne's grandfather had once had an affair with the music hall star and somewhat risqué singer Marie Lloyd. His was what John Osborne saw as the golden age, the turn of the century, when audiences knew Kipling and Shakespeare, and the Bible was still in beautiful English. Osborne's anger was in defense of old values of courage and honor. It was often unreasonable, wonderfully ill considered and always, as he wrote of Tennessee Williams's plays, "full of private fires and personal visions worth a thousand statements of a thousand politicians."

A Memory of John Osborne
Arnold Wesker

The English produce some of the world's finest writers. It amazes me how since the ground in which they seed contains little nourishment other than the stony bitchiness of literary commentators. English writers don't grow because their roots are fed but because they blow pollen to one another. Each time I experience an exhilarating play I'm reminded of the writer I could be. The best of my colleagues endow me with self-respect. Critics and peripheral literati demoralise. They enjoy blood and clowns—writers who flail or amuse them.

Kingsley Amis amuses them by allowing himself to be photographed for the press with his head and arms locked in medieval stocks. John Osborne was the kind of writer who flailed them. They tingled to his vitriol. A London journalist wrote about him:

> ... if he were nice no one would want to know. We are more diverted by his outbursts and professional enemy-making than his theatrical skills.

John always "wanted to own a bit of England." He achieved that dream with the purchase of The Hurst, a house in Shropshire set in vast grounds. It was there he wrote the second volume of his autobiography, *Almost a Gentleman*. "Almost" because, presumably, though not to the Manor born yet to the Manor aspired. "I am," he is quoted as saying, "absolutely besotted with this country and always have been."

That passion inspired one of the most extraordinary outbursts ever uttered by an English writer. In 1961 he wrote an open "Letter To My Fellow Countrymen" printed in the Socialist weekly, *Tribune*, and picked up by every major daily newspaper. It drew blood from the nation. "This is a letter of hate..." it began, and ended, "... Damn you, England. My hate will outrun you yet. I wish it could be eternal." "To be tentative," he later declared euphemistically, "was beyond me." It is a letter about which interpretations and theses will be written endlessly. Ostensibly an attack on the government for its nuclear arms policy yet it carried his image of a gentle, just, commonsensical England being poisoned by opportunistic men in commercial and political life.

The first volume of autobiography, *A Better Class of Person*, was published in 1981. Well written, honest, it distressed some critics who read what they imagined to be a heartless character assassination of his mother. They misread it. She seems to have been a woman with little generosity of spirit. He grew up fighting the erosiveness of her sour disparagements, and in the process of describing them found pity, the hallmark of art.

The critics' misreading of John's work began with *Look Back in Anger*, which is not about anger but about a love affair that fails because of the absence of generosity of spirit. Such misreading highlights a major question yet to be explored for an answer: to what extent does journalism help or distort our perception of the world? In the second volume of the autobiography, which begins with the appearance of *Look Back* at the Royal Court Theatre in May 1956, John tells a story about the Court's part-time press officer:

> ... George Fearon. He was overpaid at £10 a week. Mr. Fearon was given a copy of the play and invited me for a drink at a pub in Great Newport Street. He equivocated shiftily, even for one in his trade, and then told me with some relish how much he disliked the play and how he had no idea how he could possibly publicise it successfully ...
> "I suppose you're an angry young man ... aren't you?" ...

A headline for the world's media was born: Angry Young Man. But not the personage. There never was an "Angry Young Man" nor any such group as "The Angry Young Men." Neither John Osborne nor we, his peers, were angry; on the contrary, we were very happy. Our work was being performed and we were earning more money in a year than in our entire lives till then. But there we were, lumped together, boxed away with a label under which we were read, studied in schools and universities around the world, and written about in countless books on British drama. The plays were not allowed to describe themselves; they were described before they were read *and were read that way!* Ill-informed interviewers still ask, as though it were the most perceptive question ever and one had not written anything else in thirty years: "Are you still angry?"—hoping for a shortcut to comprehension. They barely escape being murdered on the spot.

Some artists are either loved or hated, others inspire a love-to-hate them. Pure or mixed emotions. Most relationships are like that. John inspired those who loved to hate him. I suspect his mischievous side enjoyed, perhaps cultivated, their loathing. As a result he was a high-flying rare bird everyone wanted to shoot down. When Tynan was appointed literary manager of the new National Theatre, he invited John to join them and "help make history." "I've already made history" he replied, not unreasonably though a touch arrogantly.

And a touch ungratefully. It was Tynan who had championed him. *Look Back in Anger*, having been rejected by twenty-five managers and agents, was dismissed by most critics of the daily newspapers. Then came the Sunday press and the line from Tynan's review which is recorded in theatre history: "I doubt if I could love anyone who did not wish to see *Look Back in Anger*." The so-called "British Theatre Revolution" was launched. In April 1956 I saw a touring production of the play. It changed my life. A few months later I began to write the first of my plays to be performed—*Chicken Soup with Barley*.

When invited to write my autobiography, I was hesitant for many reasons, not least because John's two volumes were so well written and I wasn't sure I could match them. When I wrote him in June 1993 sharing my fears he replied:

> I'm glad you're doing yr autobiography. It's so difficult, but I think you will find it an exhilarating experience. I wish I cd do mine over again. I learned a lot from it. First that AB is really a work of fiction, and one shd approach as if it were a novel (which, after all, so many first novels are). Facts are secondary. It's *your* dream, no one else's. Facts are secondary, feelings are all. You don't have to be fair, least of all, objective. But I mustn't lecture *you*. But, as I say, it's like recapturing a dream.

The rest of his letter confessed to a quality of misery that left me feeling concerned. His play *Inadmissible Evidence* had just been badly produced at the National Theatre.

> ... I feel utterly dispirited and without any hope either for the present or future. If it weren't for Helen, I'd take a weekend in Brighton, jab 400 units of insulin into myself (always have enough in the fridge) and walk out into the sea.
>
> The "production" of *Inadmissible* has been the most bitter, ignominious experience of my life. Director (nice woman, but ...)

feeble. No authority and full of fashionable "expressionist" shit. Leading actor a TV star of monumental ego and *minuscule* talent—a familiar combination. I was *banned* from the theatre and never spoken to not by *anyone*. When I asked the "director" of the National: wd he have treated Noel, Beckett, Miller, or indeed Harold with such open, public contempt, he just apologised most perfunctory, adding that he thought the actor was "convincing" (like the butler and the housemaid in Act One!). It's accepted that writers are treated like shit. . . .

On 20 June 1994 the Queen held what I think is a biannual gathering at Buckingham Palace of some 800 of the great and good. Among the writers present were Harold Pinter, Antonia Fraser, David Hare, Paul Johnson, David Lodge, John and myself. He was in much better spirits. My diary records:

> I told him how pleased I was that things were looking up for him and asked what was it precisely that had changed. He mumbled something about how Jill Bennett, his last wife, had persistently told him everybody out there had hated him.
> "And you know, if someone keeps telling you that you begin to believe them. So suddenly I find that everyone is being kind to me . . ."
> But I never got to understand in which way and about what.

I heard later that he was happier because his plays were being revived. Poor bloody playwrights—what else? *Look Back in Anger* in Manchester; *A Patriot for Me* by the Royal Shakespeare Company; and a commission to write for TV a play on Purcell and The Restoration.

On 3 December John briefly noted the Buckingham Palace evening with delightful and poetic inaccuracy to amuse the readers of his column in *The Spectator*. He was sweet about everyone:

> . . . It was equally surprising to meet three playwright friends there. They were just as startled to see me, and each other. Each was unnerved to discover that he was not the only dramatist present and that his cover, consequently, had been blown. All quickly, and separately, confided that they had been persuaded to attend by their wives. Hare was with his enchanting new wife, Wesker reunited with his trusty old one and Pinter with the delectable Antonia, who certainly looked at home in the Throne Room. Now, if I am clamped by the tabloids

as an old Tory blimp, they (Hare, Pinter, Wesker) are just as crudely cast as Liberal-Lefties, and it took a good few glasses of excellent champagne for us all to agree we were having a spiffing time. Wesker and I ended up dancing down the Mall. I could almost hear George Devine dismissively spitting out the dottel from his pipe.

My own diary, less lyrical but more accurate, reads:

> We drove them to their hotel, The Cadogan, in Sloane Street. "It was where Oscar Wilde was arrested" John informed us, "and where Lily Langtry lived. She bought the place.". . . Outside their hotel John, in dinner suit and black bow tie, performed for us a little farewell hop-skip-and-tap-dance routine as we drove off. The Entertainer!

"Facts are secondary," he'd written; "feelings are all."
The palace was the last time we met. Three weeks later he died.

EULOGY FOR JOHN OSBORNE

David Hare

A memorial service was held for John Osborne at St. Giles-in-the-Fields in Covent Garden on June 2, 1995. This is the text of the address delivered at the service.

"I've an idea. Why don't we have a little game? Let's pretend that we're human beings and that we're actually alive. Just for a while. What do you say? Let's pretend we're human."

It took the author's sudden death last Christmas Eve and his burial in a Shropshire churchyard, just a few miles from the blissful house he shared with his beloved Helen, to wake his own country into some kind of just appreciation of what they had lost. It is impossible to speak of John without using the word "England." He had, in some sense, made the word his own. Yet it is no secret that latterly John had imagined the local eclipse of fashion that is inevitable in his profession to be sharper and more hurtful than ever before.

However, in the flood of heartfelt and often guilty appreciation which followed on his death, he would have been astonished to see publicly acknowledged what he most surely knew all along: that the world is full of people who feel strangely rebuked by those who dare to live far freer, more fearless, even more reckless lives than the ones we are able to lead ourselves. Of all human freedoms the most contentious is the freedom not to fear what people will think of you. It still shocks people when you claim the right to hate with the same openness with which you love. But even the stage carpenter at the Theatre Royal Brighton who liked regularly to greet the visit of each of John's plays with the words "Oh blimey, not you again" would have admitted that the man who wrote "Don't be afraid of being emotional. You won't die of it" had all along been possessed of an enviable courage.

"It's deep honesty which distinguishes a gentleman," he wrote on one occasion; "he knows how to revel in life and have no expectations—and fear death at all times." On another: "I have been upbraided constantly for a crude, almost animal inability to dissemble." Or, as his mother, the famous Nellie Beatrice put it, after watching him act: "Well, he certainly puts a lot into it. Poor kid."

Central to any understanding of John's extraordinary life—five marriages, twenty-one stage plays, and more flash clothes than anyone can count—is the striking disparity between his popular reputation as a snarling malcontent, the founding member of the Viper Gang Club, and the generous, freespirited man that most of us in this church knew and loved. What he called his "beholden duty to kick against the pricks" concealed from public view a man whom we all adored as an incomparable host, an endlessly witty and caring friend, and one of the best prospects for gossip and enchantment I have ever met in my life.

He had, in Dirk Bogarde's happy phrase, a matchless gift for "uncluttered friendship." His postcards alone were worth living for. To a man writing from America to ask him the meaning of life, his typically courteous reply ran, in whole: "Wish I *could* help you with the meaning of life. J.O." To me, a colleague consoling him on some routine professional humiliation, he wrote from his beautiful home: "Never mind. I lift my eyes to the blue remembered hills, and they call back: 'shove off.'" To an Australian student, astonished to get an answer to his card saying he wanted to be a playwright: "All I can say is trust your own judgement. Don't be discouraged by anyone. The only ally you will have is yourself."

It is hardly surprising that right until the end of his life students and young people continued to write him. The whole world knew that it was John who established the idea that it would be to the stage that people would look for some sort of recognizable portrait of their own lives. It would not be from this country's then-weedy novels, nor from its still-shallow and mendacious journalism that people would expect strong feeling or strong intelligence, but from its often-clumsy, untutored living theatre. Free from the highbrow pieties of the university on one side, and from the crassness of what came to be called the media on the other, the theatre alone could celebrate John's approved qualities of joy and curiosity. It could also affront his deadly enemy, opinion.

And for many years, ridiculously, this central claim of John's, his ruling belief in the theatre's unique eloquence held and kept its authority. "On that stage," he said of the little space behind the proscenium arch at the Royal Court Theatre, "you can do anything." John knocked down the door and a whole generation of playwrights came piling through, many of them not even acknowledging him as they came, and a good half of them not noticing that the vibrant tone of indignation they could not wait to imitate was, in John's case, achieved only through an equally formidable measure of literary skill.

John was too sensible a man to make extravagant claims for what he achieved. He knew better than anyone that the so-called revolution attributed to him was on the surface only. The counter-revolutionary enemy was waiting, preparing to send relentless waves of boulevard comedies, stupid thrillers, and life-threatening musicals over the top, in order to ensure that the authenticity and originality of John's work would remain the exception rather than the rule. Nobody understood the tackiness of the theatre better than John. After all, he had played Hamlet on Hayling Island, not so much, he said, as the Prince of Denmark, as more like a leering milkman from Denmark Hill. Yet behind him there remains the true legend of a man who for some brief period burnished the theatre's reputation with the dazzle of his rhetoric.

"I love him," he wrote of Max Miller, "because he embodied a kind of theatre I admire most. 'Mary from the Dairy' was an overture to the danger that (Max) might go too far. Whenever anyone tells me that a scene or line in a play of mine goes too far in some way then I know my instinct has been functioning as it should. When such people tell you that a particular passage makes the audience uneasy or restless, then they seem (to me) as cautious and absurd as landladies and girls-who-won't."

There is in everything John writes a love for the texture of real life, a reminder of real pleasures and real pains. "I never," he wrote, in what I once claimed was his most characteristic statement, "had lunch in Brighton without wanting to take a woman to bed in the afternoon." When he heard that my own theatre company, Joint Stock, had gone on a mass outing to Epsom Races to research a play about Derby Day, his scorn was terrifying. He said when he was a young actor everyone he knew went to the Derby anyway, to enjoy it, not to bloody well research it.

It is fashionably said of John's work that he experienced a decline in the last twenty years of his life. There was nothing he resented more in later years than being asked what he was writing at the moment. Nobody, he said, asked an accountant whose accounts they were doing at the moment. Nor indeed did they ask: done any accounting lately? As he himself remarked, it is invariably those who have detested or distrusted your work from the outset who complain most vehemently of their sense of betrayed disappointment at your subsequent efforts.

Yet in making this familiar observation, critics ignore or take for granted the two exceptional, illuminating volumes of autobiography, which prove—if proof were needed—that his celebrated gift for analysing the shortcomings of others was as nothing to his forensic capacity for making comedy from his own failings. If he could be hard on others, he could be almost religiously brutal on himself. They also omit to mention what it was John declined from: a ten-year period, the last ten years of his great friend George Devine's life, in which he wrote *Look Back in Anger*, *The Entertainer*, *A Patriot for Me*, *Luther*, and *Inadmissible Evidence*. Oh yes, John Osborne declined. He declined in the sense that an unparalleled, mid-century period of dramatic brilliance remained precisely that. Unparalleled.

"A real pro is a real man, all he needs is an old backcloth behind him and he can hold them on his own for half an hour. He's like the general run of people, only he's a lot more like them than they are themselves, if you understand me."

The words are Billy Rice's, and yet they apply as much to John—more like us than we are ourselves, if you understand me—as to any music-hall comedian.

"Oh heavens, how I long for a little ordinary human enthusiasm. Just enthusiasm—that's all. I want to hear a warm, thrilling voice cry out Hallelujah! . . . Hallelujah! I'm alive!"

It is a sad fact of John's life that in the country he loved one is judged either to be clever or to be passionate. There is in the condescension of many English people to one another an automatic assumption that the head and the heart are in some sort of opposition. If someone is clever, they are usually called cold. If they are emotional, they are usually called stupid. Nothing bewilders the English more than someone who exhibits great feeling and great intelligence. When, as in John's case, a person is abundantly gifted with both, the English response is to take in the washing and bolt the back door.

John Osborne devoted his life to trying to forge some sort of connection between the acuteness of his mind and the exceptional power of his heart. "To be tentative was beyond me. It usually is." That is why this Christian leaves behind him friends and enemies, detractors and admirers. A lifelong scourge of prigs and puritans, whether of the Right or of the Left, he took no hostages, expecting from other people the same unyielding, unflinching commitment to their own view of the truth which he took for granted in his own. Of all British playwrights of the twentieth century he is the one who risked most. And, risking most, frequently offered the most rewards.

For many of us life will never be quite the same without the sight of that fabulous whiskered grin, glimpsed from across the room. Then John heading towards us, fierce, passionate, and fun.

BIBLIOGRAPHY

Patricia D. Denison and Michal Lemberger

PRIMARY SOURCES

Stage

A Bond Honoured. [Lope De Vega, *La Fianza Satisficha*, adapted by John Osborne.] London: Faber and Faber, 1966.
Déjàvu. London: Faber and Faber, 1991.
The Devil Inside. [Written in collaboration with Stella Linden.] Staged at Theatre Royal, Huddersfield, 1950. Unpublished.
The End of Me Old Cigar. London: Faber and Faber, 1975.
The Entertainer. London: Faber and Faber, 1957.
Epitaph for George Dillon. [Written in collaboration with Anthony Creighton.] London: Faber and Faber, 1958.
Four Plays: "West of Suez," "A Patriot for Me," "Time Present," "The Hotel in Amsterdam." New York: Dodd, Mead, 1972.
Hedda Gabler. [Henrik Ibsen, adapted by John Osborne.] London: Faber and Faber, 1972.
Inadmissible Evidence. London: Faber and Faber, 1965.
Look Back in Anger. London: Faber and Faber, 1957.
Look Back in Anger and Other Plays. Collected Plays, Vol. I [*Look Back in Anger, Epitaph for George Dillon, The World of Paul Slickey, Déjàvu*]. London: Faber and Faber, 1993.
Luther. London: Faber and Faber, 1961.
A Patriot for Me. London: Faber and Faber, 1966.
Personal Enemy. [Written in collaboration with Anthony Creighton.] Staged Harrogate 1955. Unpublished.
"The Picture of Dorian Gray": A Moral Entertainment. [Oscar Wilde, adapted by John Osborne.] London: Faber and Faber, 1973.
A Place Calling Itself Rome. [Based on Shakespeare's *Coriolanus*.] London: Faber and Faber, 1973.
Plays for England: "The Blood of the Bambergs" and "Under Plain Cover." London: Faber and Faber, 1963.
A Sense of Detachment. London: Faber and Faber, 1973.
Strindberg's "The Father" and Ibsen's "Hedda Gabler." [August Strindberg and Henrik Ibsen, adapted by John Osborne.] London: Faber and Faber, 1989.
A Subject of Scandal and Concern. London: Faber and Faber, 1961.
Time Present and The Hotel in Amsterdam. London: Faber and Faber, 1968.
Watch It Come Down. London: Faber and Faber, 1975.
West of Suez. London: Faber and Faber, 1971.
The World of Paul Slickey. London: Faber and Faber, 1959.

Film

The Charge of the Light Brigade. A Woodfall production in 1968; directed by Tony Richardson; screenplay by John Osborne and Charles Wood.

The Entertainer. A Woodfall production in 1960; directed by Tony Richardson; screenplay by John Osborne and Nigel Kneale.

Inadmissible Evidence. A Woodfall production in 1968; directed by Anthony Page; screenplay by John Osborne.

Look Back in Anger. A Woodfall production in 1959; directed by Tony Richardson; screenplay by Nigel Kneale with additional dialogue by John Osborne.

Tom Jones. A Woodfall production in 1962; directed by Tony Richardson; screenplay by John Osborne. Scripts: London: Faber and Faber, 1964 (Osborne's script) and New York: Grove Press, 1964 (final film version).

Television

Almost a Vision. Unpublished. Transmitted by ITV, 1 September 1976.

"A Better Class of Person" [An Extract of Autobiography for Television] and "God Rot Tunbridge Wells" [An Account of George Frideric Handel]. London: Faber and Faber, 1985.

"The Gift of Friendship": A Play for Television. London: Faber and Faber, 1972.

"Jill and Jack": A Play for Television. London: Faber and Faber, 1975.

"The Right Prospectus": A Play for Television. London: Faber and Faber, 1970.

Very Like a Whale. London: Faber and Faber, 1971.

"You're Not Watching Me, Mummy" and "Try a Little Tenderness": Two Plays for Television. London: Faber and Faber, 1978.

Nonfiction

Almost a Gentleman: An Autobiography, Vol. II, 1955–1966. London: Faber and Faber, 1991.

"The American Theatre." Encore 19 (March–April 1959): 17–21.

"At Home." Independent 4 April 1994, Feature: 17.

Review of At the Royal Court by Richard Findlater. New Standard 4 April 1981.

Review of Autobiography by Noël Coward. Tatler June 1986.

"Berliner Ensemble." Times 5 September 1963: 13D.

A Better Class of Person: An Autobiography, Vol. I, 1929–1956. London: Faber and Faber, 1981.

The British Playwrights' Mafia. Sunday Times Magazine 16 October 1977. [Included, among others, Rodney Ackland, John Arden, Alan Bennett, Robert Bolt, Bill Bryden, Edward Bond, Christopher Hampton, Peter Nichols, Arnold Wesker, and Charles Wood.]

"Come On In: The Revolution Is Only Just Beginning." Tribune 27 March 1959: 11. [On British theatre and the Royal Court Theatre.]

Damn You, England: Collected Prose. London: Faber and Faber, 1994. [Collection from more than thirty years of journalism, letters, profiles, and book reviews; writings included in this bibliography, as well as other nonfiction not included here.]

"Diary." Spectator 13 July 1985: 7. 20 July 1985: 7. 27 July 1985, 7. 3 August 1985: 7. 30 May 1992: 7. 6 June 1992: 6. 13 June 1992: 6. 20 June 1992: 7. 17 April 1993: 6. 24 April 1993: 7. 1 May 1993: 7. 4 December 1993: 6. 11 December 1993: 7. 18 December 1993: 8. 7 May 1994: 7. 14 May 1994: 6. 21 May 1994: 7. 3 December 1994: 8. 17 December 1994: 8.

"The Diary of a Somebody." Review of The Orton Diaries. Ed. John Lahr. Spectator 29 November 1986: 31–32.

"Dr. Agostinho Neto." Times 2 October 1961: 13D.

"*The Entertainer.*" *Writers' Theatre.* Eds. Keith Waterhouse and Willis Hall. London: Heinemann, 1967. 51.

"The Enthusiasm of a Young Critic." Review of *François Truffaut: Letters* ed. by Gilles Jacob and Claude Givray. *Spectator* 23 December 1989: 73.

"The Epistle to the Philistines." *London Tribune* 13 May 1960: 9. Rpt. in *John Osborne: "Look Back in Anger," A Casebook.* Ed. John Russell Taylor. 62–63. [On the monarchy.]

"The Fallen Idol." Review of *Songs My Mother Taught Me* by Marlon Brando, with Robert Lindsey. *Spectator* 8 October 1994: 48–49.

"Final Victory to the Silk Dressing-Gown." Review of *Noël Coward* by Clive Fisher. *Spectator* 2 May 1992: 31.

Foreword. *Look Back in Anger.* London: Evans Bros., 1957. 2–4.

Foreword. *Low Life* by Jeffrey Barnard. London: Duckworth, 1986.

"Friendship—But Money Comes into It, Too." *Evening Standard* 23 April 1960.

"Golden Moments with a Person." Review of *Difficulties with Girls* by Kingsley Amis. *Spectator* 1 October 1988: 34–35.

"A Great Englishman." Review of *John Betjeman: Letters, Vol. 1, 1926–1951* ed. by Candida Lycett Green. *Spectator* 23 April 1994: 30–31.

"Great Sighs of Today." *Spectator* 22 December 1984: 24–25. [On the language of the Anglican Church's alternative service book.]

Review of *The Honourable Beast: A Posthumous Autobiography* by John Dexter. *Sunday Telegraph* 30 June 1993: Books, 11.

"In Love with the Productions of His Time." Review of *Kicking against the Pricks* by Oscar Lewenstein. *Spectator* 4 June 1994: 32.

"Inside the Monstrous Concrete Piety." Review of *The National: A Dream Made Concrete* by Peter Lewis. *Spectator* 5 January 1991: 21.

"Intellectuals and Just Causes: A Symposium." *Encounter* 29 September 1967: 3–4. [On politics, protest, and Vietnam.]

Introduction to *The Father* [1988]. *Strindberg's "The Father" and Ibsen's "Hedda Gabler."* London: Faber and Faber, 1989. ix–xii.

Introduction to *Hedda Gabler* [1972]. *Strindberg's "The Father" and Ibsen's "Hedda Gabler."* London: Faber and Faber, 1989. 53–54.

Introduction. *International Theatre Annual, Number Two.* Ed. Harold Hobson. London: Calder, 1957. 9–10.

Introduction. *"Look Back in Anger" and Other Plays: Collected Plays, I.* London: Faber and Faber, 1993.

Introduction. *"The Picture of Dorian Gray": An Adaptation.* London: Faber and Faber, 1973.

"A Letter to My Fellow Countrymen." *London Tribune* 18 August 1961: 11. Rpt. in *John Osborne: "Look Back in Anger," A Casebook.* Ed. John Russell Taylor. 67–69. ["Damn You, England," on Cold War escalation.]

Letter. *Spectator* 12 April 1957: 486.

Letter. *Times* 2 September 1968: 7. [Retracts 1961 "Damn you, England."]

Letter. *Times* 18 April 1991. [*Déjàvu* and star actors.]

Review of *The Letters of Brendan Behan* ed. by E. H. Mikhail. *Sunday Telegraph* 2 February 1992: 114.

Review of *The Life of Kenneth Tynan* by Kathleen Tynan. *New York Review of Books* 34 (3 December 1987): 5.

"Looking Back in Affection." Review of *A Sense of Direction: Life at the Royal Court* by William Gaskill. *Spectator* 3 December 1988: 37–39.

"Mafia Maestro." *The Listener* 10 June 1982. [On being a TV critic.]

Review of *The Magic Lantern: An Autobiography* by Ingmar Bergman and Joan Tate. *New York Review of Books* 35 (27 October 1988): 16.

"Max Miller." *Observer* 19 September 1965.

"My Jubilee Year." *Observer.* 6 February 1977: 25, 27. [Autobiographical reflections.]

"My Vote." *Observer.* 6 October 1974: 23. [Labour "with an even emptier heart than usual."]
Review of *No Bells on Sunday: The Journals of Rachel Roberts* ed. by Alexander Walker. *Observer* 16 September 1984.
Review of *The Noël Coward Diaries.* Eds. Graham Payn and Sheridan Morley. *New York Times Book Review* 3 October 1982.
"A Nice Guy Who Hasn't Finished Yet." Review of *Timebends: A Life* by Arthur Miller. *Spectator* 5 December 1987: 41–42.
Obituary: John Dexter. *Observer* 1 April 1990.
Obituary: Tony Richardson. *Observer* 17 November 1991.
"On Being in the Big Time and Away from Dreary Old Britain." *Daily Mail* 5 July 1958.
"On Critics and Criticism." *Sunday Telegraph* 28 August 1966: 6. Rpt. in *John Osborne: "Look Back in Anger," A Casebook.* Ed. John Russell Taylor. 69–71. [On theatre critics, finances of *A Bond Honoured* and *A Patriot for Me.*]
On the Halls. *Observer* 20 April 1975. [Music halls and *The Entertainer.*]
"On the Thesis Business and the Seekers After Bare Approximate: On the Rights of the Audience and the Wink and the Promise of the Well-Made Play." *Times* 14 October 1967: 20C. [On theatre studies and John Russell Taylor's *The Rise and Fall of the Well-Made Play.*]
"On the Writer's Side." *At the Royal Court.* Ed. Richard Findlater. London: Amber Lane, 1981. 19–26.
"Out, Damned Spoto! Out, I Say." Review of *Laurence Olivier* by Donald Spoto. *Spectator* 19 October 1991: 42–43.
Review of *Peter Hall's Diaries: The Story of a Dramatic Battle* ed. John Goodwin. *Sunday Times* 25 September 1983.
"The Pioneer at the Royal Court: George Devine." *Observer* 23 January 1966: 11.
"Playwrights and South Africa." *Times* 16 May 1968: 13E.
"A Princeling Among Players." Review of *Denholm Elliott: Quest for Love* by Susan Elliott, with Barry Turner. *Spectator* 24 September 1994: 45.
"Replies to a Questionnaire." *Sight and Sound* 26 (Spring 1957): 180–85. [On "commitment" in the arts.]
Report of the Joint Committee on Censorship of the Theatre, 1967 (House of Lords Committee, 29 November 1966).
"Revolt in Cuba." *Times* 19 April 1961: 13E. [Letter to the editor signed by others.]
"Royalty and Royalties." *Spectator* 5 June 1993: 30–32. [Review of books on the royalty.]
"Schoolmen of the Left." *Observer* 30 October 1960.
"Sex and Failure." *Observer* 20 January 1957. Rpt. in *The Beat Generation.* Eds. Gene Feldman and Max Greenberg. New York: Citadel, 1958. [On the plays of Tennessee Williams.]
"The Shabby End to a Theatrical Dream." *Observer* 6 July 1986: 8. [On the National Theatre.]
"The Sonny Side of the Street." Review of *Bernard Shaw: Volume I, The Search for Love. Spectator* 24 September 1988: 27–28.
"Superman? A Look Back in Anguish." *Guardian* 23 June 1977: 12. [On Bernard Shaw.]
Telegram. *Times* 9 June 1966: 14. [*A Bond Honoured* and theatre critics.]
"That Awful Museum." *Twentieth Century* 169 (February 1961): 212–16. Rpt. in *John Osborne: "Look Back in Anger," A Casebook.* Ed. John Russell Taylor. 63–67. [Conversation with Richard Findlater on the theatre, the National Theatre, audiences, stage spaces, *Look Back in Anger, The Entertainer,* and *Luther.*]
Review of *The Theatres of George Devine* by Irving Wardle. *Observer* 28 May 1978.
"They Call It Cricket." *Declaration.* Ed. Tom Maschler. New York: MacGibbon and Kee, 1957. 61–84. Rpt. in part in *Playwrights on Playwriting.* Ed. Toby Cole.

London: MacGibbon and Kee, 1960. 140–44. [Key statements on the Anglican Church, royalty, politics, and Osborne's early life.]

"This Monumental Swindle Called the Common Market." *Tribune* 12 October 1962: 5.

"Threat to a Theatre for Nottingham." *Times* 4 June 1960: 7D.

"Transatlantic Air Race." *Times* 12 May 1969: 11.

"Trial of Two Rolling Stones: Informing the Police." *Times* 4 July 1957: 11C.

"Up Jumped a Playwright." *Guardian* 14 July 1977: 12. [On Australia.]

"A Weakness for Causes." *Time* 90 (8 September 1967): 45. [On writing letters on behalf of political causes.]

"What's Wrong at the National." Review of *Peter Hall's Diaries*. *Sunday Times* 25 September 1983: 43.

"A Working Man." *Times* 2 September 1968: 7D.

"The Writer in His Age." *London Magazine* 4 (May 1957): 47–49. Rpt. in *John Osborne: "Look Back in Anger," A Casebook*. Ed. John Russell Taylor. 59–62. [On "commitment" in the arts.]

Interviews

Alvarez, A. "John Osborne and the Boys at the Ball." *New York Times* 28 September 1969, II: 1, 6. [*A Patriot for Me*.]

Armory, Mark. "Jester Flees the Court." *Sunday Times Magazine* 24 November 1974: 34, 36.

Appleyard, Bryan. "A Stance that Never Faltered." *Times* 11 May 1983: 16.

Barber, Lynn. "Bad Behaviour." *Independent on Sunday* 2 February 1992, Review Supplement: 9.

Booth, John. "Rebel Playwright." *New York Times* 2 November 1958, II: 3.

Bragg, Melvyn. "A Line-up of One-liners." *Observer* 8 June 1986.

Brahms, Caryl. "The Vein of Anger Is Still There." *Guardian Weekly* 24 August 1974: 18.

Cagerne, Walter, ed. *The Playwrights Speak*. New York: Walter Wager, 1967. 127–28. [A BBC "Face to Face" interview.]

Chesshyre, Robert. "Fifty is a Young Age for an Angry Man." *Observer* 18 November 1979: 52.

Chisholm, Anne. "Writing for Television Is Like Writing Short Stories." *Radio Times* 17–23 October 1970.

Coleman, Terry. "Osborne without Anger." *Guardian* 12 August 1971.

Davies, Hunter. "I Need to be Reminded I Was Once Alive." *Independent* 26 April 1994: 21.

Dempsey, David. "Most Angry Fella." *New York Times Magazine* 20 October 1957: 22, 25–27.

Devlin, Polly. "John Osborne." *Vogue* June 1964: 98–99, 152, 168.

Dewhurst, Keith. "What Osborne Saw West of Suez." *Evening Standard* 6 December 1971.

Dunn, Christine. "Interview with John Osborne." *Daily Mail* 21 May 1976: 1.

Edwards, Sydney. "Osborne, the Little Englander." *Evening Standard* 30 July 1971.

Findlater, Richard. "The Angry Young Man." *New York Times* 29 September 1957, II: 1, 3.

Funke, Lewis. *Playwrights Talk About Writing*. Chicago: Dramatic Publishing Co., 1975. 197–216. [1968 interview.]

"Good Natured Man." *New Yorker* 26 October 1957: 36–37.

Gourlay, Logan, ed. *Olivier*. London: Weidenfeld and Nicolson, 1973. 145–56.

Grove, Valerie. "A Better Class of Osborne." *New Standard* 6 March 1981.

———. "No Mistake, The View Is Still Unmellowed." *Sunday Times* 30 July 1989: B7A.

Hancock, Robert. "Anger." *Spectator* 5 April 1957: 438–39.

Hardy, Rebecca. "Look Back in Remorse: An Uncharacteristic Morning After Feeling for John Osborne." *Daily Mail* 29 September 1992: 15.

Howell, Georgina. "Look Back in Candour." *Sunday Times* 13 October 1991, 4: 1A.

Hussey, Charles. "Osborne Looks Forward in Anger." *New York Times Magazine* 25 October 1964: 71–72, 74, 76, 78, 81.

"John Osborne." *Olivier*. Ed. Logan Gourlay. London: Weidenfeld and Nicolson, 1973. 145–56.

John Osborne in Conversation with Dilys Powell. Tape, British Council Literature Study Aids, 1977. [March 1976 interview.]

"John Osborne, in Conversation with Iain Johnstone, Takes a Black View of Film Work." *The Listener* 3 July 1969: 17.

Lee-Potter, Lynda. "He Made Me Realize That Loving Is The Best Way To Live." *Daily Mail* 27 January 1995: 20–21. [Interview with Helen Dawson Osborne.]

"Osborne the Romantic." *Times* 28 August 1970: 6.

"Stephen Pile Calls on John Osborne." *Sunday Times* 14 August 1983: 33.

"Talk with a Playwright." *Newsweek* 24 February 1958: 62.

Tynan, Kenneth. "John Osborne Talks to Kenneth Tynan." *Observer* 30 June 1968: 21.

———. "John Osborne Talks to Kenneth Tynan." *Observer* 7 July 1968: 21.

———. "John Osborne Talks to Kenneth Tynan—Candidly." *Atlas* 16 (September 1968): 53–57. [Condensed rpt. of 30 June and 7 July 1960 Tynan interviews; on the theatre, TV, film, social issues, *Look Back in Anger, The Entertainer,* and *Time Present.*]

Wager, Walter, ed. "John Osborne." *The Playwrights Speak*. New York: Dell, 1967. 90–109. London: Longmans Green, 1967. 71–86. [TV interview with John Freeman, January 1962.]

Watts, Stephen. "Playwright John Osborne Looks Back—And Not in Anger." *New York Times* 22 September 1963, II: 1.

Weatherby, W.J. "Middle Age of the Angry Young Men." *Sunday Times Magazine* 1 March 1981: 32–33.

White, Lesley. "More in Sorrow Than in Anger." *Sunday Times* 7 June 1992: 6–7.

SECONDARY SOURCES

Criticism

FULL-LENGTH STUDIES

Banham, Martin. *Osborne*. Edinburgh: Oliver and Boyd, 1969.

Banham concludes that it is most appropriate to measure Osborne not so much in terms of individual plays but in the larger framework of a serious exploration of social and moral issues. Plays examined include *Look Back in Anger, The Entertainer, Epitaph for George Dillon, The World of Paul Slickey, A Subject of Scandal and Concern, Luther, Plays for England, Inadmissible Evidence, A Patriot for Me, A Bond Honoured, Time Present,* and *The Hotel in Amsterdam*. Select bibliography and list of first British productions.

Carter, Alan. *John Osborne*. Edinburgh: Oliver and Boyd, 1969. 2nd ed. 1973.

Carter describes Osborne's work as provocatively honest and his plays as experiments that ask questions rather than provide answers. Emphasis on private and public voices. Analysis of plays from *Look Back in Anger* (1956) to *Very Like a Whale* (1971). First performances list. Appendix of selections from the Osborne Symposium, Royal Court, 1966. Bibliography.

Duytschaever-Sneppe, Josée. *John Osborne*. Bruges: Brouwer, 1972.

Duytschaever-Sneppe offers a 60-page monograph with brief readings of *Look Back in Anger, Epitaph for George Dillon, The Entertainer, The World of Paul Slickey, A Subject of Scandal and Concern, Luther, Plays for England, Inadmissible*

Evidence, A Patriot for Me, A Bond Honoured, Time Present, and *The Hotel in Amsterdam.* Structural analysis and overview of Osborne's work. Select bibliography. In German.

Ferrar, Harold. *John Osborne.* New York: Columbia UP, 1973.

Ferrar offers a 48-page monograph on Osborne's brand of realistic dramaturgy, which Ferrar situates in the main currents of social and theatrical history of the mid-1950s. Critical commentary, often cursory, on plays from *Look Back in Anger* (1956) to *West of Suez* (1971). Select bibliography.

Gasparetto, Pier F. *Invito alla Lettura di John Osborne.* Milan: Mursia, 1978.

Gasparetto reviews the life of Osborne, examines thematic structure in his plays, and summarizes critical reception of his work. Readings of *Look Back in Anger, The Entertainer, Epitaph for George Dillon, The World of Paul Slickey, A Subject of Scandal and Concern, Luther, Plays for England, Inadmissible Evidence, A Patriot for Me, A Bond Honoured, Hedda Gabler, A Place Calling Itself Rome, The Picture of Dorian Gray, Time Present, The Hotel in Amsterdam, The Right Prospectus, Very Like a Whale, The Gift of Friendship, Jill and Jack, West of Suez, A Sense of Detachment, The End of Me Old Cigar,* and *Watch It Come Down.* Chronology. Good bibliography. In Italian.

Goldstone, Herbert. *Coping with Vulnerability: The Achievement of John Osborne.* Washington, D.C.: UP of America, 1982.

Goldstone examines Osborne's work twenty-five years after *Look Back in Anger,* asserts that the first fifteen years overshadow the last ten, and concludes by comparing Osborne's characters to Ibsen's, Chekhov's, and Pinter's characters—all of whom, he argues, exhibit conflicting feelings about self-worth. Chapters on *Epitaph for George Dillon, Look Back in Anger, The Entertainer, Luther, Inadmissible Evidence, A Patriot for Me, A Bond Honoured, Time Present, The Hotel in Amsterdam, West of Suez, A Sense of Detachment,* and *Watch It Come Down.* Bibliography includes selected reviews of productions.

Hafner, Dieter. *"Tom Jones": Fieldings Roman und Osbornes Drehbuch: Untersuchugen zu einem Medienwechsel.* Bern: Francke Verlag, 1981.

Hafner provides a thorough, detailed analysis of *Tom Jones,* the screenplay by John Osborne based on the novel by Henry Fielding. Chronology, synopsis, scene by scene comparison, production credits, production story, and bibliography. In German.

Hayman, Ronald. *John Osborne.* Heinemann: London, 1968. 92 pp. Expanded version, New York: Frederick Ungar, 1972.

Hayman draws attention to Osborne's solitary heroes who isolate themselves from society, yet who oddly epitomize social conditions in England, and whose monologues dictate the rhythm and structure of the plays. Chapters on *Epitaph for George Dillon, Look Back in Anger, The Entertainer, The World of Paul Slickey, A Subject of Scandal and Concern, Luther, Plays for England, A Patriot for Me, Inadmissible Evidence, A Bond Honoured, Time Present* and *The Hotel in Amsterdam,* and *West of Suez.* Chronology, stage production lists, cast lists of London premieres and New York productions, and bibliography.

Hinchliffe, Arnold. *John Osborne.* Boston: Twayne, 1984.

Hinchliffe provides a thorough overview of Osborne's life and work. A critical reevaluation of Osborne's career and an examination of twenty-five years of his work, from *Look Back in Anger* (1956) to *A Better Class of Person* (1981). Chronology and select bibliography with annotations.

Kiesel, Hedwig. *Martin Luther—ein Held John Osbornes "Luther": Kontext und Historischer Hintergrund.* Frankfurt: Lang, 1986.

Kiesel situates *Luther* in its historical and dramatic context. 120-page monograph in the Anglo-American Studies series. Focus on reception of the play, contemporary playwrights, history plays in England, and detailed historical background of the play. Brief readings of *A Subject of Scandal and Concern* and *A Patriot for Me.* Addendum with 26 July 1961 Theatre Royal Nottingham program for *Luther* and historical documents on Luther. Good bibliography. In German.

Odajima, Yuji. *John Osborne.* Tokyo: Kenkyusha, 1970.

Odajima investigates key features of Osborne's "new" drama, with a focus on *Look Back in Anger* monologues and Jimmy Porter as anti-hero and outcast in pursuit of love. Good photographs. Select bibliography of criticism written in English, criticism written in Japanese, and translations of Osborne's work. In Japanese.

Page, Malcolm. *File on Osborne.* London: Methuen, 1988.

Page has compiled a valuable survey of Osborne's work from *The Devil Inside* (1950) to *God Rot Tunbridge Wells* (1985). An excellent checklist includes summaries of the plays, detailed performance history, excerpts from reviews, and selected comments by Osborne on his work. Brief chronology and select bibliography with some helpful annotation.

Prater, Eugene Greeley. *An Existential View of John Osborne.* Pine Hill: Freeman, 1993.

Prater categorizes Osborne's work as existentialist drama with characters caught in a dilemma of choices, conditioned by meaninglessness or driven by the faith of self-confidence. An examination of Osborne's plays within an existentialist quandary: confrontation of boredom, inauthenticity, alienation, and loss of motivation and care. Brief analyses of the plays and separate chapters on staging and language. Select bibliography and glossary.

Taylor, John Russell, ed. *John Osborne: "Look Back in Anger," A Casebook.* London: Macmillan, 1968.

Taylor has complied a very useful, often-cited collection of essays, reviews of first performances, selected writings by Osborne, critical studies, and contemporary perspectives. Select bibliography of studies of the modern literary scene.

Trussler, Simon. *John Osborne.* Longmans Green, 1969.

A 39-page study. See Trussler's book-length study, *The Plays of John Osborne.*

Trussler, Simon. *The Plays of John Osborne: An Assessment.* London: Victor Gollancz, 1969.

Trussler focusses on Osborne's instinctive craftsmanship as he presents detailed analyses of Osborne's first dozen plays, from *Look Back in Anger* to *The Hotel in Amsterdam* (1964). A critical methodology that critiques the plays not only as literary texts but also as works for the theatre. Comments on Osborne's journalism, a brief chronology, cast lists, and a bibliography.

Van De Perre, H. *John Osborne, Boze Jonge Man.* The Hague: Tielt, 1962.

Van De Perre examines on the early work of Osborne, whom he describes as "a rebel with a cause," in a 112-page monograph. Concise cultural history and play analysis, theatre reviews and critical commentary, and selected Osborne prose. Well chosen photographs. Brief annotated bibliography. In Dutch.

Articles, Chapters, and Sections

Abirached, Robert. "Le Jeune Théâtre Anglais." *Nouvelle Revue Française* 29 (February 1967): 314–21.

Acheson, James, ed. *British and Irish Drama Since 1960.* New York: St. Martin's Press, 1993. 33, 103, 190, 193 [*Look Back in Anger*]; 43 [*Luther*].

Adania, Alf. "Osborne azi, la Amsterdam." *România Literara* 30 (January 1969): 22.

Adell, Alberto. "Lope, Osborne y Los Críticos." *Insula* (Madrid) 22 (June 1967): 7.

Ahrends, Günter. "A Sense of Detachment." *Anglo-Americansche Shakespeare-Bearbeitungen des 20. Jahrhunderts.* Darmstadt: Wissenschaftliche Buchgeselleschaft, 1980. 68–80.

Ahrens, Rüdiger. "History and the Dramatic Context: John Osborne's Historical Plays." *Fu Jen Studies: Literature & Linguistics* (Tapei) 16 (1983): 49–75.

Ahuja, Chaman. "Luther, An Archetype: Role of Anger in Evolution." *Literary Criterion* 14, iii (1979): 40–51.

Aland, Kurt. "John Osbornes Lutherschauspiel." *Martin Luther in der Modernen Literatur: Ein Kritischer Dokumentarbericht.* Berlin: Eckhart, 1973.

Albert, D. "John Osborne's *Luther*: A Study in Human Inadequacy." *Scholar Critic* 7–8 (1987): 10–14.

Allsop, Kenneth. *The Angry Decade.* London: Peter Owen, 1958. 96–132, 135–40. [*Look Back in Anger* and *The Entertainer*; biographical material and theatre reviews.]

Alvarez, A. "Anti-Establishment Drama." *Partisan Review.* 26 (Fall 1959): 606–11.

Amis, Kingsley. "Why Lucky Jim Turned Right." *What Became of Jane Austen? and Other Questions.* New York: Harcourt Brace Jovanovich, 1971. 200–11.

Amory, Mark. "Jester Flees the Court." *Sunday Times Magazine* 24 November 1974: 34.

Anderson, Michael. "From Anger to Detachment." *Anger and Detachment: A Study of Arden, Osborne, and Pinter.* London: Pitman, 1976. 21–49. [*Look Back in Anger* to *The End of Me Old Cigar*, playlists, and select bibliography.]

Anikist, A. "Ot Osborna k Mersu." *Teatar* 6 (1969): 147–57.

Ansorge, Peter. "No People Like Show People." *Plays and Players* 14.5 (1967): 60–63.

Arden, John. "A Bond Honoured." *Times* 11 June 1966: 11.

Armistead, Claire. "Return of the Churlish Mysogynist." *Guardian* 11 June 1992, Features: 25.

Athanason, Arthur Nicholas. "John Osborne." *Dictionary of Literary Biography, 13, British Dramatists since World War II.* Ed. Stanley Weintraub. Detroit: Gale Research, 1982. 371–92.

———. "John Osborne." *Concise Dictionary of British Literary Biography, Vol. 7, Writers after World War II, 1945–60.* Detroit: Gale Research, 1991. 231–54.

Aymard, Valerie. "Duty and Patriotism Clad in Shining White." *Coriolan: Théâtre et Politique.* Eds. Jean-Paul Debax and Yves Peyre. Toulouse: Serv. des Pubs., de Toulouse–Le Mirail, 1984. [*A Patriot for Me.*]

Balakian, Nona. "The Flight from Innocence." *Books Abroad* 33 (Summer 1959): 260–70.

Banerjee, A. "A Modern Hamlet: Jimmy Porter in *Look Back in Anger*." *Hamlet Studies: An International Journal of Research on "The Tragedie of Hamlet, Prince of Denmarke"* 15, 1–2 (Summer–Winter 1993): 81–92.

Barber, Lynn. "Let's Hear It for the Great John Osborne." *Independent* 4 October 1992, Editorial: 23.

Barbour, Thomas. "Theatre Chronicle." *Hudson Review* 11 (Spring 1958): 118–20.

Barker, Clive. "*Look Back in Anger*—The Turning Point." *Zeitschrift für Anglistik und Amerikanistik* 14 (1966): 367–71.

Bas, Georges. "Alfred Redl, Le Juif Galicien: Thématique et Technique dans *A Patriot for Me* de John Osborne." *Études Anglaises* 30 (October–December 1977): 440–54.

———. "Fonction et Signification d'un Personnage Secondaire dans *A Patriot for Me* de John Osborne: Le 'Judge Advocate' Jaraslav Kunz, ou Le Vrai Bon Patriote." *Caliban* (Toulouse) 15 (1978): 55–67.

Baumgart, Wolfgang. "Die Gegenwart des Barocktheaters." *Archiv für das Stadium der Neueren Sprachen und Literaturen,* 113/198 (1961): 65–76.

Baxter, Kay M. *Contemporary Theatre and the Christian Faith.* New York: Abington, 1967. 79–88. [*Look Back in Anger, The Entertainer,* and *Luther.*]

Beaven, John. "Unlucky Jim." *Twentieth Century* 160 (July 1956): 72–74. [*Look Back in Anger* and Tennessee Williams's *Streetcar Named Desire*; Jimmy Porter and Kingsley Amis's *Lucky Jim.*]

Bentley, Eric. *The Life of the Drama.* New York: Atheneum, 1964. 287–88.

Berge, Marit. "Jimmy Porter—Osborne's Hedda Gabler." *Essays in Honour of Kristian Smidt.* Ed. Peter Bilton et al. Oslo: University of Oslo, Institute of English Studies, 1986. 202–12.

Bergonzi, Bernard. *Wartime and Aftermath: English Literature and Its Background, 1939–60.* Oxford: Oxford UP, 1993. 138, 153–57, 163, 169, 178.

Bertinetti, Paolo. *Teatro Inglese Contemporaneo.* Rome: Savell, 1979. 30–45.

Beyer, Manfred. "Pathei Mathos: Das Moderne Englische Drama und die Tradition des 'Lehrhaften Leidens.'" *Arbeiten aus Anglistik und Amerikanistik* 16.2 (1991): 225–41.

Bierhaus, E.G. "No World of Its Own: *Look Back in Anger* Twenty Years Later." *Modern Drama* 19 (March 1976): 47–55.

Billington, Michael. "The Cartoon Image Is a Potential Angry Brigade Member." *Guardian* 18 December 1973: 10.

———. "Cri de Coeur of an Eloquent Misfit." *Guardian* 11 June 1992: 25.

———. "Evidence of Anger." *Guardian* 18 June 1993, 4: 5.

———. *The Modern Actor.* London: Hamish Hamilton, 1973. 162–71.

———. "Noises Off: A Major Talent for Crucifixion." *Guardian* 25 January 1994, Features: 5.

———. "A Prisoner of Dissent." *Guardian* 27 December 1994, Features: T4.

Blau, Herbert. *The Impossible Theatre.* New York: Macmillan, 1964. 213–20. [*The Entertainer* and *Look Back in Anger.*]

Bode, Carl. "Redbrick Cinderellas." *College English* 20 (April 1959): 331–37. [Osborne, Amis, and Wain.]

Böker, Uwe. "*Look Back in Anger* im Kontext von John Osbornes Dramenkonzeption und Ideologie." *Literatur für Leser* 4.1 (1982): 33–44.

Bonnerot, Louis. "John Osborne." *Études Anglaises* 10 (1958): 378–91.

Bradbrook, M.C. *English Dramatic Form: A History of Its Development.* New York: Barnes and Noble, 1965. 178, 186–88.

Brady, Mark. "Looking Back at the Language of Anger." *Four Fits of Anger: Essays on the Angry Young Men.* Undine: Camponatto, 1986.

Brahams, Caryl. "The World of John Osborne." *John O'London's* 26 November 1959: 292.

Brown, G.E. "Music Hall References in John Osborne's *Look Back in Anger.*" *Notes & Queries* 23 (July 1976): 310.

Brown, Georgina. "Beside Himself." *Independent* 10 June 1992, Arts: 18. [Interview with Tony Palmer, director of *Déjàvu.*]

Brown, Ivor. "The High Froth." *Drama* 87 (Winter 1967): 32–34.

Brown, John Russell. "John Osborne: Theatrical Belief, *Look Back in Anger, The Entertainer, Luther, Inadmissible Evidence* and Other Plays." *Theatre Language: A Study of Arden, Osborne, Pinter, and Wesker.* London: Penguin, 1972. 118–57.

———, ed. *Modern British Dramatists: A Collection of Critical Essays.* Englewood Cliffs, NJ: Prentice-Hall, 1968. ["*Look Back In Anger*" by A.E. Dyson (rpt. *Critical Quarterly,* 1959) and "The Ascension of John Osborne" by Charles Marowitz (focus on *Luther,* rpt. *Tulane Drama Review,* 1962). Introduction,

background material, chronology, and select bibliography.]
Browne, E. Martin. "A Look Round the English Theatre: Summer and Fall, 1966." *Drama Survey* 5 (Winter 1966–67): 297.
Browne, Terry. *Playwrights' Theatre: The English Stage Company at the Royal Court.* London: Pitman, 1975. 22+.
Bruno, Edoardo. "Il Teatro Inglese." *Teatrosessanta: Tradizione, Avanguardia (note sul teatro in Italia negli anni sessanta).* Rome: Bulzoni, 1977. 45–61.
Brustein, Robert. *Seasons of Discontent.* New York: Simon and Schuster, 1965. 196–200. [*Luther.*]
———. "Theatre Chronicle." *Hudson Review* 12 (Spring 1959): 98–101. [*Epitaph for George Dillon.*]
———. *The Theatre of Revolt.* Boston: Little, Brown, 1964. 27, 316.
———. *The Third Theatre.* New York: Knopf, 1969. 146–48. [*Inadmissible Evidence.*]
Bryden, Ronald. "The Entertainer." *Plays and Players* February 1975: 22–23.
———. "*Look Back in Anger.*" *Observer* 3 November 1968.
———. *The Unfinished Hero.* London: Faber and Faber, 1969. 76–80, 81–85.
Buskens, John. "De Humorist: John Osborne—K.N.S. Antwerpen." *Vlaamse Gids* 52.6 (1968): 13.
Byczkowska, Ewa. "The Structure of *Look Back in Anger.*" *Acta Universitatis Wratislaviensis.* 233 (1974): 51–58.
Cairns, David, and Shaun Richards. "No Good Brave Causes? The Alienated Intellectual and the End of Empire." *Literature and History* 14.2 (Autumn 1988): 194–206.
Calisher, Hortense. "Will We Get There by Candlelight?" *Reporter* 4 November 1965: 38+.
Carey, John. "Almost a Gentleman." *Sunday Times,* 3 November 1991, 7: 1.
Carnall, Geoffrey. "Saints and Human Beings: Orwell, Osborne, & Gandhi." *Essays Presented to Amy G. Stock, Professor of English, Rajasthan University, 1961–65.* Jaipur: Rajasthan University Press, 1965. Rpt. in *John Osborne: "Look Back in Anger," A Casebook.* Ed. John Russell Taylor. 129–37. [*Look Back in Anger* and *Luther.*]
Carter, A.V. "John Osborne: A Re-Appraisal." *Revue Belge de Philologie et d'Histoire* 44 (1966): 971–76.
Cave, Richard Allen. *New British Drama in Performance on the London Stage, 1970 to 1985.* New York: St. Martin's Press, 1988. 101+. [*The End of Me Old Cigar, Look Back in Anger, Luther, A Sense of Detachment, Watch It Come Down, West of Suez.*]
Chambers, Colin, and Mike Prior. "John Osborne: The Curate's Ego." *Playwrights' Progress: Patterns of Postwar British Drama.* Oxford: Amber Lane, 1987. 124–34. [*Inadmissible Evidence.*]
Chiari, J. *Landmarks of Contemporary Drama.* London: Jenkins, 1965. 109–15.
Ciarletta, Nicola. "Dall'abiura al Desengano: Osborne tra Lutero e Leonido." *Agnus Voluntario: Dalla "Persona" ala Persona.* Rome: Bulzoni, 1974. 338–50.
Churchill, Randolph. "Portrait of the Artist as an Angry Young Gentleman." *Encounter* 10 (January 1958): 66–68.
Clum, John M. *Acting Gay: Male Homosexuality in Modern Drama.* New York: Columbia UP, 1992. [*A Patriot for Me, Look Back in Anger.*]
———. "'A Culture That Isn't Just Sexual': Dramatizing Gay Male History." *Theatre Journal* 41 (1989): 169–89.
Clurman, Harold. *Lies Like Truth.* New York: Macmillan, 1958. 167, 190–92.
———. "Look Back in Anger." *The Nation* 185 (9 October 1957): 272.
———. *The Naked Image.* New York: Macmillan, 1966. 101–04.
Codignola, Luciano. "Il Nuovo Teatro Inglese." *Il Teatro della Guerra Fredda e Altre Cose.* Urbino: Argalia, 1969. 141–61.

Cohn, Ruby. *Currents in Contemporary Drama*. Bloomington: Indiana UP, 1969. 5–6, 12–15, 123–24, 209.

———. *Retreats from Realism in Recent English Drama*. Cambridge: Cambridge UP, 1991. 19–22, 25–28.

——— and Bernard Dukore, eds. *Twentieth Century Drama: England, Ireland, the United States*. New York: Random House, 1966. 542–44.

Colquitt, Betsy. "Editorial: The Limited View of *Look Back in Anger*." *Descant* 4 (Fall 1959): 2, 48.

Combres, Claude. "Osborne's Imagery in *Look Back in Anger*." *Caliban* (Toulouse) 15 (1978): 35–54.

Cooke, Alistair. "An Angry Young Man on Broadway." *Manchester Guardian* 3 October 1957.

Corina, Leslie. "Still Looking Back." *New Republic* 10 February 1958: 22.

Corrigan, Robert W. "Anger and After: A Decade of British Theatre." *The Theatre in Search of a Fix*. New York: Delacorte, 1973. 301–15.

———. Introduction. *The New Theatre in Europe*. New York: Dell, 1968.

Corsani, Mary. *Il Nuovo Teatro Inglese*. 3rd. ed. Milan: Mursia, 1982. 14–26.

Darricarrère, Jacqueline. "Nuevo Brote de Arte Dramático en Inglaterra." *Revista de Occidente* 35 (February 1966): 217–25.

Davies, Alistair, and Peter Saunders. "Context of English Literature: Literature, Politics, and Society." *Society and Literature, 1945–1970*. Ed. Alan Sinfield. New York: Holmes & Meier, 1983.

De Jongh, Nicholas. *Not in Front of the Audience: Homosexuality on Stage*. London: Routledge, 1992. 3, 52–53, 90, 93, 107, 108, 105–19.

———. "A Patriot in the Closet." *Guardian* 28 March 1992: 14.

———. "The Secret Gay Love of John Osborne." *Evening Standard* 24 January 1995: 12.

Deleanu, Horia. "John Osborne si 'Tinierii Furiosi.'" *Dileme si Pseudodileme*. Bucharest: Eminescu, 1972. 239–53.

Dempsey, D. "Most Angry Fella." *New York Times Magazine* 20 October 1957: 22, 25–27.

Deming, Barbara. "John Osborne's War Against the Philistines." *Hudson Review* 11 (Autumn 1958): 410–19. [*Look Back in Anger* and *The Entertainer*.]

Dennis, Nigel. "Out of the Box." *Encounter* 17 (August 1961): 51–53. [*Luther*.]

Denny, Neville. Afterword. *Luther* by John Osborne. London: Faber and Faber, 1971. 158–70.

Denty, Vera D. "The Psychology of Martin Luther." *Catholic World* 194 (November 1961): 99–105.

Ditsky, John. "Jimmy Porter and the Gospel of Commitment." *Ariel* 8 (April 1977): 71–84.

———. "Osborne's Gospel of Commitment: *Look Back in Anger*." *The Onstage Christ: Studies in the Persistence of a Theme*. London: Vision, 1984. 111–22.

Dixon, Graham A. *Still Looking Back: The Deconstruction of the Angry Young Man in "Look Back in Anger" and "Déjàvu."* *Modern Drama* 37.3 (Fall 1994): 521–29.

Dobree, Bonamy. "No Man's Land." *Swanee Review* 65 (1957): 309–16.

Doménech, Ricardo. "El Teatro Inconformista de John Osborne y Arnold Wesker." *El Teatro, Hoy: Doce Crónicas*. Madrid: Cuadernos para el Diálogo, 1966.

Doty, Gresdna A., and Billy J. Harbin, eds. *Inside the Royal Court Theatre, 1956–1981, Artists Talk*. Baton Rouge: Louisiana State UP, 1990. 3+.

Downer, Alan S. "Total Theatre and Partial Drama: Notes on the New York Theatre, 1965–66." *Quarterly Journal of Speech* 12 (October 1966): 225–36. [*Inadmissible Evidence* and *Death of a Salesman*.]

Driver, Tom F. *Romantic Quest and Modern Query*. New York: Delacorte, 1970. 455–56.

Droll, Morton. "The Politics of Britain's Angry Young Men." *Western Political Quarterly* 12 (June 1959): 555–57.

Dukore, Bernard. "Portrait of a Would-Be Artist." *Western Speech* 30 (Spring 1966): 68–81. [*Epitaph for George Dillon.*]

Duncan, Ronald. "A Preface to the Sixties." *London Magazine* 7 (July 1960): 15–19. [Relation to Shaw and Ibsen.]

Dupee, F.W. "Isn't Life a Terrible Thing, Thank God." *Partisan Review* 25 (Winter 1958): 122–26. Rpt. as "England Now—Ariel or Caliban" in Dupee, *"The King of the Cats" and Other Remarks on Writers and Writing*. New York: Farrar, Strauss and Giroux, 1965. 196–200. [*Look Back in Anger.*]

Dyer, Geoff. "Hot Air from Puffing Johnny." 30 April 1994, Features: 29.

Dyson, A.E. "*Look Back in Anger.*" *Critical Quarterly* 1 (Winter 1959): 318–26. Rpt. in *Modern British Dramatists: A Collection of Critical Essays*. Ed. John Russell Brown. 47–57.

Edgar, David. "The Diverse Progeny of Jimmy Porter." *The Second Time as Farce: Reflections on the Drama of Mean Times*. London: Lawrence & Wishart, 1988. 137–42.

Egan, Robert G. "*Anger* and the Actor: Another Look Back." *Modern Drama* 32.3 (September 1989): 413–24.

Elsom, John. "A Bond with Nahum Tate." *London Magazine* 6 (November 1966): 73–76. [*A Bond Honoured.*]

———. *Post-War British Theatre*. London: Routledge & Kegan Paul, 1976. 72–81. [To *The End of Me Old Cigar.*]

———. *Post-War British Theatre Criticism*. London: Routledge & Kegan Paul, 1981. 74–80.

Esslin, Martin. "Brecht and the English Stage." *Tulane Drama Review* 11 (Winter 1966): 63–70.

———. "John Osborne: Entwicklung eines Rebellen." *Jenseits des Absurden: Aufsätze zum Modernen Drama*. Vienna: Europa, 1972. 97–104.

———. *Reflections: Essays on Modern Theatre*. Garden City, NY: Doubleday, 1969. 78, 81, 84–85, 167. [*Luther.*]

———. *The Theatre of the Absurd*. Garden City, NY: Doubleday, 1969. 101–02, 379.

———. "Where Angry Young Men Led." *New York Times* 8 May 1966, II: 4–5.

Evans, Gareth Lloyd. *The Language of Modern Drama*. London: Dent, 1977. 102–13.

———. "The Seven Lives of Jimmy Porter." *Manchester Guardian Weekly* 30 June 1966: 13.

Evans, Gareth, and Barbara Lloyd. *Plays in Review, 1956–1980*. London: Batsford Academic and Educational, 1985. [*Look Back in Anger, The Entertainer, West of Suez.*]

Faber, M.D. "The Character of Jimmy Porter: An Approach to *Look Back in Anger.*" *Modern Drama* 13 (May 1970): 67–77.

Findlater, Richard. "The Case of P. Slickey." *The Twentieth Century* 167 (January 1960): 29–38.

———. *The Future of the Theatre*. London: Fabian Society, 1959.

———, ed. *At the Royal Court: 25 Years of the English Stage Company*. London: Amber Lane, 1981.

Flint, Martha, and Charlotte Garrard. "*Le Diable et Le Bon Dieu* and an Angry Young Luther." *Journal of European Studies* 2 (1972): 247–55.

Fraser, G.S. *The Modern Writer and His World*. Harmondsworth: Penguin, 1964. 223–33. [Relation to Brecht and Tennessee Williams.]

Freedman, Morris. *The Moral Impulse*. Carbondale: U of Southern Illinois P, 1967. 116–17. [Jimmy Porter and Tennessee Williams's Kowalski (*Streetcar Named Desire*).]

Gale, Steven H. "John Osborne: Look Forward in Fear." *Essays on Contemporary British Drama*. Eds. Hedwig Bock and Albert Wertheim. Munich: Max Hüeber, 1981. 5–29. [*A Patriot for Me.*]

Garstenauer, Maria. "A Selective Study of English History Plays in the Period between 1960 and 1977." *Inst. für Anglistik & Amerikanistik, Univ. Salzburg.* Poetic Drama & Poetic Theory Series 15. Salzburg: 1985.
Gasciogne, Bamber. *Twentieth Century Drama.* New York: Hutchinson, 1962. 196–98. [*Luther.*]
Gaskill, William. "Farewell to a Passionate Man." *Financial Times* 31 December 1994, Arts: IX.
Gassner, John. *Dramatic Soundings.* New York: Crown, 1968. 612–14.
———. *Theatre at the Crossroads.* New York: Holt, Rinehart and Winston, 1960. 173–77.
Gersh, Gabriel. "The Theatre of John Osborne." *Modern Drama* 10 (September 1967): 137–43.
Gianakaris, C.J. "Theatre of the Mind in Miller, Osborne, and Shaffer." *Renascence* 30 (Autumn 1977): 33–42.
Gimeno Giménez, Luisa M. "Los Héroes de John Osborne: Psicología del Rebelde." *Estudios de Filología Inglesa* 1 (1976): 41–53.
Gindin, James. *Postwar British Fiction.* Berkeley: U of California P, 1963. 51–64.
Goetsch, Paul. "Zwei Versionen der Selbstdeutung: Osbornes Stück *Look Back in Anger* und seine Autobiographie *A Better Class of Person.*" *Phantasie und Deutung: Sychologisches Verstehen von Literatur und Film.* Ed. Wolfram Mauser et al. Würzburg: Konigshausen & Neumann, 1986. 239–52.
Goldie, Terry. "Dolls and Homes and rthe Anger of Reality." *World Literature Written in England* 19 (1980): 203–12. [*Look Back in Anger.*]
Gomez, Christine. "Bells and Trumpets, Bears and Squirrels: A Note on Some Recurring Images in *Look Back in Anger.*" *Scholar Critic* 7–8 (1987): 1–9.
———. "The Dramatic Presentation of Incest as a Vehicle of Social Criticism in John Osborne's *Under Plain Cover* and *A Bond Honoured.*" *Indian Scholar* 7 (1985): 11–20.
———. "The Malcontent Outsider in British Drama—Jacobean and Modern." *The Aligarh Journal of English Studies* 12.1 (April 1987): 53–74.
———. "Profaning the Sacred: The Juxtaposition of Incest and Marriage in Ford, Ibsen and Osborne." *The Aligarh Critical Miscellany* 2.1 (1989): 74–84.
Göring, Michael. "Luther und die Reformation als Gegenstand des Historischen Dramas der Gegenwart." *Literaturwissenschaftliches Jahrbuch im Aftrage der Görres-Gesellschaft* 28 (1987): 263–82.
Graef, Hilda. "Why All This Anger?" *Catholic World* 188 (November 1958): 122–28. [*Look Back in Anger.*]
Granger, D. "Themes for New Voices." *London Magazine* 3 (December 1956): 41–47.
Grindin, James. *Postwar British Fiction.* Berkeley: University of California Press, 1963. 51–64. Rpt. in *John Osborne: "Look Back in Anger," A Casebook.* Ed. John Russell Taylor. 183–85. [*Look Back in Anger*, Wesker.]
Gross, Robert F. "Running Out of Words: *Inadmissible Evidence.*" *Words Heard and Overheard: Main Text in Contemporary Drama.* New York: Garland, 1990. 29–55.
Guerrero Zamora, Juan. "Osborne o *Much Ado about Nothing:* Socialmente Hablando." *Historia del Teatro Contemporáneo.* IV. Barcelona: Flors, 1967. 12–26.
Gullì Pugliatti, Paola. "The Distribution of Implicit Information in The Opening Scenes of Dramatic Texts." *Lingua e Stile* 16 (1981): 481–93.
Hague, Angela. "Picaresque Structure and the Angry Young Novel." *Twentieth Century Literature* 32.2 (1986): 209–20.
Hahnloser-Ingold, Magrit. *Das Englische Theater und Bert Brecht: Die Dramen von W.H. Auden, John Osborne, John Arden in ihrer Beziehung zum Epischen Theater von Bert Brecht und den Gemeinsamen Elisabethanischen Quellen.*

Bern: Francke, 1970. 129–73.
Haigh, Kenneth. "Master of the Tirade; Appreciation, John Osborne." *Guardian* 27 December 1994, Features: T5.
Hall, Stuart. "Beyond Naturalism Pure." *Encore* (November–December 1961): 12–19. Rpt. in *The Encore Reader* and *New Theatre Voices of the Fifties and Sixties*. Eds. Charles Marowitz, Tom Milne, and Owen Hale. 212–20. [Wesker, Arden, and Osborne.]
Haltresht, Michael. "Guilt and Expiation in John Osborne's Plays." *Cithara* 16.1 (1976): 33–39.
———. "Sadomasochism in John Osborne's 'A Letter to My Fellow Countrymen.'" *Notes on Contemporary Literature* 4 (Fall 1975): 10–12.
Hammerschmidt, Hildegara. "*Luther.*" *Das Historische Drama in England (1956–1971): Erscheinungsformen und Entwicklungstendenzen*. Weisbaden: Humanitas, 1972. 105–39.
Hancock, Robert. "Anger." *Spectator* 5 April 1957: 438–39. [Reply by Osborne in *Spectator* 13 April 1957.]
Harben, Niloufer. *Twentieth-Century English History Plays*. Totowa, NJ: Barnes & Noble, 1988. 188–212.
Hardwick, Elizabeth. "Theater in New York." *New York Review of Books* 6 June 1966: 5–6. [*Inadmissible Evidence*.]
Hare, Carl. "Creativity and Commitment in the Contemporary British Theatre." *Humanities Association Bulletin* 16 (Spring 1965): 21–28.
Harris, Paul. "The Daughter John Osborne Tried to Forget." *Daily Mail* 16 January 1995: 3.
Hartley, Anthony. "Angry Romantic." *Spectator* 18 May 1957: 688.
Hartley, Walter. "Useful Criticism." *Times* 15 June 1966: 13D.
Harwood, Ronald. *A Night at the Theatre*. London: Methuen, 1982. 135–51. [*The World of Paul Slickey*.]
Hayman, Ronald. *British Theatre Since 1955*. Oxford: Oxford UP, 1979. 34–38.
Heilman, Robert B. *Tragedy and Melodrama: Versions of Experience*. Seattle: U of Washington P, 1966. 138, 145–48, 297–98. [*Look Back in Anger* and *Inadmissible Evidence*.]
Herbert, Jocelyn. "The Price of Loyalty; Appreciation, John Osborne." *Guardian* 27 December 1994, Features: T5.
Hewison, Robert. *In Anger: Culture in the Cold War, 1945–60*. London: Weidenfeld & Nicolson, 1981.
Hidalgo, Pilar. *La Ira y la Palabra: Teatro Inglés Actual*. Madrid: Capsa, 1978. 17–42.
Hilton, Frank. "Britain's New Class." *Encounter* 10 (February 1958): 59–63. [*Look Back in Anger*.]
Hinchliffe, Arnold P. *British Theatre, 1950–1970*. Oxford: Blackwell, 1974. 45–76.
———. "Whatever Happened to John Osborne?" *Contemporary English Drama*. Ed. C.W.E. Bigsby. Stratford-upon-Avon Studies 19. London: Arnold, 1981. 53–63.
Hobson, Harold. "*Look Back in Anger*." *Sunday Times* 13 May 1956.
———. "Political Slant." *Drama* 165.5 (1987): 17–18.
Hirst, D.L. *Comedy of Manners*. London: Methuen, 1979. 81–96. [Plays since *Time Present*.]
Hollis, Christopher. "Keeping Up With the Rices." *Spectator* 18 October 1957: 504–05.
Holloway, John. "Tank in the Stalls: Notes on the School of Anger." *Hudson Review* 10 (Autumn 1957): 424–29.
Hopkins, Nick. "Angry Man of the Theatre Dies." *Daily Mail* 26 December 1994: 1–2.
Howard, Philip. "Angry Old Codgers." *Times* 10 June 1992: 16C.
Hughes, Catherine. "John Osborne's Generation Gap." *America* 11 October 1969: 292–97. [To *Time Present*.]
Huizinga, J.H. "*Look Back* Looked Back On." *New Review* 3, 29 (August 1976): 59–62.

Hunter, G.K. "The World of John Osborne." *Critical Quarterly* 3 (Spring 1961): 76–81. [*The World of Paul Slickey*.]
Huss, Roy. "John Osborne's Backward Half-Way Look." *Modern Drama* 6 (May 1963): 20–25. [*Look Back in Anger*.]
———. "Social Drama as Veiled Neurosis: The Unacknowledged Sadomasochism of John Osborne's *Look Back in Anger*." *The Mindscapes of Art: Dimensions of the Psyche in Fiction, Drama, and Film*. Rutherford, NJ: Fairleigh Dickinson UP, 1986. 121–34.
Hussey, Charles. "Osborne Looks Forward in Anger." *New York Times* 25 October 1964, VI: 71.
I[hlenfeld], K[urt]. "Osborne's Luther." *Eckart Jahrbuch* (1961–62): 312–15.
Iley, Chrissy. "Relationship of the Week." *Sunday Times* 29 January 1995: Features.
Innes, Christopher. "John Osborne: The Rhetoric of Social Alienation." *Modern British Drama, 1890–1990*. Cambridge: Cambridge UP, 1992. 98–113.
Jackson, Kevin. "Jimmy, Don't Be A Hero." *Independent* 14 November 1991: 23.
"John Osborne." *Daily Telegraph* 27 December 1994: 23.
"John Osborne." *New York Times* 27 December 1994: A15+.
"John Osborne." *Times* 27 December 1994, Features: 15.
"John Osborne." *Washington Post* 27 December 1994, Metro: D4.
"John Osborne: A Symposium." London: Royal Court Theatre, 1966. Rpt. in *John Osborne: "Look Back in Anger," A Casebook*. Ed. John Russell Taylor. 185–86. [Retrospective ten years after *Look Back in Anger*; comments by Alan Sillitoe, Peter Brook, Angus Wilson, John Arden, Tony Richardson, George Steiner.]
Karrfalt, David H. "The Social Theme in Osborne's Plays." *Modern Drama* 13 (May 1970): 78–82.
Kato, Kyohei. "An Essay on John Osborne." *Collected Essays by Members of the Faculty*, no. 13. Kyoritsu, Japan: Kyoritsu Women's Junior College, 1969. In Japanese.
Kaul, R.K. "The Origins of Osborne's Pacificism." *Rajesthan University Studies in English* 7 (1974): 49–59.
Kaur, Bhagwan. "Look Back in Anger: A Feminist Approach." *Panjab University Research Bulletin (Arts)* 21.1 (April 1990): 71–80.
Kemp, Peter. "Tantrums and Teddy Bears." *Times Literary Supplement* 19 June 1992: 18.
Kennedy, Andrew K. "Old and New in London Now." *Modern Drama* 11 (February 1969): 437–46. [*Time Present* and *The Hotel in Amsterdam*.]
———. *Six Dramatists in Search of a Language: Studies in Dramatic Language*. Cambridge: Cambridge UP, 1975. 192–212. [Shaw, Eliot, Beckett, Pinter, Osborne, Arden.]
Kerr, Walter. *The Theatre in Spite of Itself*. New York: Simon & Schuster, 1963. 129–31. [Rpt. of earlier review of *Look Back in Anger*.]
———. *Tragedy and Comedy*. New York: Simon & Schuster, 1967. 325–27.
Kershaw, John. "John Osborne: A Modern Romantic" and "*Look Back in Anger*: Language and Character." *The Present Stage*. London: Fontana, 1966. 21–33, 34–41.
King, Seth S. "Britain Damned by John Osborne." *New York Times* 19 August 1961, 4: 1.
Kitchin, Laurence. "Redbrick Luther" and "The Wages of Sex." *Drama in the Sixties: Form and Interpretation*. London: Faber and Faber, 1966. 185–91. [*Luther* and *Inadmissible Evidence*.]
———. *Mid-Century Drama*. London: Faber and Faber, 1960. 99–101, 104–06. Extract rpt. in *John Osborne: "Look Back in Anger," A Casebook*. 179–83.
———. "Realism in the English Mid-Century Drama." *World Theatre* 14 (January–February 1965): 17–26.
———. "Theatre—Nothing But Theatre." *Encounter* 10 (April 1958): 39.

Klotz, Günther. *Britische Dramatiker der Gegenwart*. Berlin: Henschel, 1982. 59–79.
Knight, G. Wilson. "The Kitchen Sink: On Recent Developments in Drama." *Encounter* 11 (December 1963): 48–54. [Relation to absurdist drama.]
Kreuzer, Ingrid. "Der Rückzug in die Höhle: John Osborne, Look Back in Anger (1956)." *Entfremdung und Anpassung: Die Literatur der Angry Young Men in England der Fünfziger Jahre*. Ed. Heinz Nyszkiewiez. Munich: Winkler, 1972. 88–97.
Kuin, J. "Religieuze Problematiek bij Schrijvers Zonder Geloof." *Roeing* 38 (1962): 34–50.
Lahr, John. "Poor Johnny One-Note." *Evergreen Review* 12 December 1968: 61–63, 93–95. Rpt. in *Up Against the Fourth Wall: Essays on Modern Theatre*. New York: Grove Press, 1970. 230–45. Rpt. in *Theatre 72*. Ed. Sheridan Morley. London: Hutchinson, 1973. 185–97. [To *The Hotel in Amsterdam* and *Time Present*.]
Landstone, Charles. "From John Osborne to Shelagh Delaney." *World Theatre* 8 (Autumn 1959): 203–16.
Langman, F.H. "The Generation That Got Lost Staying Home: A Letter to Jimmy Porter." *Theoria* 11 (1958): 29–30.
Laurien, Hanna R. "*Epitaph for George Dillon*." *Zeitgenössche Englische Dichtung: Einfürung in die Englische Literaturbetrachtung mit Interpretation, III: Drama*. Frankfurt: Hirsch, 1968. 170–81.
Leech, Clifford. *The Dramatist's Experience*. New York: Barnes and Noble, 1970. 140.
Leslie, P. "The Angry Young Man Revisited." *Kenyon Review* 27 (Spring 1965): 344–352. [*Look Back in Anger*.]
Levin, Bernard. "How His Genius Struck Me." *Times* 27 December 1994, Features: 12.
Lewis, Allen. *The Contemporary Theatre*. New York: Crown, 1971. 315–35. [To *The Hotel in Amsterdam*.]
Lewis, Peter. "The Lamp Still Burns." *Sunday Telegraph* 7 June 1992, Arts: 114.
Leyburn, Ellen D. "Comedy and Tragedy Transposed." *Yale Review* 53 (Summer 1964): 553–62. [Relation to Miller and Williams.]
Lipp, Solomon. "The 'Little Man' in Paradise." *Mosaic* 10, iv (1977): 15–22.
"*Look Back in Anger* in Sweden." *Times* 13 May 1957: 14B.
Lukic, Darko. "'Novi Val' Engleske Drame Na Primjeru Djela: *The Entertainer* (*Zabavljac*) Johna Osbonea." *Poz* 30 (1988): 221–37.
Lumley, F. "The Invective of John Osborne." *New Trends in Twentieth Century Drama*. London: Barrie and Rockliff, 1967. 221–32. [To *A Bond Honoured*.]
Lutz, Bruno Von. "Das Britische Empire in Ausgewählten Englischen Dramen der Gegenwart: Kritik und Nostalgie." *Literatur in Wissenschaft und Unterricht* 17 (1984): 21–35.
Magee, Bryan. *The New Radicalism*. London: Secker and Warburg, 1962. 180.
Mander, John. *The Writer and Commitment*. London: Secker and Warburg, 1961. 179–88. Extract rpt. in *John Osborne: "Look Back in Anger," A Casebook*. Ed. John Russell Taylor. 143–49.
Mannes, Marya. "A Question of Timing." *Reporter* 14 November 1957: 38.
Marowitz, Charles. "The Ascension of John Osborne." *Tulane Drama Review* 7 (Winter 1962): 175–79. Rpt. in *Modern British Dramatists*. Ed. John Russell Brown. 117–21. Rpt. in *John Osborne: "Look Back in Anger," A Casebook*. Ed. John Russell Taylor. 161–65. [To *Luther*.]
———. *Confessions of a Counterfeit Critic*. London: Eyre Methuen, 1973. [*George Dillon*, *Plays for England*, *A Bond Honoured*.]
Marowitz, Charles, Tom Milne, and Owen Hale, eds. *The Encore Reader: A Chronicle of the New Drama*. London: Methuen, 1965. Reissued as *Theatre Voices of the Fifties and Sixties: Selections from Encore Magazine, 1956–1963*. London: Methuen, 1981. [Selected criticism, very useful background material.]

Martin, Graham. "A Look Back at Osborne." *Universities and Left Review* 7 (Autumn 1959): 37–40.
McCarthy, Mary. "A New Word." *Harper's Bazaar* April 1958: 176–78. Rpt. in *Sights and Spectacles*. London: Heinemann, 1959. 184–96. Rpt. in *John Osborne: "Look Back in Anger," A Casebook*. Ed. John Russell Taylor. 150–60. [*Look Back in Anger* and *The Entertainer*, relation to Shaw.]
———. "Odd Man In." *Partisan Review* 26 (Winter 1959): 100–06. [*Epitaph for George Dillon*; relation to Genet and O'Neill.]
Medwin, Michael. "Passion for Honesty; Appreciation, John Osborne." *Guardian* 27 December 1994, Features: T5.
———. "Verdict on Osborne." *Observer* 4 July 1965: 17. [*A Patriot for Me*.]
Mennemeier, Franz N. *Das Moderne Drama des Auslandes*. 3rd ed. Düsseldorf: Bagel, 1976. 135–46.
Metwally, Abdalla A. "Jimmy Porter, the Angry Young Man." *Studies in Modern Drama*, II. Beirut: Beirut Arab U, 1971. 68–96.
Mihályi, Gábor. *Végjáték*. Budapest: Gondolat, 1971. 139–53.
Miller, Karl. "Second Opinion, 2: John Osborne." *Sunday Times Magazine* 20 November 1966: 83, 86.
Millgate, Michael. "A Communication: A Good Word for England." *Partisan Review* 24 (Summer 1957): 428–31. [Jimmy Porter and Kingsley Amis's *Lucky Jim*.]
———. "An Uncertain Feeling in England." *New Republic* 9 September 1957: 16–17.
Milne, Tom. "The Hidden Face of Violence." *Encore* 7.1 (1960): 14–20. Rpt. in *Modern British Dramatists*, ed. John Russell Brown, 38–46, and *The Encore Reader*, eds. Charles Marowitz, Tom Milne, and Owen Hale. 116–24. [Relation to Eliot, Fry, and Pinter.]
———. "*Luther* and *The Devils*." *New Left Review* 12 (November–December 1961): 55–57.
"Mr. Osborne Looks On In Anger." *Times* 9 June 1966: 14D.
Morgan, Edwin. "That Uncertain Feeling." *The Encore Reader*. Ed. by Charles Marowitz, Tom Milne, and Owen Hale. London: Methuen, 1965. 52–56. Rpt. in *John Osborne: "Look Back in Anger," A Casebook*. 138–42. [Relation to Miller and Williams.]
"Moscow Looks Back in Anger." *Times* 19 December 1969: 7E.
Mortimer, John. "The Angry Young Man Who Stayed That Way." *New York Times* 8 January 1995, Arts: 5, 32.
———. "Looking Back at John Osborne and a Lifetime of Anger." *International Herald Tribune* 11 January 1995, Feature.
Murphy, Brian. "Jimmy Porter's Past: The Logic of Rage in *Look Back in Anger*." *Midwest Quarterly* 18 (July 1977): 361–73.
Nathan, David. "John Osborne—Is His Anger Simmering?" *The Curtain Rises*. Comp. Dick Richards. London: Frewin, 1966. 244–47.
Neumann, Fritz-Wilhelm. "*Look Back in Anger*: Psychoanalyse und Solzialer Kontext." *Anglistik & Englischunterricht* 7 (February 1979): 27–38.
Nicoll, Allardyce. "Somewhat in a New Dimension." *Contemporary Theatre*. Eds. John Russell Brown and Bernard Harris. Stratford-upon-Avon Studies, no. 4. London: Arnold, 1962. 77–95. Rpt. in *John Osborne: "Look Back in Anger," A Casebook*. Ed. John Russell Taylor. 177–79. [Relation to earlier dramatists.]
Nichols, Peter. "Always the Intruder." *Guardian* 31 December 1994, Features: 31.
Nightingale, Benedict. "Come Back, Jimmy; All is Unforgiven." *Times* 15 June 1992: 12.
———. "The Fatality of Hatred: On John Osborne." *Encounter* 58. 5 (May 1982): 63–70.
———. "Osborne's Old Times." *New Statesman*, 27 August 1971: 277.
———. "Outing the Real John Osborne." *Times* 28 January 1995: Features.
Novick, Julius. *Beyond Broadway*. New York: Hill and Wang, 1968. 150.
O'Brien, Charles H. "Osborne's *Luther* and the Humanistic Tradition." *Renascence*

21 (Winter 1969): 59–63.

O'Connor, John J. "The Three Faces of John Osborne." *Audience* 6 (Spring 1969): 108–13. [*Epitaph for George Dillon, Look Back in Anger*, and *The Entertainer*.]

Oppel, Horst. "John Osborne: *Look Back in Anger*." In *Das Moderne Englische Drama: Interpretationen*. Berlin: Erich Schmidt, 1963. 316–30.

Orr, John. "The Absence of Tragedy in the English Theatre." *Tragic Drama and Modern Society: Studies in the Social and Literary Theory of Drama from 1870 to the Present*. London: Macmillan, 1981. 241–62.

"Osborne's Anger." *New Yorker* 20 February 1995: 18+.

"Osborne's Random Sortie." *Times* 23 January 1968: 81.

Osztovits, Levente. "John Osborne." *Az Angel Irodalom a Huszadik Században*, III. Eds. Laszlo Báti and István Kristó-Nagy. Budapest: Gundolat, 1970. 231–52.

Owen, Michael. "The Truth About Johnny O." *Evening Standard* 10 June 1993: 29. [Trevor Eve on *Inadmissible Evidence* at the National Theatre.]

Page, Anthony. "Inadmissible Epitaph." *Guardian Supplement* 6 June 1992: 12–13.

Pálffy, István. "The Dialectics of Experience and Intention in Contemporary English Drama." *Studies in English American* (Budapest) 4 (1978): 229–42.

———. "Az Élmény és Szándék Dialektikája a Modern Angol Drámában." *Filológiai Közlöny* 24 (January–March 1978): 30–36.

———. "John Osborne: Harag és Formakeresés." *Az új Angol Dráma—mint a 'Valóság Drámája.'* Budapest: Akadémiai, 1978. 85–123.

Palmer, Helen H., and Anne Jane Dyson. *European Drama Criticism*. Hamden, CT: Shoestring Press, 1968. 305–10.

Parsons, Sandra, Keith Waterhouse, and Lynda Lee-Potter. "Angry with Everyone—Especially Women." *Daily Mail* 27 December 1994: 32–33.

Pasquier, Marie, et al. *Le Nouveau Théâtre Anglais*. Paris: Colin, 1969. 102–29.

Peinert, Dietrich. "'Bear' and 'Squirrel' in John Osborne's *Look Back in Anger*." *Literatur in Wissenschaft und Unterricht* (Kiel) 1 (1968): 117–22.

Peel, Marie. "Power and Pattern v. Morality 1. Poetry and Drama." *Books and Bookmen* 18.1 (1972): 38–42.

———. "Violence in Literature." *Books and Bookmen* 17.5 (1972): 20–24. [*Look Back in Anger*.]

Pérez Gallego, Cándido. *Literatura y Reveldía en la Inglaterra Actual: Los "Angry Young Men," un Movimiento Social de los Años Cincuenta*. Madrid: Consejo Superior de Investigaciones Cientificas, Instituto Miguel de Cervantes, 1968. 129–43.

Pfister, Manfred. "Music Hall und Moderne Drama: Populäre Komik als Medium und Thema im Zeitgenössischen Englischen Theater." *Anglistentag 1980, Giessen: Tagungsbeiträge und Berichte im Auftrage des Vorstandes*. Ed. Herbert Graves. Grossen-Linden: Hoffmann, 1981. 117–38. [*The Entertainer*.]

Platz, Norbert H. "Coriolan und das Persönliche in der Politik: John Osbornes *A Place Calling Itself Rome*." *Anglo-Amerikanische Shakespeare-Bearbeitungen des 20. Jahrhunderts*. Ed. Horst Priessnitz. Darmstadt: Wissenschaflitche, 1980. 190–202.

———. "*Inadmissible Evidence*." *Das Zeitgenössche Englische Drama: Einfürung, Interpretation*. Eds. Klaus D. Fense and Norman Platz. Frankfurt: Athenäum, 1975. 179–98.

Playfair, Giles. "Phoney War." *Spectator* 17 June 1966: 754.

Popkin, Henry. "Brechtian Europe." *Drama Review*, 12 (Fall 1967): 156–57. [*Luther*.]

———. "Theatre II." *Kenyon Review* 20 (Spring 1958): 309–10. [*Look Back in Anger*.]

———. "Williams, Osborne, or Beckett?" *New York Times Book Review* 13 November 1969: 32–33, 119–21.

Post, Robert M. "The Outsider in the Plays of John Osborne." *Southern Speech Communication Journal* 39 (Fall 1973): 63–75.

Price, Martin. "The London Season." *Modern Drama* 1 (May 1958): 53–59. [*The Entertainer.*]

"Profile: John Osborne." *Observer* 17 May 1959.

"Putting Drama in Touch with Contemporary Life: Two Years of the English Stage Company." *Times* 19 March 1958: 3B.

Raab, Michael. "*The Entertainer*: die Music Hall als Symbol für England." "*The Music Hall Is Dying*": *Die Thematisierung der Unterhaltungsindustrie im Englischen Gegenwartsdrama.* Tübingen: Niemeyer, 1989. 134–62.

Rabey, David I. *British and Irish Political Drama in the Twentieth Century: Implicating the Audience.* Basingstoke: Macmillan, 1986. 78–84.

Raby, Astria. "John Osborne: Tres Variaciones Sobre un Tema." *Atenea* 417 (1967): 37–59.

Rillie, John A.M. "*The Entertainer.*" *Insight IV: Analyses of Modern British and American Drama.* Ed. Hermann J. Weiand. Frankfurt: Hirschgraben, 1975. 94–102.

Roberts, Mark. *The Tradition of Romantic Morality.* London: Macmillan, 1973. 1–26, 78–84. [*Look Back in Anger.*]

Roberts, Philip. *The Royal Court Theatre, 1965–1972.* London: Routledge & Kegan Paul, 1986. 5+.

Robinson, David. "*Look Back in Anger.*" *Sight and Sound* 29, 3–4 (Summer–Autumn 1959): 122–5, 179.

Robson, W.W. *Modern British Literature.* London: Oxford UP, 1970. 116, 157–58.

Rogers, Daniel. "*Look Back in Anger*—to George Orwell." *Notes & Queries* 9 (1962): 310–11.

———. "'Not for Insolence, But Seriously': John Osborne's Adaptation of *La Fianza Satisfecha.*" *Durham University Journal* 29 (1968): 146–70. [*A Bond Honoured.*]

Rogoff, Gordon. "Richard's Himself Again: Journey to an Actor's Theatre." *Tulane Drama Review* 11 (Winter 1966): 29–40.

Rollins, Ronald G. "Carroll and Osborne: Alice and Alison in Wild Wonderland." *Forum* (Houston) 7 (Summer 1969): 16–20.

Roy, Emil. *British Drama Since Shaw.* Carbondale: U of Southern Illinois P, 1972. 100, 106, 115, 123–24, 128. [*Inadmissible Evidence.*]

Rupp, Gordon E. "John Osborne and the Historical Luther." *The Expository Times* 73 (February 1962): 147–51. [Erik Erickson's *Young Man Luther.*]

———. "Luther and Mr. Osborne." *Cambridge Quarterly* 1 (Winter 1965–66): 28–42.

Rusinko, Susan. "John Osborne: An Angry Young Man." *British Drama 1950 to the Present: A Critical History.* Boston: Twayne, 1989. 35–46.

Rutherford, Malcolm. "Kitchen-Sink Nostalgia." *Encounter* 73, 4 (November 1989): 74–75.

Sahl, Hans. "John Osborne." *Welt und Wort* 14 (1959): 36–37.

Saltzman, Arthur M. "John Osborne." *Critical Survey of Drama.* Vol. 4. Ed. Frank N. Magill. Englewood Cliffs, NJ: Salem Press, 1985. 1428–37.

Sarcevic, Petar. "Bijes i zvuk Johna Osbornea." *Ruk* 15 (1969): 163–70.

Schäfer, Karl K. "*Look Back in Anger.*" *Hundlung im Neueren Britischen Drama: Eine Untersuchung an Dramen der Fünfziger und Sechziger Jahre.* Frankfurt: Fischer, 1985. 86–101.

Schmidt, William E. "John Osborne, British Playwright, Dies at 65." *New York Times* 27 December 1994: A15.

Schulz, Dieter. "Ritual und Spiel in John Osborne's *Look Back in Anger.*" *Sprachkunst: Beiträge zur Literaturwissenschaft* 9, 1 (1978): 171–82.

Schwanitz, Dietrich. "John Osborne: *The Entertainer*—und John Osborne, The Entertainer." *Englisches Drama von Beckett bis Bond.* Ed. Henrick F. Plett. Munich: Fink: 1982. 100–17.

Scott-Kilvert, Ian. "The Hero in Search of a Dramatist: The Plays of John Osborne."

Encounter 11 (December 1957): 26-30.

Selz, Jean. "John Osborne et Jimmy Porter." *Les Lettres Nouvelles* 61 (June 1958): 908-11.

Servadio, Gaia. "Il Dandy con il Metra Spara Salve." *La Fiers Litteraria* 1 August 1968: 14.

Seymour, Alan. "Maturing Vision." *London Magazine* 5 (October 1965): 75-79. [*A Patriot for Me.*]

―――. "Osborne V.C." *London Magazine* 5 (May 1965): 69-74. [*Epitaph for George Dillon.*]

Shayon, Robert Lewis. "*Luther*, Whose Identity Crisis?" *Saturday Review* 17 February 1968: 42.

Sherry, Ruth Forbes. "Angry Young Men." *Trace* (May-June 1960): 33-37.

Shostakov, D. "Monologi Dzhona Osborne." *Inostranaya Literatura* 7 (1967): 112-16.

Sierig, Hartmut. "Der Junge Mann Luther." *Narren und Totentänzer: Eine Theologische Interpretation Moderner Dramatik*. Hamburg: Argentur des Rauben Hauses, 1968. 172-84.

Sigal, Clancy. "Looking Back Without Anger." *Commonweal* 8 (May 1970): 186-88.

Sinfield, Alan. "The Theatre and Its Audiences." *Society and Literature, 1945-1970*. Ed. Alan Sinfield. New York: Holmes & Meier, 1983. 173-97.

Sked, Alan. "A Patriot for Whom?: Colonel Redl and a Question of Identity." *History Today* 36 (July 1986): 9-14.

Slavina, M.N. "Rechevaia Kharakteristika Personazhei v Sotsiolisticheskom Aspekte." *Vestnik Leningradskogo Universiteta. Seriia Istorii, Iazyka i Literatury* 3 (July 1987): 111-13. [*The Entertainer.*]

Spacks, Patricia Meyer. "Confrontation and Escape in Two Social Dramas." *Modern Drama* 11 (May 1968): 61-72. [*Look Back in Anger* and *A Doll's House.*]

Spalter, Max. "Five Examples of How to Write a Brechtian Play That Is Not Really Brechtian." *Educational Theatre Journal* 27 (May 1975): 220-35. [*Luther.*]

Spanos, William V. *The Christian Tradition in Modern British Verse Drama*. New Brunswick, NJ: Rutgers UP, 1967. 336-37. [Relation to Eliot and Fry.]

Spencer, Lois. "*Look Back in Anger.*" *Insight II: Analyses of Modern British Literature*. Eds. John V. Hagopian and Martin Dolch. Frankfurt: Hirsch, 1970. 277-84.

Spender, Stephen. "London Letter: Anglo-Saxon Attitudes." *Partisan Review* 25 (Winter 1958): 110-16. [Relation to Dylan Thomas.]

―――. "Notes from a Diary." *Encounter* 7 (August 1956): 71.

―――. "Notes from a Diary." *Encounter* 11 (December 1958): 75-77.

Stefanov, Vasil. "Spoluki na Mladostta. Piesata 'Osborne ses Gnjai Nazad' vav Varnenskija Dramat Teatar." *Teatar* 21.3 (1968): 43-44.

Stoll, Karl H. "Osbornes Charaktere." *Harold Pinter: Ein Beitrag zur Typologie des Neuen Englischen Dramas*. Düsseldorf: Bagel, 1977. 182-96.

Stoppard, Tom. "'A Very Satirical Thing Happened to Me on the Way to the Theatre Tonight." *Encore* 10 (March-April 1963): 33-36. [*Under Plain Cover.*]

Stratmann, Gerd. "Der Böse Zauber der Verhältnisse: Formen und Funktion der Mythisierung im Modernen Englischen Drama." *Poetica* 9.1 (1977): 62-97.

Stroman, B. "Maarten Luther en John Osborne." *Vlaamse Gids* 45 (September 1961): 633-35.

―――. "Tweërlei Aftotendheid." *Vlaamse Gids* 49 (November 1965): 746-47.

Styan, J.L. *The Dark Comedy: The Development of Modern Comic Tragedy*. 2nd ed. Cambridge: Cambridge UP, 1968. [*The Entertainer*, *Look Back in Anger*, and *Luther.*]

Sundrann, Jean. "The Necessary Illusion." *Antioch Review* 18 (Summer 1958): 236-44. [*The Entertainer.*]

"Sweete Alisoun." *Times Literary Supplement* 25 (January 1957): 49.

Takada, Mineo. "A Non-U-Intelligenstia Dramatist." *Annual Reports of Studies*. Vol.

23. Kyoto: Doshisha Women's College of Liberal Arts, 1972. 146-88.
Taylor, John Russell. "John Osborne." *Anger and After: A Guide to the New British Drama*. London: Methuen, 1962. 39-66. Review ed., Methuen, 1969. Review extract rpt. in *John Osborne: "Look Back in Anger," A Casebook*. Ed. John Russell Taylor. 75-96. [To *Plays for England: The Blood of the Bambergs* and *Under Plain Cover*.]
———. *The Angry Theatre*. New York: Hill and Wang, 1962. 39-57.
———. "British Drama of the Sixties." *On Contemporary Literature*. Ed. Richard Kostelanetz. New York: Avon, 1964. 90-96.
———. "*Inadmissible Evidence.*" *Encore* 9 (November-December 1964): 43-46. Rpt. in *John Osborne: "Look Back in Anger," A Casebook*. Ed. John Russell Taylor. 96-100.
———. "Ten Years of the English Stage Company." *Tulane Drama Review* 11 (Winter 1966): 120-31. [Decade following *Look Back in Anger*.]
Tetzeli von Rosador, Kurt. *Das Englische Geschichtsdrama seit Shaw*. Heidelburg: Winter 1976. 268-78.
Thomas, Michael. "Translator's Dilemma." *Plays and Players* 13.6 (1966): 53.
Toschi, Gastone. *Angoscia e Solitudine Nel Teatro Contemporaneo*. Fossano: Esperienze, 1970. 101-14.
Trilling, Ossia. "The New English Realism." *Tulane Drama Review* 7 (Winter 1962): 184-93.
———. "The Young British Drama." *Modern Drama* 111 (September 1960): 168-77.
Trussler, Simon. "British Neo-Naturalism." *The Drama Review* 23 (Winter 1968): 130-36. [Influence on Wesker and others.]
———. "His Very Own Golden City: Interview." *Tulane Drama Review* 11 (Winter 1966): 192-202. [Interview with Arnold Wesker.]
———. "John Osborne." *British Writers, Supplement 1*. New York: Scribners, 1987. 329-40.
———. "John Osborne." *Dramatists: Great Writers of the English Language*. Vol. 3. Ed. James Vinson. New York: St. Martin's Press, 1979. 449-52.
Tschudin, Marcus. "Luther." *A Writer's Theatre: George Devine and the English Stage Company at the Royal Court*. Bern: Lang, 1972. 183-216.
Tynan, Kenneth. "Men of Anger." *Holiday* 23 (April 1958), 92-93, 177, 181-82, 184. Rpt. as "The Angry Young Movement" in *Tynan on Theatre*.
———. "A Phony or a Genius?" *Observer* 16 February 1958: 12. Rpt. in *Curtains: Selections from the Drama Criticism and Related Writings*. New York: Atheneum, 1961. 205-207. [*Epitaph for George Dillon*.]
———. *Tynan on Theatre*. Harmondsworth: Penguin, 1964. 130-32, 173-76, 205-07. [*Look Back in Anger*, *The Entertainer*, and *Epitaph for George Dillon*.]
———. *Tynan Right and Left*. New York: Atheneum, 1967. 5-6, 77-79, 109-10.
———. *A View of the English Stage, 1944-1965*. London: Methuen, 1975. 11+.
———. "The Voice of the Young." *Observer* 13 May 1956: 11. [Famous positive review of *Look Back in Anger*.] Rpt. in *Curtains*. New York: Atheneum, 1961. 130-32.
Valette, Jacques. "Lettres Anglo-Saxonnes: La Souete Anglaise et le Théâtre de John Osborne." *Mercure de France* 333 (June 1958): 342-46.
Van der Veen, Adriaan. "Boze Jongelieden in een Zich Vernieuwend Engeland." *Vlaamse Gids* 43 (April 1959): 232-36.
Van Lokhorst, Emmy. "Toneelkroniek: *Wrok Tegen Het Verleden*." *De Gids* 120.112 (1957): 404-07.
Wagener, Christel. "John Osbornes Dramenschaffen: Thesen zu einer Kritik seiner Entwicklung bis 1973." *Political Developments on the British Stage in the Sixties and Seventies*. Rostock: Wilhelm-Pieck U, 1976. 110-15.
Wandor, Micheline. *Carry on, Understudies*. London: Routledge & Kegan Paul, 1981. 140-41, 147-48.

———. "Heroism, Cries of Manhood and the Kitchen Sink: *Look Back in Anger* and *A Patriot for Me* by John Osborne." *Look Back in Gender: Sexuality and the Family in Post-War British Drama*. London: Methuen, 1987. 8–18.
Ward, A.C. *Twentieth-Century English Literature*. London: Methuen, 1964. 11, 138, 140. [*Look Back in Anger*.]
Wardle, Irving. "Looking Back on Osborne's Anger." *New Society* 1 July 1965: 22–23.
———. "Osborne and the Critics." *New Society* 16 June 1966: 22–23.
———. "Revolt Against the West End." *Horizon* 5 (January 1963): 26–33.
———. "The World of John Osborne." *Times* 6 July 1968: 18E.
———. *The Theatres of George Devine*. London: Cape, 1978. [On the Royal Court Theatre.]
Watson, George. "Osborne, Pinter, Stoppard." *British Literature Since 1945*. Basingstoke: Macmillan, 1991. 145–74.
———. "Osborne, Pinter, Stoppard: A Playful Look at London since 1956." *Virginia Quarterly Review: A National Journal of Literature and Discussion* 62 (Spring 1986): 271–84.
Watt, David. "Class Report." *Encore* (September 1957). Rpt. in *The Encore Reader*. Eds. Charles Marowitz, Tom Milne, and Owen Hale. 56–61. [*Look Back in Anger*.]
Weise, Wolf D. *Die 'Neuen Englishchen Dramatiker in Ihrem Verhältnis su Brecht: Unter Besoonderer Berücksichtugung von Wesker, Osborne, und Arden*. Bucharest: Gehlen, 1969. 111–40.
Weiss, Samuel. "Osborne's Angry Young Play." *Educational Theatre Journal* 12 (December 1960): 285–88. [*Look Back in Anger*.]
Wellwarth, George E. "John Osborne: 'Angry Young Man'?" *The Theatre of Protest and Paradox*. New York: New York UP, 1964. 222–34. Rpt. in *John Osborne: "Look Back in Anger," A Casebook*. Ed. John Russell Taylor. 117–28. [Two Plays for England: Blood of the Bambergs, and Under Plain Cover.]
Wendal, Karl H. "John Osborne." *Englische Literatur der Gegenwart in Einzeldarstellungen*. Ed. Horst W. Drescher. Stutgart: Kröner, 1970. 377–406.
Wesker, Arnold. "Center 42: The Secret Reins." *Encounter* 25 (March 1962): 3–6. [*Look Back in Anger*.]
———. "An Entertainer's Farewell." *Guardian* 11 January 1995, Features: T14.
West, Atlick. "John Osborne." *Filologiai Kozlony* 9 (January–June 1963): 129–34.
Whiting, John. "*Luther*." *London Magazine* 1 (October 1961): 57–59. Rpt. in *John Whiting on Theatre*. London: Alan Ross, 1966. 37–44.
Williams, Melvin G. "Looking Backward: Osborne's *Luther*." *Occasional Review* 6 (Summer 1977): 87–94.
Williams, Raymond. "*Look Back in Anger*." *Drama from Ibsen to Brecht*. New York: Oxford UP, 1969. 318–22.
———. "The New English Drama." *Twentieth Century* 170 (1961): 168–80. Rpt. in *Modern British Dramatists*. Ed. John Russell Brown. 26–37.
———. "Recent English Drama." *The Modern Age*. Ed. Boris Ford. Harmondsworth: Penguin, 1964. 487–88, 501–07. [Osborne and the Royal Court Theatre.]
Wilson, A. "New Playwrights." *Partisan Review*, 25 (Fall 1959): 631–34.
Winkler, Elizabeth H. "The Ambivalence of Popular Culture . . . : John Osborne." *The Function of Song in Contemporary British Drama*." Newark, DE: Delaware UP, 1990. 228–35.
Wiszniowska, Marta. "Re-interpreting Osborne." *Studia Anglica Posnaniensia* 12 (1980): 143–49.
Wohlfahrt, Paul. "'Berliner Westwochen' mit Osborne's *Luther*." *Begegnung* 18 (September 1963): 262.
Wolf, Matt. "Beyond 'Anger.'" *Chicago Tribune* 19 July 1992, Arts: 20.
Worsely, T.C. "Minority Culture." *New Statesman* 26 January 1957: 97.
Worth, Katharine J. "The Angry Young Man: John Osborne." *Experimental Drama*.

Ed. William A. Armstrong. London: G. Bell, 1963. 147–68. Rpt. in *John Osborne: "Look Back in Anger," A Casebook*. Ed. John Russell Taylor. 101–16. [To *Luther*; relation to Shaw and Galsworthy.]

———. *Revolution in Modern English Drama*. London: Bell, 1973. 67–85. [Osborne, Shaw, and Coward]

———. "Shaw and John Osborne." *The Shavian*. 2 (October 1964): 29–35.

"Wrath at the Helm?" *Times* 26 May 1969: 7C.

Wyatt, Woodrow. *Distinguished for Talent*. London: Hutchinson, 1958. 116–22. [*Look Back in Anger*.]

Young, Wayland. "London Letter." *Kenyon Review* 17 (Autumn 1956): 642–47.

Zapf, Hubert. "Abstrakte Gesellschaft und Modernes Englisches Drama: Das Beispiel von John Osbornes *Look Back in Anger*." *Forum Modernes Theater*, 1.1 (1986): 35–55.

———. "John Osborne, *Look Back in Anger*: Die Exposition der Problematik." *Das Drama in der Abstraken Gesellschaft: zur Theorie und Struktur des Modernen Englischen Dramas*. Tübingen: Niemeyer, 1988. 61–86.

Zyl, John van. "Film Adaptation as an Interpretation of a Play: The Case of *Look Back in Anger*." *South African Theatre Journal* 3.2 (September 1989): 4–18.

Dissertations

Andrucki, Martin E. "Confused Voices: A Study in Social Ideas and Dramatic Form in the Plays of John Osborne and Clifford Odets." *American Doctoral Dissertations* AAC0295295 (Harvard U 1975).

Athanason, Arthur Nicholas. "John Osborne: From Apprenticeship to Artistic Maturity." *Dissertation Abstracts International* 33: 6898A–12A (Pennsylvania State U 1972).

Brohaugh, Clair Bernhardt. "John Osborne and the Theme of Authority." *Dissertation Abstracts International* 36: 8068A–12A (U of Nebraska 1975).

Brookbank, Charles D. "The Theme of Boredom in Selected Modern Dramas." *Dissertation Abstracts International* 32:5929A–10A (U of Minnesota 1971).

Brown, Christy Lynn. "Alienation Versus Commitment: The Role of the Artist Figure in Contemporary British Drama." *Dissertation Abstracts International* 43:2675–08A (Indiana U 1982).

Budd, Dirk Ronald. "The Vicissitudes of the Osborne Protest from 1956 to 1964." *Dissertation Abstracts International* 30:1163A–03A (U of Pennsylvania 1968).

Conlon, Patrick Owen. "Social Commentary in Contemporary Great Britain, as Reflected in the Plays of John Osborne, Harold Pinter, and Arnold Wesker." *Dissertation Abstracts International* 29:3713A–10A (Northwestern U 1968).

Cosgrove, James Daniel. "The Rebel in Modern Drama (Ibsen, Brecht, Eliot, Shaw, Osborne)." *Dissertation Abstracts International* 49:2864–10A (St. John's U 1988).

Gamber, Cayo Elizabeth Dumais. "No Place Like Home: Feminism, Semiotics, and Staged Space." *Dissertation Abstracts International* 52:0546–02A (George Washington U 1991).

Gilliard, Bari Lynn. "Men in Crisis: Vision and Form in John Osborne's Major Plays." *Dissertation Abstracts International* 36:1526A–3A (U of Utah 1975).

Hinchey, James Francis. "John Osborne as a Social Critic and Dramatic Artist: The Theme of Isolation and Estrangement in His Works." *Dissertation Abstracts International* 32:6977A–12A (U of Wisconsin 1972).

Lee, Sandra Marie. "John Osborne and the Ironic Comedy of Failure: A Study of Comic Subject and Techniques." *Dissertation Abstracts International* 36:320A–1A (Loyola U 1975).

Mixon, Harold Dean. "An Analysis of Four Plays by John Osborne as Social Drama." *Eureka* (OColQ) 1817763 (Florida State U 1963).

Moore, Robert Barry. "The Published Stage Plays of John Osborne, 1956–1968: A Critical Exploration." *Dissertation Abstracts International* 32:7123–12A (U of Denver 1971).
Orley, Ray. "The Separated Self: Alienation as a Major Theme in the Plays of John Osborne, Arnold Wesker, and Harold Pinter, 1956–1971." *Dissertation Abstracts International* 37:5445–09A (U of California, Berkeley, 1976).
Reader, Robert Dean. "Illusion and Reality: An Approach to the 'History Play' Using *Luther* by John Osborne as the Model." *Dissertation Abstracts International* 46:3537–12A (U of Michigan 1986).
Soliman, Mohammad Fathi. "Modes of Communication in Modern English Drama with Special Reference to John Osborne, Harold Pinter and Arnold Wesker." *Dissertation Abstracts International* 51:0171–01A (U of Keele, U.K., 1987).
Strane, Robert Erskine. "Gasconade for the End of the World: The Plays of John Osborne." *American Doctoral Dissertations* AAC1239151 (Yale 1966).
Van Niel, Pieter January "The Plays of John Osborne—The Experiments and the Results." *Dissertation Abstracts International* 33:4576–08A (Stanford U 1972).

Bibliographies

Adelman, Irving, and Rita Dworkin. *Modern Drama: A Checklist of Critical Literature on Twentieth Century Plays*. Metuchen, NJ: Scarecrow Press, 1967. 236–38.
Bailey, Shirley Jean. "John Osborne: A Bibliography." *Twentieth Century Literature*, 7 (1961): 118–120.
Carpenter, Charles A. "John Osborne." *Modern Drama Scholarship and Criticism 1966–80: An International Bibliography*. Toronto: U of Toronto P, 1986. 110–11. [Thorough, with many non-English sources.]
Coleman, Arthur, and Gary R. Tyler. *Drama Criticism*. Denver: Swallow Press, 1966. 169–71.
Harris, Richard Hough. *Modern Drama in America and England, 1950–1970: A Guide to Information Services*. Detroit, MI: Gale Research Co., 1982. 393–401. [Annotated, early material.]
King, Kimball. *Twenty Modern British Playwrights: A Bibliography, 1956–1976*. New York: Garland, 1977. 85–124. [Thorough, annotated.]
Northouse, Cameron, and Thomas P. Walsh. *John Osborne: A Reference Guide*. Boston: G.K. Hall, 1974. [Annotated.]
Palmer, Helen H., and Dyson, Anne J. "John James Osborne." *European Drama Criticism*. Hamden, CT: Shoestring Press, 1968: 305–10.
Salem, James M., ed. *A Guide to Critical Reviews. Part 3: British and Continental Drama from Ibsen to Pinter*. Metuchen, NJ: Scarecrow Press, 1968. 178–81,
Stoll, Karl-Heinz. *The British Drama: A Bibliography with Particular Reference to Arden, Bond, Osborne, Pinter, Wesker*. Bern: Lang, 1975.

Contributors

Ronald Bryden reviewed the first productions of John Osborne's plays of the 1960s for the *New Statesman* magazine and, subsequently, for the London *Observer*. He is an Emeritus Professor of the Graduate Centre for the Study of Drama at the University of Toronto.

William W. Demastes is Associate Professor and Director of Graduate Studies of English at Louisiana State University, Baton Rouge. He is author of *Beyond Naturalism: A New Realism in American Theatre* (1988) and *Clifford Odets: A Research and Production Sourcebook* (1991) and has written articles on modern drama in such journals as *Modern Drama, Theatre Journal*, and *New Theatre Quarterly*. He is editing a series of books entitled *Modern Dramatists Research* and *Production Sourcebooks*. In addition, he is editing a four-volume series on modern American, British, and Irish playwrights, and is putting together a collection of essays on American Dramatic Realism.

Patricia D. Denison teaches at Barnard College, Columbia University, in the departments of English and Theatre. She has published articles on modern and Victorian drama in *Modern Drama* and an essay on James Herne in *Realism and the American Dramatic Tradition*. She has recently completed a book on Arthur W. Pinero and late-nineteenth-century British drama.

David Galef teaches British literature at the University of Mississippi. He has published essays on Conrad, Forster, Joyce, Woolf, T.S. Eliot, and others. His book, *The Supporting Cast: A Study of Flat and Minor Characters*, was published by Pennsylvania State UP in 1993.

Luc M. Gilleman is an Assistant Professor at Smith College. His dissertation is entitled "Sense and System: A Contextual Study of Language-Oriented Realistic Plays in Postwar Britain," and his articles on Harold Pinter and John Osborne appeared in the Belgian journal *De Vlaamse Gids* and in *Post-War Literatures in English*. He has also written about Julian Beck and Eric Bentley for the *American National Biography*.

Robert Gordon is Senior Lecturer in Drama at Goldsmith's College, University of London. He has worked as a professional actor and director and in 1990 appeared in *MerryGoRound: A Chekhov Quartet* in London, Moscow, and Yalta. He is the author of *Red Earth*, a play about women's experiences of apartheid, performed in London in 1985, and *Waterloo Road*, presented at the Young Vic Studio in 1987. Publications include articles on Orton, Rattigan, Wycherley, Congreve, Simon Gray, and Pinter. His book on Tom Stoppard was published in the Macmillan *Text and Performance* series in 1991. His current research is on theatre in post-apartheid South Africa.

David Graver is an Assistant Professor of English and Comparative Literature at Columbia University where he teaches courses on modern drama and literary theory. He is the author of *Aesthetics Disturbance: Anti-Art in Early Twentieth-Century Avant-Garde Drama* (U of Michigan P). His articles on twentieth-century drama and theatre have appeared in *PMLA*, *The Drama Review*, *Theatre Journal*, *Performing Arts Journal*, *New Theatre Quarterly*, and *British Writers Supplement II* (Scribners). He is currently writing a book on Post-Imperial British Historical Drama.

Robert F. Gross is Director of Theatre and Associate Professor of English and Comparative Literature at Hobart and William Smith Colleges. He is the editor of *Christopher Hampton: A Casebook* and the author of *Words Heard and Overheard* and *S.N. Behrman: A Research and Production Sourcebook*.

David Hare began in 1971 one of the longest associations of any playwright with a contemporary theatre. Since *Plenty* in 1978, the National Theatre in London has presented ten of his plays, including *The Secret Rapture*, *Racing Demon*, and *Skylight*.

Mark Hawkins-Dady, currently freelance writer and editor, has carried out research on selected productions at Britain's National Theatre. He is series editor of *International Dictionary of Theatre* (3 vols., St. James Press), of which Volumes 1 (*Plays*) and 2 (*Playwrights*) were published in 1992 and 1993. He has also contributed articles to *New Theatre Quarterly* and other publications.

Kimball King is Professor of English at the University of North Carolina. He is General Editor of Garland Publishing Inc.'s *Casebook* series and Garland's *Studies in Modern Drama* series. His book-length publications in drama include *Twenty Modern British Playwrights* (1977), *Ten Modern Irish Playwrights* (1979), and *Ten Modern American Playwrights* (1981), as well as *Sam Shepard: A Casebook* (1989).

John Mortimer is a playwright, novelist, and former practicing barrister. He has written many film scripts as well as stage, radio, and TV plays; the Rumpole plays won him the British Academy Writer of the Year award. Several of his books, including *Summer Lease*, *Paradise Postponed*, *Titmuss Regained*, and *Under the Hammer*, have been made into successful TV series. He lives with his wife and two daughters in what was once his father's house in the Chilterns.

Austin E. Quigley, currently Dean of Columbia College, is the H. Gordon Garbedian Professor of English and Comparative Literature at Columbia University. The author of *The Pinter Problem* and *The Modern Stage and Other Worlds*, he has published many articles on modern drama, literary theory, and linguistic theory. His most recent book is on the problematics of literary theory.

Sheila Stowell teaches in the Department of Theatre at the University of Victoria. Recent publications include *A Stage of Their Own: Feminist Playwrights of the Suffrage Era* (Manchester UP 1992; Michigan UP paperback 1994) and (with Joel Kaplan) *Theatre and Fashion: Oscar Wilde to the Suffragettes* (Cambridge UP 1994).

Arnold Wesker is the author of 34 stage plays, and sundry stories and scripts, many of which are translated throughout 16 languages. Century–Random House have just published his autobiography, *As Much As I Dare*.

Index

Addison, John, 94
Adventure Story (Terence Rattigan), 126
Albee, Edward, 30, 87
All about Eve (Joseph Mankiewicz, dir.), 95
Allsop, Kenneth, 77, 89
Almost a Gentleman, 5, 6, 78, 89, 175, 179, 185, 187
Altman, Robert, 167
Amis, Kingsley, 11, 30, 187
Anglo-Saxon Attitudes (Angus Wilson), 17
Arden, John, 69, 112, 125, 126
Aristotle, 72, 88, 114, 117
Armistead, Claire, 175, 176, 180
Armory, Mark, 62, 63
Armstrong's Last Good Night (John Arden), 125
Asprey, Robert, 161, 162, 163
Attenborough, Richard, 11
Auden, W(ystan) H(ugh), 161

Balakian, Nona, 89
Bakhtin, M(ikhail) M(ikailovich), 154
Bancroft, Anne, 167
Barber, Lynn, 179
Barker, Howard, 126
Barnes, Peter, 114
Bateson, Gregory, 75, 88, 89
The Beatles, 9, 129
Beatrice, Nellie, 179, 194
Beaumont, Binkie, 3
Beavin, Janet Helmick, 88
Beckett, Samuel, xv, xvi, 21, 23, 27, 30, 31, 133, 141, 142, 144, 190
Behan, Brendan, 113
Behrman, S(amuel) N(athaniel), 160–61
Bennett, Alan, 114, 126
Bennett, Jill, 5, 179, 190
Berliner Ensemble, 113, 120

A Better Class of Person, 16, 24, 175, 179, 185, 188
Beyond the Fringe (Alan Bennett and Jonathan Miller), 16
Billington, Michael, 144, 171, 173, 178, 179, 180
The Birthday Party (Harold Pinter), 113
Blamires, Harry, 87
The Blood of the Bambergs, 162
Bogarde, Dirk, 194
Bolt, Robert, 126
Bond, Edward, 69, 87, 126
Bosch, Hieronymus, 124
Boscolo, Luigi, 89
Bowen, Elizabeth, 17
Bowles, Peter, 113
Brando, Marlon, 61
Brecht, Bertolt, xx–xxi, 40, 68, 93, 94, 113, 115, 120–22, 124, 126, 144
Brenton, Howard, 35
Brideshead Revisited (Evelyn Waugh), 17
British Playwrights' Mafia, 185
Brook, Peter, 92
Brown, John Russell, 74, 88
The Browning Version (Terence Rattigan), xix, 92
Bryden, Ronald, xiv, xv, xxiii, 88, 94, 113
Bunker, Archie, 171
Burgess, Guy, 158–62
Bunyan, John, 10, 11
Burton, Richard, xvii, 61, 62, 63
But for Whom Charlie (S.N. Behrman), 160
Butler, Robert, 143
Butley (Simon Gray), 177

Carey, John, 179
Carrington, Dora DeHoughton, 19
Carter, Alan, 72, 77, 82, 88, 89

Cecchin, Gianfranco, 89
Chesterton, G(ilbert) K(eith), xxv, 11, 185
Chicken Soup with Barley (Arnold Wesker), 189
Chilton, Charles, 11, 114
Churchill, Caryl, 114
Churchill, Winston, 7, 16, 93
City Sugar (Stephen Poliakoff), 114
Cloud Nine (Caryl Churchill), 114
Cockburn, Claud, 160
Comedians (Trevor Griffiths), 114
Comedy Theatre, 167, 172
Congreve, William, 152
Coveney, Michael, 173
Coward, Noël, xix, 3, 92, 104, 113, 114, 183, 190
Craige, Betty Jean, 88
Creighton, Anthony, xxvi, 28
Cromwell (David Storey), 126
Cukor, George, 95
The Custard Boys (John Rae), 16

Daniels, Sarah, 126
D'Arcy, Margaretta, 126
D'Aubignac, Abbé, 74, 88
Dawson, Helen, xxvi, 178, 185, 189, 193
Death of a Salesman (Arthur Miller), 93
DeBanzie, Brenda, 95, 101, 109
Defoe, Daniel, 10
Déjàvu, xiv, xvi, xvii, xxiv, 3–6, 7, 17, 19, 35, 52–58, 167–74, 175,177, 178, 179, 180
DeJongh, Nicholas, xxvi, 142
Delaney, Shelagh, 113
Demastes, William, xiii, xvii
D'Emilio, John, 161
Dempsey, David, 62
De Profundis (Oscar Wilde), 161
Devine, George, 93, 113, 183, 184, 191, 196
Dingo (Charles Wood), 114
Dollimore, Jonathan, 162, 164
The Doll's House (Henrik Ibsen), 167
Donne, John, xiii
Dylan, Bob, 174
Dyson, A(nthony) E(dward), 80, 89

Eden, Anthony, 103
Egan, Peter, 172
Eliot, George, 10
Eliot, T.S., xiii, xxvi, 21, 25
Elsom, John, 119, 126
The End of Me Old Cigar, xv, 30–31
English Stage Company, 16, 113
The Entertainer, xiv, xv, xix–xx, 4, 5, 10–12, 17, 24, 91–114, 127, 178, 180, 184, 196
Entertaining Mr Sloane (Joe Orton), 114
Epitaph for George Dillon, 28
Erickson, Eric, 116, 125
Eve, Trevor, xxii, 129–33, 137, 138, 140, 143, 144, 178

Faber, M(el) D., 84, 88, 89
Farleigh, Lynn, 178
Fearon, George, 188
Ferrar, Harold, 164
Ferreira, Antonio, 88, 89
Finney, Albert, 119, 184
Forget-me-not Lane (Peter Nichols), 114
Fraser, Antonia, 190

Gale, Stephen, 88, 164
Galef, David, xv, xviii, xx
Galileo (Bertolt Brecht), 120–21, 126
Garnett, Alf, 171
Gascoigne, Bamber, 89
Gaskill, William, 120
Genet, Jean, 157
The Gift of Friendship, 4, 32
Gilleman, Luc, xviii–xix
Gilliatt, Penelope, 5, 179
The Go-Between (L.P. Hartley), 17
God Rot Tunbridge Wells, 175
Goldman, James, 87
Goldstone, Herbert, 32, 161, 163
The Good Person of Setzuan (Bertolt Brecht), 120
Gordon, Robert, xix–xx
The Graduate (Mike Nichols, dir.), 167
Grant, Steve, 143
Graver, David, xx–xxi
Graves, Robert, 13
Gray, Simon, 177
Greene, Graham, 159
Griffiths, Trevor, 114
Gross, John, 132, 143, 170, 173
Gross, Robert, xxii–xxiv, 162
Grove, Valerie, 179
The Gut Girls (Sarah Daniels), 126

H (Charles Wood), 114
Habeas Corpus (Alan Bennett), 114
Hague, Angela, 21
Haigh, Kenneth, xvii, 61, 62, 63
Hamlet (William Shakespeare), 92, 169
Hammer, Stephanie Barbé, 149, 163, 164
Harben, Niloufer, 119, 125
Hare, David, xxv, 35, 114, 190, 191
Hartley, L(eslie) P(oles), 17

Hassan, Ihab, xvi, 53, 59
Hawkins-Dady, Mark, xxi–xxii
Hayman, Ronald, xvii, 62, 149, 163
Heartbreak House (George Bernard Shaw), 109
The Heat of the Day (Elizabeth Bowen), 17
Hédelin, François. *See* Abbé D'Aubignac
Hegel, Georg Wilhelm, 117
Heidegger, Martin, 21
Henry V (William Shakespeare), 92
Herbert, Jocelyn, 120
Hewison, Robert, 159
Hill, Christopher, 11
Hinchliffe, Arnold, 61, 125, 153
Hirst, David, 151, 152
Hobsbawm, Eric, 11
Hoffman, Dustin, 167
Holden, Anthony, 113
The Hotel in Amsterdam, xiv, xv, 13, 18, 27–29, 180
Howard, Philip, 178
Huss, Roy, 88

The Iceman Cometh (Eugene O'Neill), 93
Inadmissible Evidence, xiv, xv, xxi–xxii, 12, 15, 18, 25–28, 127–46, 162, 177, 178, 184, 189, 196
The Island of the Mighty (John Arden and Margaretta D'Arcy), 126

Jackson, Don, 88
Jaspers, Karl, 21
Jellicoe, Ann, 113
Jingo (Charles Wood), 114
Joint Stock, 195
Johnson, Paul, 190
Johnson, Samuel, xxv, 185

Kafka, Franz, 129, 144
Karpf, Anne, 90
Kemp, Peter, 173, 180
Kennedy, Andrew, 74, 88
Kermode, Frank, 159
Kierkegaard, Sören, 21
King, Kimball, xxiv–xxv, xxvi
Kipling, Rudyard, 186
Knight, G. Wilson, 88

Langtry, Lily, 191
Larkin, Philip, 11
Laughton, Charles, 126
Lawrence, D(avid) H(erbert), 10, 11
Leavis, F(rank) R(aymond), 10
Le Carré, John, 159, 160
Lee-Potter, Lynda, xxvi

Left-Handed Liberty (John Arden), 125
Leigh, Vivien, 92
"A Letter of Hate," 185
"Letter to My Fellow Countrymen," 187. *See* "A Letter of Hate"
Lillo, George, xxii, 147, 148, 163
Lilly, Emma, 172
The Lion in Winter (James Goldman), 87
Littlewood, Joan, 11, 30, 113, 114
Lloyd, Marie, 11, 185
Lodge, David, 190
The London Merchant (George Lillo), xxii, 147–49, 163, 164
Long Day's Journey into Night (Eugene O'Neill), 93, 101
Look Back in Anger, xiii, xiv, xvi–xix, xxiv, xxv, xxvi, 4, 6–10, 16–17, 18, 22–24, 35–54, 56, 58, 61–69, 71–90, 91, 94, 97, 101, 106, 113, 119, 124, 168–69, 171, 172, 173, 174, 175, 177, 178, 180, 183, 184, 188, 189, 190, 196
"Look Back II," xvi, 167. *See* Déjàvu
Loot (Joe Orton), 114
The Lord Chamberlain, xiv, xxiv, 16, 169
Lustig, Vera, 172, 173
Luther, xx–xxi, 17, 24, 115–26, 180, 184, 196
Lyotard, Jean-François, xvi, 53, 59
Lyric Theatre, Hammersmith, 113

MacInnes, Colin, 11
Maclean, Donald, 158–162
The Madness of George III (Alan Bennett), 126
A Man for All Seasons (Robert Bolt), 126
Mankiewicz, Joseph, 95
Martin, Graham, 88
Marwick, Arthur, 156
Maugham, Somerset, 13
McCarthy, Mary, 29
Melon (Simon Gray), 177
Miller, Arthur, 113, 184, 190
Miller, D(avid) A., 155, 164
Miller, Max, 92, 108, 195
Millett, Kate, 90
Milton, John, xiii
Morley, Sheridan, 143, 170, 173
Mortimer, John, xxv

National Theatre, 127, 129, 130, 131, 141, 142, 144, 146, 175, 177, 178, 189, 190
Nichols, Peter, 114
Nightingale, Benedict, 74, 88, 180, 185

O'Brien, Edna, 30
Oedipus at Colonus (Sophocles), 167
Oh, Calcutta! (Kenneth Tynan), 14
Oh, What a Lovely War! (Charles Chilton and Joan Littlewood), 11, 114
Old Vic Theatre, 92
Olivier, Laurence, 3, 5, 91–95, 98–100, 107–08, 111, 112, 113, 127, 175, 184
1 Henry IV (William Shakespeare), 170
O'Neill, Eugene, 110
"On the Thesis Business," 25
Oppel, Horst, 84, 89
Orton, Joe, 9, 69, 114, 175
Osborne, Helen Dawson. *See* Helen Dawson
Osborne, Nellie Beatrice. *See* Nellie Beatrice
Osborne, Nolan, 172
O'Toole, Peter, 174, 178

Page, Anthony, 179
Page, Bruce, 158, 159, 160, 164
Page, Malcolm, 125
Palazzoli, Maria, 80, 89
Palmer, Tony, 169, 170, 172, 174
A Patriot for Me, xv, xxii–xxiv, xxvi, 17, 25, 125, 126, 147–165, 180, 184, 190, 196
Pequigney, Joseph, 164
Peter, John, 143
Philby, Kim, 158–62, 164
Pinter, Harold, 9, 69, 72, 75, 81, 85, 113, 190, 191
Pirandello, Luigi, 68, 93
Piscator, Erwin Friedrich, 124
The Player (Robert Altman, dir.), 167
Poliakoff, Stephen, 114
Poppy (Peter Nichols), 114
The Portrait of Dorian Gray (Oscar Wilde), 154
Potter, Stephen, 9
Prata, Guiliana, 89
Priestley, J(ohn) B(oynton), 13, 114
Purcell, Henry, xxvi, 190

Querelle (Jean Genet), 157
Quigley, Austin, xvi, xvii, 75, 81, 88, 89

Rae, John, 16
Rank, Arthur, 16
Rattigan, Terence, xix, 5, 38, 39–40, 73, 74, 86, 92, 114, 126, 183
Redgrave, Vanessa, 18
Red Peppers (Noël Coward), xix, 92, 113
A Resounding Tinkle (N. F. Simpson), 112
Restoration (Edward Bond), 126

Richardson, Tony, 5, 6, 18, 95, 113, 120, 184
Richard II (William Shakespeare), 17
Richard III (William Shakespeare), 92
Riddle, Jimmy, 167
The Rise of the Meritocracy (Michael Young), 8, 9, 14, 156
Robeson, Paul, 3
Ross, Katharine, 167
Ross (Terence Rattigan), 5, 126
Royal Court Theatre, 16, 71, 91, 94, 95, 99, 112, 113, 118, 120, 127, 156, 172, 175, 183, 188, 194
Royal Exchange Theatre, Manchester, xxvi
Royal Shakespeare Company, xxvi, 190
The Ruling Class (Peter Barnes), 114
Rupp, E(rnest) G(ordon), 125
Rutherford, Malcolm, 173

Sanders of the River (Edgar Wallace), 3
Sartre, Jean Paul, 21, 31
Saturday Night and Sunday Morning (Karl Reisz, dir.), 95
Saved (Edward Bond), 87
Schulz, Dieter, 84, 89
Sedgwick, Eve Kosofsky, 159
Sedgwick, Peter, 88
Segal, Lynne, 156
Selz, Jean, 88
A Sense of Detachment, xv, 14, 30
Separate Tables (Terence Rattigan), 38, 39–40, 73
Serjeant Musgrave's Dance (John Arden), 125
"Sex and Failure," 32
Scott-Kilvert, Ian, 89
Shakespeare, William, xiii, 17, 92, 99, 117, 119, 169, 172, 186
Shands, Harley, 89
Shaw, George Bernard, 155, 183
Shuttleworth, Ian, 172, 173
Sillitoe, Alan, xiii, 69
Simon, Neil, 177
Simpson, N(orman) F(rederick), 112
Sinfield, Alan, 156
Sloman, Roger, 131
Smith, Bessie, 184
Smith, Neil, 143
Spacks, Patricia, 89
Spencer, Charles, 172
A Star Is Born (George Cukor, dir.), 95
State of Revolution (Robert Bolt), 126
Staten, Harry, 31
Stoppard, Tom, 35
Storey, David, 30, 126

Stowell, Sheila, xxiv
Strachey, Lytton, 19
A Streetcar Named Desire (Tennessee Williams), 61, 62, 93
Strindberg, August, 95
A Subject of Scandal and Concern, 25
Sweet Saturday Night (Colin MacInnes), 11

Table by the Window (Terence Rattigan), 72–74, 86
Taylor, John Russell, 32, 77, 88, 93, 126
Taylor, Paul, 143
Teeth 'n' Smiles (David Hare), 114
"That Awful Museum," 58, 63, 88
Thatcher, Margaret, 19
Theatre Royal, Brighton, 193
Theatre Royal, Stratford East, 113
Theatre Workshop, 30
"They Call It Cricket," 29, 72, 87, 88
Thiher, Alan, 21, 23
This Sporting Life (Karl Riesz, dir.), 95
Thompson, E(dward) P(almer), 11
Time Present, xiv, 12, 13, 18
Titus Andronicus (William Shakespeare), 92
Tolstoy, Leo, 19
Tom Jones, 5
Tonight at 8:30 (Noël Coward), 113
Townsend, Pete, 174
Trevis, Di, xxii, 127, 139, 143, 144
Trussler, Simon, xv, 23, 125, 126, 127, 145
Twain, Mark, 6
Twelfth Night (William Shakespeare), 170
2 Henry IV (William Shakespeare), 170
Tynan, Kenneth, 14, 73, 88, 89, 91, 94, 97, 113, 116, 119, 125, 169, 173, 184, 189

Under Plain Cover, 157
Ure, Mary, 5

Van Lockhorst, Emmy, 89
Very Like a Whale, 30, 175
Victory (Howard Barker), 126
Vinegar Tom (Caryl Churchill), 114
Viper Gang Club, 194

Von Wright, Georg Henrik, 22, 23

Wager, Walter, 23
Wain, John, 30
Waiting for Godot (Samuel Beckett), 20, 27
Wall, Max, 94, 113
Wall, Mickey, 21
Wallace, Edgar, 3
Wandor, Michelene, 89
The Waste Land (T. S. Eliot), 25
Watch It Come Down, 13, 14, 15, 19
The Waters of Babylon (John Arden), 112
Watzlawick, Paul, 80, 82, 88, 89
Waugh, Evelyn, 4, 17
The Waves (Virginia Woolf), 27
Wesker, Arnold, xxv, xxvi, 30, 113, 125, 127, 190, 191
"Wesker Trilogy" (Arnold Wesker), 125
West of Suez, xv, 13, 15, 18, 28–29, 30, 180
What the Butler Saw (Joe Orton), 114
White, Lesley, 174, 177
Who's Afraid of Virginia Woolf? (Edward Albee), 87
Wilde, Oscar, xxv, 152, 154, 161, 176, 191
Wilden, Anthony, 90
Williams, Stephen, 88
Williams, Tennessee, 32, 61, 62, 110, 184, 186
Williamson, Nicol, xxii, 127, 142, 143–45
Wilson, Angus, 17
Wilson, Harold, 12, 128
Wittgenstein, Ludwig, xv, 21–27, 29, 31, 32, 75
Wordsworth, William, 11
Wood, Charles, 114
Woolf, Virginia, 27
Worth, Katharine, 25
"Writing for the Theatre" (Harold Pinter), 72

Young, Michael, 8–9, 14, 156
Young, Wayland, 89
You're Not Watching Me, Mummy, 175

Zeifman, Hersh, 58–59
Zimmerman, Cynthia, 59

For Product Safety Concerns and Information please contact our EU representative GPSR@taylorandfrancis.com
Taylor & Francis Verlag GmbH, Kaufingerstraße 24, 80331 München, Germany